PERSPECTIVES IN MUSIC THEORY

Second Edition

PERSPECTIVES IN MUSIC THEORY

AN HISTORICAL-ANALYTICAL APPROACH

Paul Cooper

Shepherd School of Music
Rice University

1817

HARPER & ROW, PUBLISHERS, New York
Cambridge Hagerstown Philadelphia San Francisco
London Mexico City São Paulo Sydney

Sponsoring Editor: Phillip W. Leininger
Project Editor: Céline Keating
Designer: T. R. Funderburk
Senior Production Manager: Kewal K. Sharma
Compositor: Music Typographers
Printer and Binder: The Murray Printing Company

PERSPECTIVES IN MUSIC THEORY: An Historical-Analytical Approach, Second Edition

Library of Congress Cataloging in Publication Data

Cooper, Paul.
   Perspectives in music theory.

   Includes index.
   1. Music—Theory. I. Title.
MT6.C7785P5 1980 781 78-26448
ISBN 0-06-041373-5

CONTENTS

PREFACE

Music theory owes its existence to actual musical practice. Without the great legacies of music literature, from Medieval chant to the sound designs of the twentieth century, not only would there be minimal need of instruments and performers, but discussion of axioms would be purely speculative as well.

Perspectives in Music Theory is a set of observations: of the nature of musical sound and of its continuity in time, of the elements of music and their multiple combinations, and of actual compositions from about 800 AD to the present. An understanding of these observations is essential to the education of the inquiring student of music.

The second edition of the text and the accompanying Workbooks, Volume I and Volume II, are designed to be used in the initial two-year sequence of study at the college level. The scope is large but the goals are specific. Among these goals are a basic familiarity with pretonal music, the acquisition of analytical techniques and writing skills as they pertain to tonal music (c. 1650-1900), and an introduction to the technical and conceptual aspects of twentieth-century music. The basic premises and the structuring of the first edition have been retained: compositional principles and stylistic observations are derived from examination of examples from major composers; historical mutations, theoretical postulates, and performance practices are viewed as interwoven and correlated phenomena. Many concepts are discussed several times, with additional information or perspective supplied on each successive occasion, as the need develops. This spiral pedagogical procedure manifestly responds to a natural learning process in that it provides for constant review of previously presented materials and thereby effects a learning reinforcement, and simultaneously presents new knowledge in portions that the student can absorb.

The new edition is substantially expanded. A more complete discussion of aesthetics, acoustics, fundamentals, the elements of music, and basic theoretical concepts has been provided. A stronger historical perspective has been formulated, and many complete compositions have been added. These modifications serve to ally theory more clearly with music as it evolved—that is, with music history. The Suggested Studies recommend the composition of short pieces utilizing a specific vocabulary, the performance of representative works in the classroom, and the analysis of diverse compositions as further creative, aural, and intellectual reinforcements.

Interspersed throughout the text are brief discussions of counterpoint, instrumentation, form in music, and performance practices. These discussions are intended as introductions, not substitutes, for thorough studies. If, however, a stimulus has been provided for the student to begin thinking about the "color of melody," the "form of harmony," and other significant aspects of music such as texture, fabric, environment, musical event and nonevent, then the author's purpose will have been wonderfully realized.

The music of Europe and the United States has a remarkable continuity, not too dissimilar to that of prose literature, from Greek antiquity to current models. And like prose literature, music during any given era—inclusive of the work of brilliant nonconformists such as Gesualdo and Ives—has a quite specific vocabulary, grammar, and syntax. The germinal processes and syntactical principles that provide logic, coherence, unity and variety, tension and repose, movement and stasis are the bases of a practical theory of Western music. The study of music theory, when viewed as the foundation of the art form, must be one of the student's more rewarding and enjoyable endeavors.

In a way, most college texts are written by students. The debt I owe my students is profound, because both editions of *Perspectives* have attempted to respond to the needs and curiosities of aspiring young musicians. I am grateful to my colleagues at the University of Michigan, where these ideas were initially proposed; to my friends at the College-Conservatory of Music, the University of Cincinnati, for the patience of a rigorous and objective five-year testing; and to the hundreds of teachers throughout Australia, Canada, Great Britain, and the United States who have shared some of my views on comprehensive musical education.

I am particularly indebted to John Baur, Tulane University; Edith Borroff, the State University of New York (Binghamton); Marcia Citron, Rice University; Margery Stomne Selden, the College of Saint Elizabeth (New Jersey); and Elliott Schwartz of Bowdoin College for their sage counsel. My fervent thanks go to Christiane Cooper for her editing, preparation of manuscript, and infinite patience for me and for the theories of music.

Paul Cooper

"Teachers open the door. . . . You enter by yourself."

—Ancient Chinese proverb

THEORETICAL CONCEPTS

"If you would understand the invisible,
look carefully at the visible."

—from the Talmud

Chapter 1

MUSICAL THEORY
MUSICAL AESTHETICS

DEFINITION

Music is the art and science of organized sound. It is manifest in every major culture; its origin as an accompaniment to ritual predates conscious scientific endeavor. Music (Gk. *mousikē* tekhne, Muses' art) may have special significance according to time or place: "Music is the noblest of arts to be used only for the glorification of God" (Andreas Werckmeister, c. 1690), or "Music is an entertainment...an innocent luxury" (Charles Burney, c. 1776). Today, a standard dictionary describes music as "an art of sound in time which expresses ideas and emotions in significant forms through the elements of rhythm, melody, harmony, and color."[1]

MUSICAL THEORY

Theory is the body of fundamental principles underlying a science or application of science. Thus musical theory encompasses the classified study of the elements of music listed above as well as technical categories such as solfeggio, counterpoint, orchestration, and form. The study also embraces acoustics, calculations of intervals,

---

[1]*The Random House Dictionary of the English Language,* ed. Jess Stein (New York: Random House, 1971).

scales, and harmonic composites in the scientific area, and the aesthetics of music as a speculative and somewhat subjective counterpart.

PURPOSE

The study of musical theory should provide the information and the incentive for applying the principles of music to the composition, performance, and historical study of the art. The development of fluent skills in notation and writing, aural-visual analysis, sight-singing and sight-reading, aural perception, and oral and expository articulation are basic and minimum goals to be attained. Theoretical studies should also assist an understanding of the development of Western music—from its sacred and secular origins to contemporary thought and practice. Theory guides the composer in the control of sound and design; it prompts the performer in the creation of sound—from the control of a specific note, through the subtleties of coloring and phrasing, to the realization of an architectural whole; finally, it provides a basis for most serious research into the discipline of music. For all these reasons theory should be considered the core of study, from which are derived the inspiration and knowledge for a continuing comprehensive and creative musicianship.

MUSICAL AESTHETICS

How may one define beauty? When does craft become art? What constitutes a musical masterpiece? These questions have prompted serious dialogue for centuries, and the arguments continue. *Aesthetics* (Gk. *aisthesis,* feeling, sensation) is generally understood as the philosophy or study of the beautiful. Among aestheticians, there are two principal views of music, which have prompted these hundreds of years of discourse. In briefest form, these views are: (1) that music is a *heteronomous* art and is capable of expressing extramusical elements, and (2) that music is an *autonomous* art and may realize only intrinsic principles and ideas.

It is immediately discernible that even a standard dictionary definition of music contains subjective views: "...expresses ideas and emotions in significant forms...." Does music express ideas? Intrinsic or extramusical? Does music express emotions or does it, rather, appeal to the emotions of the performer or listener? And finally, must the form be a significant one? The form of folk melody consisting of two four-measure phrases $\overset{A}{\overbrace{\qquad}_{4}}\ \overset{A'}{\overbrace{\qquad}_{4}}$ may not be significant but nonetheless may serve as the appropriate conveyor of a text narrative. In the *History of Aesthetics,*[2] Bosanquet states:

[2]Bernard Bosanquet, *History of Aesthetics* (New York: Macmillan, 1908).

The one true aesthetic principle recognized by Hellenic antiquity in general [is that] beauty consists in the imaginative or sensuous expression of unity in variety. . . . The relation of whole to part—a slightly more concrete expression for unity in variety—has never been more perfectly elucidated or more justly appreciated than by Plato and Aristotle. . . . Moreover the relation of the one to the many or of the part to the whole is represented in comparative purity by geometric figures, or again by rhythmic or spatial intervals that bear numerical relation to one another. And for this reason Greek philosophy is inclined to select form, ratio, or proportion as the pure and typical embodiment of beauty.

A brief historical summation of some significant contributions to musical aesthetics is provided by Willi Apel in the *Harvard Dictionary of Music*.[3]

In the sixth century B.C., Pythagoras commented that music was an expression of universal harmony, which is also realized in mathematics and astronomy. Plato, about 400 B.C., concluded that music was a most appropriate conveyer of social and political education. The great Roman statesman and philosopher Boethius (died A.D. 524) made three divisions of music:

Musica mundana (the Pythagorean harmony of the universe)
Musica humana (the harmony of the soul and body)
Musica instrumentalis (music as actual sound)

About 1619, Kepler correlated musical tones and intervals with the movements of the planets and their astrological functions; two hundred years later, Schopenhauer countered by speculating that music is the purest incarnation of the absolute will and the expression of human feelings in their abstract interpretation of metaphysical ideas.

At various times music has been thought of as an oratorical art, as a poetry of lesser clarity, as form moving in sounds. There is no one prevailing aesthetic of music in the late twentieth century; rather, since 1950, the function and very purpose of the art have been subjected to considerable scrutiny. "Advances in modern technology have precipitated a crisis for art, as for society, of such dimensions that our old notions of what constitutes art, how it should be made, and so on, are rapidly becoming or have already become, obsolete."[4] Yet, despite changing aesthetic perceptions, some guidelines are clearly discernible. Great masterpieces of music, which serve the student as a basis for the learning of technique, performance practice, and style for performers and scholars and as comparative models for composers, seem to embody a remarkable set of balances:

[3]Willi Apel, *Harvard Dictionary of Music* (Cambridge, Mass.: Harvard University Press, 1944).

[4]Christopher Ballantine, "Towards an Aesthetic of Experimental Music," *The Musical Quarterly* (April 1977): pp. 224-46.

THE PHYSIOLOGICAL COMPONENTS OF MUSIC (What? and How?)

The logic of note-to-note progression or succession and the control of each of the elements (rhythm, melody, harmony, and color) that, collectively, produce the whole are fundamental requisites of music composition. These are the physiological aspects of the craft of the composer. One cannot imagine the B Minor Mass of Bach, Beethoven's *Eroica* Symphony, or Stravinsky's *Sacre du Printemps* existing in any state other than the one of technical perfection they exemplify and share with a vast list of works from the past and present.

THE PSYCHOLOGICAL COMPONENTS OF MUSIC (Where? and When?)

Gesture, phrase or phrase equivalent, musical event, and climax are psychological aspects of a composition. Their balance is critical to a listener's response. The ability—or lack thereof—to perceive relationships of sound in time is in large part attributable to this complex phenomenon. Numerous writers have explored the relationship of art (music) to mathematics and, by inference, its significance to psychological balance. These ideas are briefly described on page 7.

THE PHILOSOPHICAL COMPONENTS OF MUSIC (Why?)

Béla Bartók addressed himself to this balance by stating, "I cannot conceive of music that expresses absolutely nothing." Assuredly Bartók and others with similar views are not speaking of program music—that is, music with an explicit scenario provided by the composer. Do the Seventh and Eighth Symphonies of Beethoven also express ideas and emotions, as do the Sixth Symphony, the *Pastorale,* complete with movement headings (provided but later regretted by the composer), and the Ninth Symphony, on Schiller's text affirming the brotherhood of man? Composers and aestheticians who hold to the heteronomous view of musical expression would reply affirmatively. This view does not, however, presuppose that musical ideas and emotions must be capable of being verbally articulated or described nor that a rationalization must be found to justify their existence.

Sound in time is essentially an abstract notion. Any suggested idea or engendered emotion obviously results in conjunction with the experiential reference of the listener. Herein lies the uniqueness of the art and science of organized sound.

PHYSICAL PROPERTIES OF SOUND

The basic materials of music are *time* and *sound.* Time provides the outer and inner dimensions of organized musical events. Sound is an inclusive term for all antonyms of silence, including noise, white noise,* and sounds in nature (ocean waves, bird calls, sonar soundings of underwater animals, etc.) as well as musical sound. It is investigated and defined in an elaborate science called *acoustics*.

TIME

In a musical composition, two aspects of time are important considerations for the student of music. In examining them, the student should remember that time becomes meaningful or significant in relation to perceivable guideposts: dark ⟶ sunrise ⟶ day ⟶ sunset ⟶ dark, or silence ⟶ sound ⟶ event ⟶ climax ⟶ sound ⟶ silence (often interrupted by applause—noise—in the concert hall!). The dimensions of a musical composition delineated by time must take into account both sound and silence.

REAL TIME

Once sound is initiated by a performance of music, *real time* is a measurable factor. The duration of a symphony, for example, might be twenty minutes. These minutes are fractions of hours and days, and of larger segments of calculated and measurable time governed by physical and cosmic principles.

Example 1

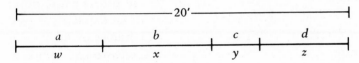

PSYCHOLOGICAL TIME

After listening to the work, the twenty-minute time span may seem to have been much shorter or much longer. Compression or expansion of events in time is a common illusion of perception, whether it applies to the listening to music, the viewing of a drama or television program, or the reconsideration of an ordinary conversation. Further, the events may be recalled in an order very different from the actual presentation—for example, the most notable and impressive events may be recalled first, with those of lesser retentional qualities following in order of effectiveness, or perhaps forgotten altogether. All these manifestations are aspects of *psychological time*.

For the composer and performer of music, then, time is a complex phenomenon to be considered and treated with utmost attention.

*A composite of all pitches, analogous to the "color" white in the spectrum.

SOUND

Not all the subdivisions of the science of acoustics need be considered in initial theoretical studies (e.g., architectural acoustics or minute pitch calculations requiring logarithmic equations). However, the basic nature of sound, together with a discussion of consonance, dissonance, and resonance, and the study of basic pitch calculations are both germane and essential.

FREQUENCY

Frequency refers to the number of vibrations per second effected by an elastic body when the equilibrium of that body is in some way disturbed. The pitch of a sound is dependent only on the frequency of the vibrations. Although "pitch" is a subjective concept in that separate individuals may hear the same pitch differently, it has an objective technical meaning and is the term most commonly used to designate a specific number of vibrations per second. For example, (A above middle C) a′ = 440. Example 2 shows only *four cycles per second* by way of illustration.

Example 2

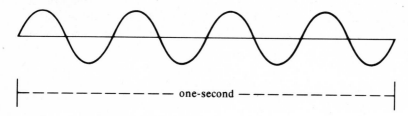

"An elastic body" is a technical phrase used to include a string secured at both ends (violin, piano, and so on) or a suspended or anchored piece of metal (cymbals, vibraphone), as well as a pipe of an organ or wind instruments in which an enclosed air column is caused to vibrate. The frequency is in inverse proportion to the length of the vibrating body. This may be demonstrated by the violin A string: open (full length) it will sound at 440 vibrations per second; when divided exactly in half it will produce an A (a″) of 880 vibrations per second.

AMPLITUDE

Amplitude is the amount of energy effecting the vibrational disturbance, or as stated in a fundamental principle of acoustics: The intensity of a sound depends on the amplitude of the vibration. It is the measurement of loud and soft. The technical term for the unit of measurement of loudness is *bel* (after Alexander Graham

Bell), and one-tenth of a bel is called a *decibel,* a thoroughly familiar term. Most musical sound will have a range from about 25 db (very soft) to 100 db for a very loud passage from a large ensemble, without mechanical amplification. Example 3 illustrates amplitude of a fading, or decaying, sound.

Example 3

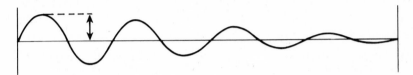

TIMBRE

Timbre refers to the quality, or color, of a tone. The difference between tones of the same pitch (A 440) produced by different instruments—such as a flute, trumpet, or violin—is a *timbral* difference and unrelated to either frequency or amplitude. Numerous acousticians have demonstrated that timbre is determined by the number and relative prominence of *overtones* or *harmonics* produced by a particular instrument. Further discussion of this phenomenon is found in Chapter 3 (overtone series) and Chapter 7 (timbre, color).

CONSONANCE AND DISSONANCE

Consonance and *dissonance* are terms used since antiquity to describe the effect of two or more simultaneous or contiguous sounds. Although certain designations such as "perfect consonances" have precise meaning in music theory, the generic terms are obviously subjective and their connotations relative rather than absolute. Some intervals that we deem consonant were regarded as dissonant in other eras. For example, an anonymous writer from the thirteenth century[5] found the following congruence quite despicable:

Example 4

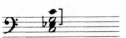

[5]*Anonymous IV,* quoted in Hugo Riemann, *History of Theory,* trans. Raymond Haggh (Lincoln, Nebraska: University of Nebraska Press, 1962), p. 162.

"Here we see such a worthless and unpleasant dissonance as the sixth [!], which in general is to be rejected. . . ." The twentieth-century theorist and composer Walter Piston observed that the history of Western music is strongly correlated to the evolution and emancipation of the dissonance. Even with this reminder, Example 5 serves to illustrate the relative aspects of the term. Observe that the same chord (X) in Example 5 might be considered either consonant or dissonant, depending on its context, behavior, and dynamic relation.

Example 5

a. Chord X is relatively "consonant"
b. Chord X is relatively "dissonant"

RESONANCE

Resonance is the term used to describe the transmission of vibrations from one sound source to another. The two entities must be capable of vibrations of the same frequency for this acoustical phenomenon to take place. An easy, demonstrable experiment illustrating resonance is to depress middle c on the piano *silently* and to strike the C an octave below. One will hear the struck C as well as the resonance transmitted to the depressed middle c. In a broader sense, the term *resonance* is also applied to the sympathetic vibrations inherent in the materials of musical instruments —for example, the sounding board of a piano or the diverse woods of a fine violin.

CHAPTER SUMMARY

1. Music is the art and science of organized sound. Musical theory encompasses the classified study of the elements of music. Musical aesthetics seeks to explain the cause and effect of sensation evoked by organized sound. Since antiquity and continuing to the present time, two principal views of aesthetics have been suggested: (1) music as a heteronomous art, and (2) music as an autonomous art. Three components of music may be described as physiological, psychological,

and philosophical. The balance of the components within a composition serves to unify the intellectual and emotional intent of the composer.

2. The basic materials of music are time (real and psychological) and sound. Sound is systematically defined in the science of acoustics. Important terms and concepts include frequency, amplitude, timbre, consonance, dissonance, and resonance.

SUGGESTED STUDIES

1. Briefly discuss one or more of the following (or similar) topics:

> Music as a Utilitarian Function
> Music as Entertainment
> The Relationship of Folk Music to Art Music
> Music as an Extension of Reality

2. Listen to a recording of an unfamiliar composition, such as a movement from a Haydn or Mozart symphony. Be prepared to discuss aspects of real versus psychological time after one hearing of the work.

3. Suggested readings:

> Suzanne Langer. *Philosophy in a New Key*. New York: Mentor, 1948. "Aesthetics of Music." In Willi Apel, ed., *Harvard Dictionary of Music*. Cambridge, Mass.: Harvard University Press, 1944.

Chapter 2

THE NOTATED PAGE
NOTATION

THE NOTATED PAGE

The signs, symbols, and words that constitute musical notation have both a specific order and a precise rendering. Observe in Example 6 the placement of the composer's name and the title, and the performance instructions (walking, **_p_**, _poco ritard._).

Example 6

SILVER MOONBEAMS

(Ablakomba, Ablakomba, Folksong)

Béla Bartók (1881-1945)

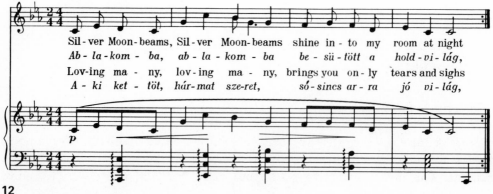

All my love I gave to one lad but I suf-fer, sad and lone-ly.
Lám én csak e - gyet sze-re-tek, még - is de so - kat szen-ve-dek,

Tell me, moon-light why my sweet-heart has be-trayed my lov-ing heart.
Ez az ál - nok bé-res le-gény csal-ta meg a szi-ve-met.

Since the time of Haydn and Mozart, most tempi have been indicated. Dynamics are placed between the staves in keyboard music, below the staff in instrumental music, and above the staff in vocal music. Braces, clefs, key signatures, and meter signatures have a standard and set order. All lines of music that are to be heard simultaneously are connected by a minimum of one vertical bar. An additional brace is employed for the keyboard or for instruments of like or identical quality. A single staff of music (e.g., a work for solo violin) has no initial bar.

Example 7

STAFF (STAVE)

Staff or *stave* refers to the five horizontal lines upon or between which the notes and rests are indicated. In general, notation represents the visual image of sound placement. The invention of the staff (four lines) is credited to Guido d'Arezzo

(c. 1000), who recommended that the lines indicate d f a c^i. A five-line staff was used as early as 1200, while the system most commonly used today dates from the late sixteenth century.

CLEFS

Clefs indicate the location of a specific pitch. Most common are the treble, or G, clef and the bass, or F, clef. The clef signs owe their origins to the Gothic letters G and F respectively and are placed on a particular *line*. C clefs (again, from the Gothic letter C) all specify *middle C*. Used very extensively in earlier music, the C clefs are retained today for viola (alto clef, C on the third line) and occasionally bassoon, trombone, and cello (tenor clef, C on the fourth line). Although all clefs are movable, in modern practice only a movable C clef is used. Middle C is *always* placed on a line, not on a space of the staff. Study Example 8 carefully; compare 8e and 8g.

Example 8

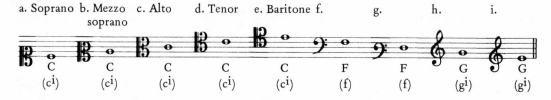

a. Soprano b. Mezzo soprano c. Alto d. Tenor e. Baritone f. g. h. i.

C (c^i) C (c^i) C (c^i) C (c^i) C (c^i) F (f) F (f) G (g^i) G (g^i)

Fluency in reading all clefs is indispensable in the study of string quartets and orchestral scores and in negotiating transpositions.

KEY SIGNATURES

A *key signature* constitutes a preinventory of pitches that require either a sharp or a flat; it traditionally indicates one of two keys: the major tonic or the minor tonic. All signs for signatures and for *accidentals* are derived from a common source—the letter *b*.

Example 9

♭ = *molle* (soft) = flat
♮ = *durum* (hard) = natural
♯ = derived from ♮ (hard) = sharp

In Example 6, Bartók uses a key signature of three flats, E♭ major or C minor (the latter in this example), to indicate pitch and scale consistency.

METER SIGNATURES

Since about 1600, *meter* or *time signatures* have been employed in notated music to indicate the number and kind of durational units (beats) contained within a measure. The most widely used are perhaps $\frac{3}{2}, \frac{2}{4}, \frac{3}{4}, \frac{4}{4}, \frac{6}{8}, \frac{9}{8}$. The upper number specifies the number of principal beats (e.g., 3 in $\frac{3}{2}$); the lower number indicates the kind of note that represents one beat (e.g., in $\frac{3}{2}$ the half note receives one beat, or in $\frac{3}{4}$ the quarter note receives one beat). In Example 6, the number of beats per measure alternates between 2 and 4; therefore Bartók has elected to place both $\frac{2}{4}$ and $\frac{4}{4}$ in the initial signature instructions.

Gregorian chant as well as other early Medieval music contained no time signatures. Rather, rhythm was determined principally by the long and short syllables of Latin texts or by imitations of those basic patterns. From about 1250, however, the complexity of composed music necessitated a more precise rendering of note values, and an elaborate system developed, which satisfactorily coped with the problem. Four signs were used $C, O, C, $ and $\odot$. In modern transcription these designations could represent $\frac{2}{4}, \frac{3}{4}, \frac{6}{8},$ and $\frac{9}{8}$* respectively.

TEMPO AND DYNAMICS

Tempo (L. *tempus,* time) refers to the rate of a given duration: ♩ = 60, or ♩ = 144. Typically, composers indicate a general rate or tempo by using designations such as *adagio* (It., slowly, softly), *allegro* (It., cheerful), *moderately slow,* or *very fast.* Dynamic indications specify sound volume. Abbreviations of Italian words such as *pianissimo* (**pp**), *fortissimo* (**ff**), *sforzato* (**sf** or **sfz**), *forte-piano* (**fp**), as well as symbols ⟨ (increasing in volume) and ⟩ (decreasing in volume) are commonly employed.

METRONOME

The *metronome* is an instrument that measures the rate of motion per minute. It was invented by Maelzel in the early nineteenth century and is commonly used by composers to indicate a very specific tempo. M.M. ♩ = 120 stands for Maelzel Metronome, with a setting of 120 oscillations per minute, with the quarter note used as the unit of measure.

*Time signatures are not arithmetical fractions; therefore proper notation is $\frac{2}{4}, \frac{6}{8}$ etc., not 2/4, 6/8 etc.

A composition in $\frac{4}{4}$ meter ($\quarternote = 120$) will require 30 measures for one minute of music:

$$\frac{4 \times X}{120} \qquad 4X = 120 \qquad X = 30$$

Similarly, 30 measures in $\frac{3}{8}$ meter at $\eighthnote = 90$ will have a duration of one minute:

$$\frac{3 \times 30}{90} = 1 \text{ (minute)}$$

NOTATION

Notation is a system of signs and symbols to represent the aural realization of music. *Neumes* (Gk. *neuma,* nod, sign) provided a basis for a notational system in the Middle Ages (c. 700 to c. 1300). A few common neumes illustrate this graphic representation:

Example 10

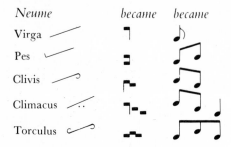

Neume	became	became
Virga		
Pes		
Clivis		
Climacus		
Torculus		

Example 11

GRADUALE VATICANUM (excerpt)

Neumatic, modern Gregorian

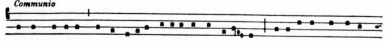

Videns Dominus flentes sorores Lazari ad monumentum, lacrimatus est coram

Judæis, et clamabat: Laza-re, veni foras: et prod-i-it ligatis manibus et pedibus,

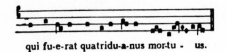

qui fu-e-rat quatridu-a-nus mor-tu - us.

MENSURAL

Common or standard notation in use today is derived from *mensural notation,* a system established by Franco of Cologne c. 1250. There were two divisions in this system:

Black mensural, from c. 1250 to 1450
White mensural, from c. 1450 to 1600

A table of equivalents shows the relation of mensural to standard notes and rests:

	Maxima	Longa	Brevis	Semibrevis	Minima	Sm[1]	F[2]	Sf[3]
Notes:								
Standard equivalents:								

[1]Sm = semiminima
[2]F = fusa
[3]Sf = semifusa

Example 12

a. Black mensural notation: excerpt from a Modena manuscript dating from about 1410*

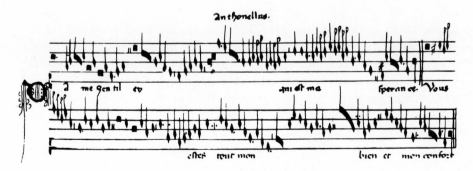

*Quoted in Donald Jay Grout, *A History of Western Music,* rev. ed. (New York: W. W. Norton, 1973), p. 88.

Example 12

b. *PARAGON DES CHANSONS* (excerpt)

White mensural, printed at Lyons, 1538 by Jacques Moderne. Composed by Pierre Certon. The example shows the superius and tenor of a part book.

Courtesy of Samuel F. Pogue.

From about 1600, and continuing for 350 years, composers provided for the gradual development of the notation system in current use. Since c. 1950 several new systems have emerged—each attempting to serve the expressive needs of the composer while solving the technical problems of the performer. Examples 13 and 14 illustrate that notation has been, and is, a constantly changing process, appropriate for the particular sound it represents.

Example 13

THRENODY: TO THE VICTIMS OF HIROSHIMA (excerpt)

Krzysztof Penderecki (1933-   )

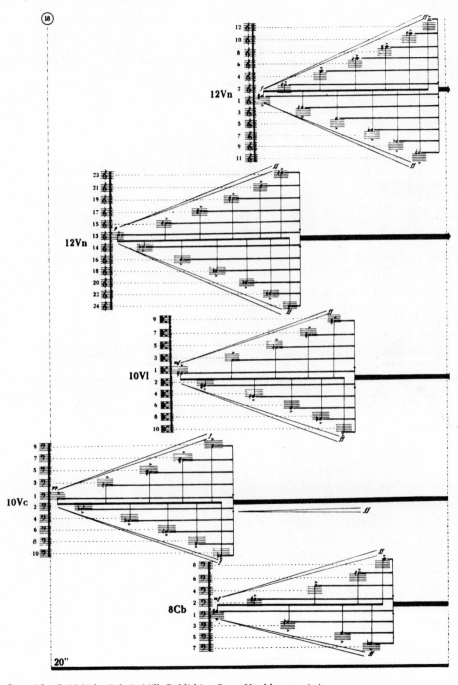

Example 14

STUDIE II

Fragment from an electronic score

Karlheinz Stockhausen (1928-   )

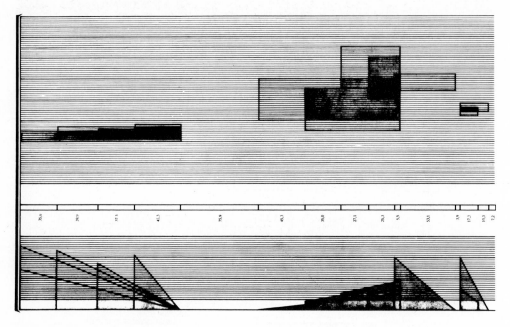

CHAPTER SUMMARY

Standard notation in current use has a specific order and a precise rendering, which the music student must master. Clefs indicate the location of a specific pitch; fluency in reading all clefs is an important skill in score reading and transposition. Key signatures provide a preinventory of pitches requiring accidentals; meter signatures indicate the durational units contained within a measure, while tempo and dynamics specify the rate of a given duration and sound volume, respectively.

In the development of notation of Western music one observes a consistent movement toward specificity—from neumes above a text to neumes on a staff, to greater rhythmic clarity in mensural notation, to explicitness in standard and some contemporary notations. Notational systems emerge, of course, in response to the expressive needs of the composers of particular eras.

SUGGESTED STUDIES

Study and compare the two notations below. Be able to discuss the similarities and differences between the two versions.

Example 15

a.

b.

(When the Lord saw the sisters of Lazarus weeping at the tomb he wept before the Jews, and cried out: 'Lazarus, come forth!' And he who had been four days dead came forth, bound hand and foot.)

The above examples are found in *The New Oxford History of Music* (London: Oxford University Press, 1954), Vol. 2, p. 118. Used by permission.

Chapter 3

HARMONIC SERIES
OCTAVE IDENTIFICATION
SCALES
INTERVALS
KEY SIGNATURES

HARMONIC SERIES (Overtone Series)

A single note consists of a *fundamental* and an additional complex of sound called the natural *harmonic series,** or *overtone series*. Very briefly explained, this is caused by the fact that the vibrating body producing the sound vibrates as a whole *and* in sections of one-half, one-third, and so on; it therefore vibrates at the frequency of its fundamental pitch *and* in multiples of that frequency (the secondary vibrations, however, have a much smaller amplitude).

The overtone series is of great interest for both practical and historical reasons. All wind instruments are constructed in accordance with the series; similarly, natural harmonics on string instruments are overtone resultants.

Example 16

= Fundamental

1 2 3 4   5 6 7 8 9 10 11 12 13 14 15 16

*The term *partials* has a similar meaning to "harmonics" and "overtones." For proper distinction, however, the fundamental is included in the calculation of partials, excluded for calculations of harmonics and overtones.

22

Both in vocal and in instrumental music, chordal formations typically take advantage of the natural phenomenon of the overtone series.

Example 17

a. Chordal formations   b. An orchestral sonority

OCTAVE IDENTIFICATION

The *octave* is considered the most perfect consonance of all intervals, with a frequency ration of 1:2 from any given initial pitch (i.e., if great C = 65.5, then small c = 131, and c′ = 262).* This relationship is a natural phenomenon that has been referred to as the "basic miracle of music." Its use is common in most music systems. Of several octave designations, the one cited in the table below is the most commonly employed:

Example 18

Contra	Great	Small	One-line	Two-line	Three-line	Four-line	Five-line
C_1							
CC	C	c	c^i	c^{ii}	c^{iii}	c^{iiii}	c^{iiiii}

Other pitches are reckoned *above* the C designations:

| a^i | D | g^{ii} | A₂ or AAA |

*Some writers cite 261.68 vibrations per second as a precise frequency for "middle c."

Since antiquity, theorists have used the overtone series as both a guide and a rationale for discussion of interval calculations, scale formations, and even such subjective items as "pleasant and unpleasant" sounds. Reduced to their *approximate* ratios to the fundamental, the notes of the C major scale, often called the "natural diatonic scale," have the following characteristics:[1]

C	D	E	F	G	A	B	c
1,	9/8,	5/4,	4/3,	3/2,	5/3,	15/8,	2

Terms such as *perfect consonance* are derived from the observation of lower ratios for the octave, perfect fifth, and perfect fourth.

Interestingly, the structure of the overtone series coincides, in a very general way, with the development of Western music:

Example 19

a. Unison singing or the singing in octaves (magadizing) in Greek music and in Ambrosian and Gregorian chant.
b. Organum (motion in parallel fourths and fifths); from c. 850. Organum is generally considered to be the origin of polyphony.
c. Triadic music; from c. 1400.
d. Addition of the chordal seventh (C E G B♭); from c. 1600.
e. Addition of the chordal ninth (C E G B♭ D); from c. 1750.
f. Use of the whole-tone scale (B♭ C D E F♯); from c. 1880.
g. Total chromaticism and the twelve-tone technique, as well as experimentation with microtones, emerging in the first part of this century.

SCALES

Scale (It. *scala,* ladder) is a term that denotes an ordered arrangement of pitch materials. Strictly interpreted, the term implies a sequence of rising pitches—usually defined within the octave. The basis of traditional Western music is the *diatonic scale* (c d e f g a b c^i), consisting of both whole tones and semitones. A scale comprising

[1]George David Birkhoff, *A Mathematical Theory of Aesthetics and Its Application to Poetry and Music* (Houston: Rice Institute Pamphlet, Vol. 29, No. 3, 1932).

only semitones results in a *chromatic,* or *duodecuple,* scale. Most scales consist of five to eight different pitches, with seven tones (heptonic) being the most usual. There is no theoretical preclusion, however, to 3-note or 11-note scales. From the twelve chromatic pitches of the octave, a myriad of scale formations are possible. Ten different scales are shown in Examples 20-22.

Example 20

Very common (the basis of Western music from c. 1600 to 1900):

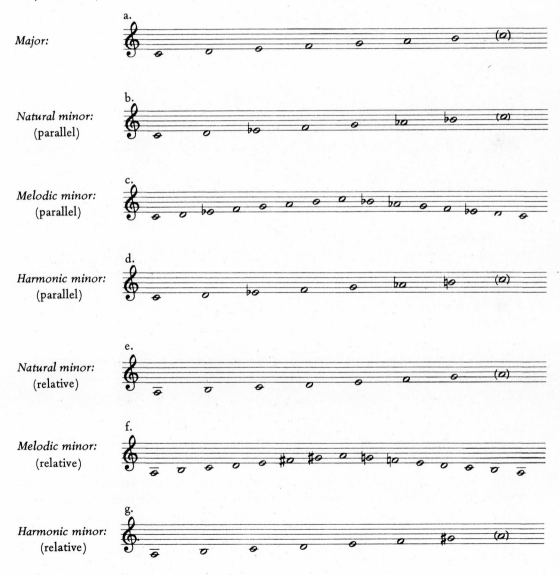

Example 21

Less common:

Pentatonic:

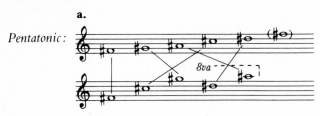

Observe that this pentatonic scale may be derived from the projection of equidistant intervals.

Gypsy (Hungarian):

Whole-tone:

Synthetic:

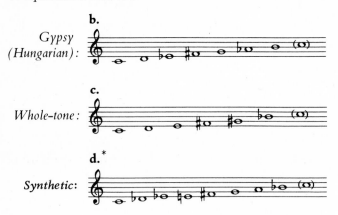

Example 22

Other formations:

Synthetic:

Synthetic:

*This expressive scale, which alternates semitones with whole tones, has an interesting evolution. In isolated instances, it is used by Liszt and Ravel; it is employed with some frequency by Bartók. The formation is sometimes referred to as the Messiaen scale, after Olivier Messiaen, who, in his writings, describes it as "a mode of limited transposition."

†Also called an "acoustical" scale. Compare to the overtone series.

INTERVALS

The distance between two pitches is called an *interval*. In calculating and describing an interval, at least four different aspects are considered:

1. The theoretical description of consonance or dissonance
2. The arithmetical distance (or difference) between two notes
3. The quality (harmonic color)
4. The indication of whether the interval is contained within an octave (simple) or is greater than an octave (compound)

CONSONANCE AND DISSONANCE

Intervals are typically described as being in one of three classes:

Perfect consonances: unisons (primes), fourths, fifths, octaves
Imperfect consonances: thirds, sixths (tenths, etc.)
Dissonances: seconds, sevenths (ninths, etc.)

DISTANCE

A facile method of determining *distance* is achieved by the use of a diatonic scale:

Example 23

prime   2nd   3rd   4th   5th   6th   7th   8ve   9th   10th   11th   12th

QUALITY

Perfect consonances may be altered to include three forms: perfect, diminished, and augmented. The *decrease* in distance by a semitone of a perfect interval results in *diminished* quality; the *increase* in distance by a semitone results in *augmented* quality.

Example 24

a.   b.

perfect 5th   diminished 5th   perfect 4th   augmented 4th

Imperfect consonances and *dissonances* may appear in four forms: augmented, major, minor, and diminished. The *increase* in distance by a semitone of a major interval results in *augmented* quality; a semitone *decrease* of a major interval results in *minor* quality; a semitone *decrease* of a minor interval results in *diminished* quality.

Example 25

major 7th   augmented 7th   major 7th   minor 7th   diminished 7th

The intervals produced from the tonic note, ascending in a major scale, are:

> *Perfect:* primes (or unisons), fourths, fifths, octaves
> *Major:* seconds, thirds, sixths, sevenths

A procedural discrepancy occurs in the intervals produced from the tonic note of the natural minor scale. One would assume that this scale would produce perfect and minor intervals; it contains also the *major* second.

> *Perfect:* primes, fourths, fifths, octaves
> *Minor:* thirds, sixths, sevenths
> *Major:* seconds

SIMPLE, COMPOUND

Any interval larger than an octave is termed *compound;* those within the octave are called *simple.* Therefore, the total description of the interval in Example 26 is: imperfect consonant, minor tenth, a compound interval.

Example 26

Two observations are in order for intervals of any kind:

1. That the first and last notes are reckoned in determining the distance: C to F is
   C D E F (= a perfect fourth), *not* D E F . . . as in measuring time.
2. That the arithmetical description remains constant regardless of chromatic alteration or visual appearance on the keyboard. All intervals in Example 27 are sixths:

Example 27

Common abbreviations for the quality of intervals are: P for perfect, A for augmented, M for major, m for minor, d for diminished.

INVERSION OF INTERVALS

Two principles are essential for determining interval inversion (i.e., c^i *down* to f):

1. The *sum* of the ascending and the descending intervals is 9 (in Example 28)

$$4 + X = 9$$
$$X = 5, \text{ or perfect fifth}$$

Example 28

$= P4 \qquad = X$

2. When an interval is inverted, the quality changes for the imperfect consonant and for the dissonant intervals:

Perfect intervals remain perfect.
Augmented intervals become diminished.
Major intervals become minor.
Minor intervals become major.
Diminished intervals become augmented.

A few illustrations will clarify these principles:

Example 29

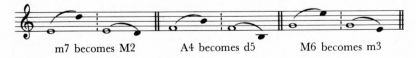

m7 becomes M2   A4 becomes d5   M6 becomes m3

AUGMENTED SECOND

In vocal music of all periods prior to the nineteenth century, the melodic interval of an *augmented second* is typically avoided.

Example 30

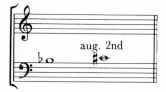

THE TRITONE (Augmented fourth, diminished fifth)

Two other intervals with the common name of *tritone* require cautious voice-leading: the augmented fourth and the diminished fifth.

Example 31

Several centuries of musical and theoretical controversy on the tritone have given the *Diabolus in Musica* a rather special reputation. Its *harmonic* use in the seventeenth and eighteenth centuries is not uncommon, however.

Example 32

a. *Von Gott will ich nicht
   lassen,* J. S. Bach

b. *Was mein Gott will,*
   J. S. Bach

KEY SIGNATURES

Key signatures result from the transposition of the C major scale to any one of the remaining eleven chromatic tones within the octave. In retaining the identical order of whole tones and semitones, two "circles of fifths" are effected.

Example 33

Ascending circle:

C   G (one sharp)   D (two sharps)

semitones between
    3-4 and 7-8
and continuing *up:* A E B F♯ C♯

Example 34

Descending circle:

C   F (one flat)   B♭ (two flats)

and continuing *down:* E♭ A♭ D♭ G♭ C♭

Observe that the two circles produce fifteen different key signatures, of which B-C♭, C♭-D♯, and F♯-G♭ have the same sound *in equal temperament.* These pairs are known as *enharmonic* equivalents.

PARALLEL AND RELATIVE MINOR

Minor scales are of two categories—*parallel* or *relative*—as determined by their relationship to the major tonic.

Example 35

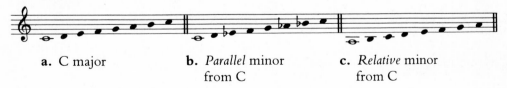

a. C major   **b.** *Parallel* minor   **c.** *Relative* minor
                                from C   from C

The relative minor takes the same key signature as major (i.e., two flats for B♭ major or g minor; four sharps for E major or c♯ minor, etc.). The relationship is calculated a minor third *below* the major tonic note. Obviously, the parallel minor signature is derived a minor third *above* the tonic note.

Semitones for the three common minor scales are given below:

Natural minor: 2-3, 5-6
Melodic minor: 2-3, 7-8 ascending; 6-5, 3-2 descending
Harmonic minor: 2-3, 5-6, 7-8

TRIADS

Triad is a term for three tones sounding simultaneously. Four species of triads are the basis of *tertian music;* these species are all derived from positioning a perfect fifth above a given note.

Example 36

Internal coloration results from the use of either a large (major) or small (minor) third. Further modification can be achieved by altering the fifth down a half step or up a half step. A facile way of remembering triad quality is shown in Example 37.

Example 37

Triads constructed on each scale degree have a particular nomenclature in tonal music. These names are applicable for any tonic, whether major or minor. Example 38 is constructed in C major.

Example 38

    I = tonic
ii = supertonic

iii = mediant
IV = subdominant
 V = dominant
 vi = submediant
vii° = subtonic, or leading tone

Observe the relationships and names:

Tonic-mediant-submediant, and
Tonic-dominant-subdominant.

Common designations for major, minor, diminished, and augmented triads are as follows:

upper-case Roman = major (e.g., I in major)
lower-case Roman = minor (e.g., ii in major or i in minor)
lower-case Roman with o = diminished (e.g., vii° in major or minor)
upper-case Roman with + = augmented (e.g., III⁺ in minor).

CHAPTER SUMMARY

A single note consists of a fundamental and an additional complex of sound called the natural harmonic series or overtone series. Wind instruments are constructed in accordance with the series; chordal formations typically take advantage of this natural phenomenon; since antiquity, theorists have used the overtone series as both a guide and a rationale for discussion of interval calculations and scale formations.

Scale is a term that denotes an ordered arrangement of pitch materials. Most Western music from c. 1600 to 1900 employs scales that are termed major or minor. Other scales, such as the pentatonic scale, are found in folk music and in non-Western musics.

The distance between two pitches is called an interval. Intervals are typically described as perfect consonances, imperfect consonances, or dissonances. They are also classified as simple and compound (within an octave and larger than an octave, respectively).

Key signatures result from the transposition of the C major scale to any one of the remaining eleven chromatic tones within the octave. *Triad* is a term for three tones sounding simultaneously. They are classified as: major, minor, diminished, and augmented.

SUGGESTED STUDIES

1. Notate the overtone series from B♭¹ to the 16th partial (see Example 16). Memorize the order of the first eight partials from any given pitch.

2. Practice octave identification at a keyboard instrument, giving precise names for each pitch (see Example 18).

3. A total command of major and minor scales is imperative. Notate, play, and sing all major and minor scales as necessary for complete fluency.

4. Practice interval recognition by analyzing any example from the text that contains two or more independent lines of music—for example, Example 48 or Example 68. Here again, fluency is essential.

5. Invent a new scale—that is, a *synthetic* scale. Compose a short piece of about 12 measures for solo flute or cello using this new scale.

Chapter 4

PITCH ORGANIZATION

Although the science of acoustics was well developed in the ancient world before 3000 B.C., specific information about the theory of Western music dates from about the time of Pythagoras in the sixth century B.C. As implied in Chapter 1, music theory has, at times in history, related strongly to such diverse fields as aesthetics, philosophy, religion, mathematics, and physical science. One observes throughout, however, a sense of continuity as well as common goals on the part of composers and theorists. Composer/theorists have sought to order the pitch materials within the octave, to explore and expand the range of pitches to be used, to bring a logic and coherence to durational and temporal aspects of musical sound, and to secure tuning systems compatible with their creative and expressive needs.

TETRACHORD (four-tones)

Greek theory considered a two-octave range called the Greater Perfect System (*systems teleion metabolon*) and "measured" in *tetrachords* from the highest to the lowest tones, with an added lowest tone to complete the two octaves.[1]

---

[1] Greek music also employed a Lesser Perfect System. See Willi Apel, *Harvard Dictionary of Music* (Cambridge, Mass.: Harvard University Press, 1944), pp. 301-304.

```
        a'⌉
        g'│ I
        f'│
       ⌈e'⌋
       │d'
 II    │c'
       ⌊b
        a⌉
        g│ III
        f│
       ⌈e⌋
       │d
 IV    │c
       ⌊B
        A
```

In the Greater Perfect System the two outer notes of the tetrachord (= four strings) were fixed, and the two inner notes were capable of being varied to produce the three genera: diatonic, chromatic, and enharmonic. The diatonic genera consisted of a stepwise filling-out of the fourth (A G F E); the chromatic genera a sesquitone (minor third) plus two semitones (A F♯ F♮ E); the enharmonic genera a ditone (major third) plus two dieses (quarter tones) giving an F♮ F↓ E.

The consonance of the fourth occupies a place of major structural importance in the formation of the Greater Perfect System. It is the smallest of the consonances, having the ratio of 4/3 in the Pythagorean system of defining interval relationships, and is consonant, because consonance in that system is determined by the excellence of the relationship existing between superparticular combinations of the numbers 1 to 4 (2/1 = octave; 3/2 = fifth; 4/3 = fourth).[2]

Aristoxenus, in the fourth century B.C., presented a sophisticated description of the three principal types of tetrachords—*enharmonic, chromatic,* and *diatonic*—in his treatise entitled *Harmonics*. Depending upon pitch placement and arrangement of whole tones and semitones, Greek modes were considered to have effect on the character, even the morality, of the listener and performer. This view is known as the *doctrine of ethos*.

The next important step in the development of Western music is the emergence of the *ecclesiastical modes*.

[2]Hugo Riemann, *History of Theory,* trans. Raymond Haggh (Lincoln, Nebraska, University of Nebraska Press, 1962), p. 340.

MODES

Differentiation is made between scale and *mode,* for classification of particular formations identified with Medieval and Renaissance music. These formations are called *Church modes.* The main period of the modal system (c. 800-1500) relied primarily on eight modes (shown below in Example 39), which are related to sacred music.

Example 39

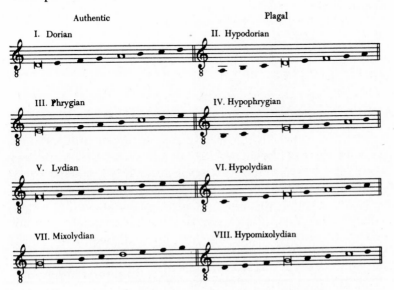

Church modes may be considered as a classification, in the ninth and tenth centuries, of a vast number of melodies known as *chant* or *plainsong.* Classification of melodies, melodic patterns, and formulae, existing in both notated and aural versions, seems to have been based on the following criteria:

1. The range (*ambitus*) of the chant, which is usually limited to an octave plus one or two additional tones.
2. The concluding tone (*finalis*), which typically produces a conclusive effect and, in a certain sense, a tonal orientation to a specific pitch. (The concept of a *confinalis* as a concluding pitch, usually a perfect fifth higher than the expected *finalis,* is observed both in theory and practice.)
3. The "reciting" tone (*psalmtone,* or *dominant*) serves as a further delineation of the characteristics of a specific mode.

Four additional modes, used in secular music but not admitted as Church modes, are included in a sixteenth-century discussion of all twelve modes, Glarean's *Dode-kachordon* (1547).

Example 40

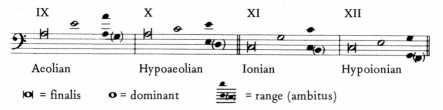

Aeolian   Hypoaeolian   Ionian   Hypoionian

◖○| = finalis   ○ = dominant   = range (ambitus)

Modes I, III, V, VII (IX, XI) are termed *authentic*.
Modes II, IV, VI, VIII (X, XII) are called *plagal*.
Modes I through VIII remain today as officially designated *Church modes*.

Current discussions of modes will include analogies to the keyboard; for example, the observation will be made that Dorian includes all the white notes of the keyboard from d to d′. A similar observation suggests that a mode is a specific octave segment of the diatonic (C major) scale with one of the pitches serving as a center tone; that is, *finalis*. Lastly, it is noted that the authentic modes are closely related to the more familiar major and natural minor scales:

Dorian: as natural minor with a raised sixth scale degree
Phrygian: as natural minor with a lowered second scale degree
Lydian: as major with a raised fourth scale degree
Mixolydian: as major with a lowered seventh scale degree

An additional two modes, *Locrian* (the white notes from b to b¹) and *Hypolocrian*, are theoretically possible but are rarely used. These "hypothetical modes" might be compared to a key signature of ten sharps.

HEXACHORD

Between the Greek system of tetrachords and our contemporary concept of octave scales is an ingenious system described by Guido d'Arezzo (b. 995), based on the *hexachord* (Gk. *hexa*, six; *chordos*, string, tone). The hexachord of Medieval theory comprised six diatonic tones, with a semitone in the middle. There were three such hexachords, as indicated below:

C hexachord, *naturale* (natural): c d e f g a
G hexachord, *durum* (hard): G A B c d e
F hexachord, *molle* (soft): f g a b♭ c¹ d¹

By a method of overlapping and the employment of the *free tone* (b-b♭), the "gam-ut" from great G to e^{ii} was ingeniously spanned.

Example 41A.

Each of the 20 pitches has a specific label. The designations are derived from reading *down* from the information given above or below the note. For example, the first note, "G," has a designation of gamma + ut (hence our word *gamut*); d^i would be D-la-sol-re, pronounced and written "Delasolre."

In order to accommodate melodic progressions which exceeded the compass of one hexachord, two (or more) hexachords were interlocked by a process of transition, called *mutation.* For instance, in order to interpret the melody: c e d g a b a, the tone g was considered as a pivot-tone, being *sol* in the lower hexachord c-a, and *ut* in the higher hexachord g-e^i. Hence, the solmization of this melody would be: ut re ut sol (= ut) re mi re.[3]

Example 41B.

SOLMIZATION

Solmization refers to music systems that designate notes by syllable names rather than by letter names.

Current practice allows for two main systems, *fixed* and *movable,* with considerable argument among musicians concerning the advantages of each. In the fixed-do

[3] Apel, *Harvard Dictionary of Music,* pp. 331-332.

system, the syllable name is invariable for any specific note; that is, all C's (C#'s, Cb's), irrespective of tonality or key signature, are called *do* (*ut* in Latin, and retained in French). In the movable-do system, *do* is always the *tonic* note when in a major key. For a minor key, two possibilities exist: la (tonic) ti do, etc., and do (tonic) re me, etc. The following example illustrates:

Example 42

```
Fixed:    re   la   fa   mi   ti (si)   do   re   la   sol   la
Movable:  do   sol  mi   re   la        ti   do   sol  fa    sol
```

The chromatic, or *inflected,* forms of the syllables are cited below:

Example 43

a. Ascending

```
do   di   re   ri   mi   fa   fi   sol   si   la   li   ti   do
```

b. Descending

```
do   ti   te   la   le   sol   se   fa   mi   me   re   ra   do
```

Sight-singing syllables emanated from the *Hymn to St. John,* quoted by Guido d'Arezzo in the eleventh century. The hymn is an exciting example of subtle musical organization.

Example 44

HYMN TO ST. JOHN

Quoted by Guido

Ut que - ant la - xis *re* - so - na - re fi - bris *Mi* - - ra

ge - sto - rum *fa* - mu - li tu - o - rum, *Sol* - ve___ pol -lu - ti

La - bi - i re - a - tum, San - cte___ *Jo* - an - nes.

The seventh syllable, *si,* was formed from the initials of Sancte Joannes, c. 1650. "That Thy servants may freely sing forth the wonders of Thy deeds, remove all stain of guilt from their unclean lips. O Saint John."

OBSERVATIONS:

1. The first note of each of the first six phrases is successively higher (C D E F G A).
2. The seventh phrase (*Sancte Joannes*) responds to gravity and provides a complete-ly satisfying cadence.*
3. The melody is *curvilinear* (i.e., exhibits gradually ascending and descending mo-tion); the real high point (*Labii*) is reached at a very specific proportional and mathematical juncture.
4. Three-note cells of varying shape permeate the total time span.
5. The numbers 3 and 7, symbolical and mystical, are to be found at every dimen-sion; for example, there are a total of 49 notes—or seven times seven.
6. Unity and variety are in perfect balance.

TWELVE-TONE

The *twelve-tone* system is primarily a technique of pitch arrangement and utili-zation devised independently by Arnold Schoenberg and Josef Hauer in the second decade of this century. The ordering of the twelve pitches contained within the octave may serve as the basis of vertical and horizontal formations in a composition. This set order is called a "row." It should be observed that the row quoted in Example 45 divides into two parts: 1-6 and 7-12, with each part, or hexachord, containing an identical interval makeup.

Example 45

---

*A musical *cadence* (L. *cadere,* to fall) is a temporary or permanent point of repose imposed by any element or combination of elements.

Ross Lee Finney's symmetrical hexachords (see Example 45) are manipulated to produce strongly tonal and functional choral parts in *Edge of Shadow*. In the following excerpt (Example 46), the instrumental parts are omitted.

Example 46

EDGE OF SHADOW (excerpt)

Text by Archibald MacLeish

Ross Lee Finney (1906-   )

Reprinted from *Edge of Shadow* by Ross Lee Finney (Peters Nr. 6192). © 1960 by Henmar Press, Inc., New York. Reprint permission granted by the publisher.

OBSERVATIONS:

1. The simultaneous use of two transpositions of the row, a perfect fifth apart, allows for a flexible treatment and manipulation.
2. The homophonic texture and the repeated pitches provide for stability and a kind of instantaneous familiarity.
3. The slow harmonic rhythm results from *prolongation* (i.e., extension in time caused by the setting of the text).
4. The passage relates in several ways to certain aspects of the chordal style of the sixteenth century, yet the totality (including the instrumental accompaniment) is decidedly, and lyrically, of this century.

---

*There are two principal ways of numbering serialized pitch: 1 through 12 and 0 through 11. 1-12 is used in most introductory discussions; 0-11 is appropriate for mathematical considerations (mod 12). Each has advantages.

TEMPERAMENT

Temperament refers to various tuning systems for the subdivision of the octave. Four principal temperaments have been used in Western music:

The *Pythagorean system,* discussed by Pythagoras c. 550 B.C., derives all tones from the interval of the *pure fifth;* e.g., F c g d^i a^i e^{ii}.

Just intonation is a system of tuning in which all intervals are derived from the pure fifth (as in the Pythagorean system) AND the *pure third.*

The *mean-tone system,* in use c. 1500, utilizes a smaller fifth so that a succession of four such fifths results in a pure third; e.g., c g d^i a^i e^{ii} (pure).

Equal temperament, as its name implies, divides the octave into twelve equal parts (semitones). Demand for the system grew in the sixteenth century and it came into common use in the early eighteenth century; its universality was not accepted, however, until about 1850. Equal temperament is the basis of most Western music performed or written today.

The composer's search for viable pitch systems and for compatible tunings for the organizations might be shown graphically as follows:

Pitch system: (organization)	Greater Perfect System	Tetrachords	Modes	Hexachords	Non Modal Secular
Temperament:	550 B.C. Pythagorean		A.D. 800	1050	1250

Pitch system:	Modes Continue	Tonal Major and Minor Scales			Chromaticism
Temperament:	1450 Mean-Tone Just	1600		1750 Equal	1850

Pitch system:	Tonal Neo Modal Chromaticism	12-Tone	Electronic
Temperament:	1900 Equal	1925	present

CHAPTER SUMMARY

Music theory has, at times in history, related strongly to such diverse fields as aesthetics, philosophy, religion, mathematics, and physical science. Within this diversity, however, one observes that composer/theorists have sought to order the pitch materials of the octave. Principal systems or "organizations" include: the Greek tetrachord and the Greater Perfect System; Medieval modes and hexachords; major and minor scales from the tonal period (c. 1600 to 1900); and the twelve-tone method of the twentieth century.

Solmization refers to music systems that designate notes by syllable names rather than by letter names.

Temperament refers to various tuning systems for the subdivision of the octave. The four principal systems include: the Pythagorean system, just intonation, the mean-tone system, and equal temperament. Equal temperament is the basis of most Western music performed or written today.

SUGGESTED STUDIES

1. Sing, play, and memorize the eight Church modes (see Example 39).
2. Be able to transpose any of the authentic modes to a different starting note—for example, Dorian from c, Lydian from d.
3. Apply syllable names to appropriate examples from the text (see particularly those of Chapter 19) and to other melodies.
4. Memorize, at the correct pitch level, the *Hymn to St. John,* Example 44.
5. Compose a short composition for your instrument using a twelve-tone row which you, or the class, have invented.

SUGGESTED READING AND LISTENING

James Murray Barbour. *Tuning and Temperament: A Historical Survey.* East Lansing, Mich.: Michigan State College Press, 1951. This book also has a three-record set, giving demonstrations of the various temperament systems discussed (Musurgia Records).

Chapter 5

ELEMENTS OF MUSIC
Rhythm

ELEMENTS OF MUSIC

The *elements* of music are the broad components of organized sound: *rhythm, melody, harmony,* and *color.** Several writers also list *texture* and *form* as elements. Perhaps a more accurate classification would designate both texture and form as resultants and compounds of one or more of the simple elements.

> *Rhythm* is a term used to describe the temporal quality (duration) of sound.
> *Melody* is a succession of pitches; by its nature it cannot be separated from rhythm.
> *Harmony* is the resultant of the simultaneous combination of two or more musical sounds.
> *Color* is a term used to identify the quality of sound produced by voices or instruments.

*Rhythm, melody, and color are discussed in some detail in Chapters 5, 6, and 7 respectively. Texture and form are introduced in Chapter 8. *Harmony,* treated in its historical context, is presented throughout the text in Parts II, III, and IV.

Texture denotes the dispositions of pitch and timbre, as well as the horizontal and vertical dimensions of sound.

Form suggests an architecture of sound, the placement and pacing of a musical event, a "sound design" in time.

RHYTHM

Rhythm denotes the organization of *time* and *duration*. All aspects of temporality relate to one or more of the general classifications of rhythm:

1. Metrical rhythm
2. Measured rhythm
3. Free rhythm

1. *Metrical rhythm:*

Each time value is a multiple or fraction of a fixed unit (beat). Normal accents recur regularly to provide systematical grouping (measure).

Example 47

CANTIGAS À MADRE (VILLANCICO)

Thirteenth century

2. *Measured rhythm:*

Each time value is a multiple or a fraction of a specified unit but without regularly recurring accents.

Example 48

BENEDICTUS

Claudio Monteverdi (c. 1567-1643)

*) o. = cf. bars. 4/5   **) o. =

E. E. 6028

3. *Free rhythm:*
No common metrical unit is provided.

Example 49

ALLELUIA

From *Vidimus Stellam*

Gregorian chant

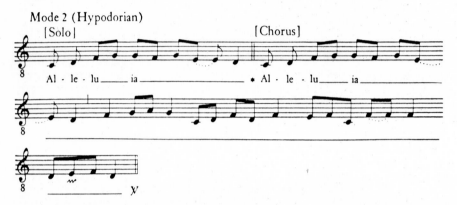

Mode 2 (Hypodorian)

RHYTHMIC MODES

Metrical schemes are derived from *modal rhythm,* introduced probably by Leoninus shortly before 1200. Rhythmic modes established the consistent repetition of simple patterns in ternary meter.

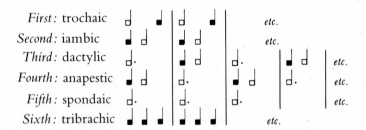

In the early fourteenth century, triple and duple rhythms became coequals—to be followed shortly by dotted rhythms, syncopations, and polyrhythms. The rhythmic complexity of polyphonic music in the late fourteenth century is paralleled only by music written since 1900.

MENSURAL NOTATION

The complexity might be explained, in part, by composers' response to and exploration of an elaborate and intricate mensural notation system. The dogma of the Trinity in the Church undoubtedly influenced numerous musical concepts, including the notational system. Initially, mensural notation provided for three aspects of time, each of which was divided into three (perfect) or two (imperfect) parts.

Mood: Perfect: ■ ■ ■

             Imperfect: ■   ■

Time: Perfect: ◆ ◆ ◆

             Imperfect: ◆   ◆

Prolation: Perfect: ♦ ♦ ♦

             Imperfect: ♦   ♦

Modification eventually produced a somewhat simpler system, illustrated in the following chart, which includes modern equivalents.

Example 50

	Tempus	*Prolatio*	*Sign*	*Example*	*Equivalents*
I	Imperfect	Imperfect	C		$=\frac{2}{4}$
II	Perfect	Imperfect	O		$=\frac{3}{4}$
III	Imperfect	Perfect	C		$=\frac{6}{8}$
IV	Perfect	Perfect	O		$=\frac{9}{8}$

An extraordinary example from the fifteenth century combines all prolations at once. (For a twentieth-century counterpart, see *George Washington's Birthday* by Charles Ives.)

Example 51

MISSA: PROLATIONUM (excerpt)

Johannes Ockeghem (c. 1425-1495)

Two metrical symbols have survived from mensural notation of the Middle Ages: **C** and **₵**.

In current practice, the *alla breve* sign (**₵**) typically signifies the halving of arithmetical ratios, resulting in a different fundamental pulse.

Example 52

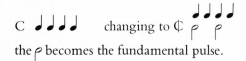

the ♩ becomes the fundamental pulse.

PERFORMANCE PRACTICE

Notated music after about 1600 contains original bar lines, placed by the composer for ease of reading by performers and to indicate consistent metrical groupings. The presence of bar lines, however, offers neither invitation nor license to accent the first beat of each measure.

Dance-derived music, whether vocal or instrumental, is typically more regular in rhythmic groupings and more constant in basic pulse, and may be, on occasion, more highly accented.

Song-derived music (again, either instrumental or vocal or a combination of the two) is quite another matter. Song-derived music will tend to be less regular rhythmically, should contain some natural elasticity of phrases and periods, and will normally not be highly accented rhythmically. The accents will be achieved by high (pitch) points, dynamics, full textures, dissonance of pitches, and so on.

Example 53

A theoretical disposition of accents, *possibly* appropriate for certain kinds of dance-derived music.

Example 54

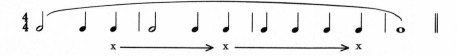

A psychological accent (thought, not executed) on the fourth beat will propel the phrase, cause the greatest amount of tension to occur in measure 3, and delineate more clearly the text (if any) and the musical structure as a whole. "Think last beat" should be a guide for the musical performance of *song-derived* literature. Further, the motto is appropriate for performance of such music from any century—whether a thirteenth-century motet or a twentieth-century cantata.

CONDUCTING PATTERNS

Conducting patterns indicate the time and (depending on the tempo) the subdivision (Example 55):

Example 55

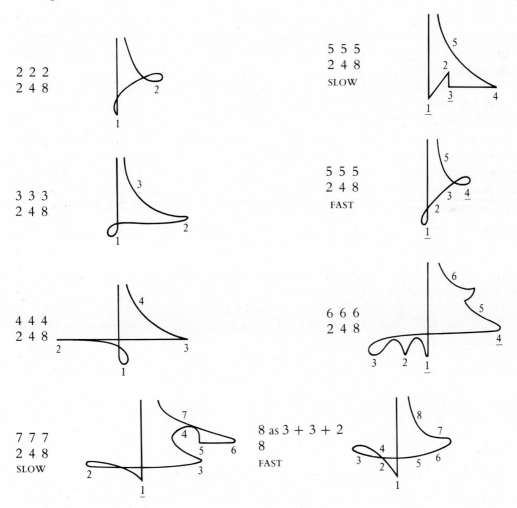

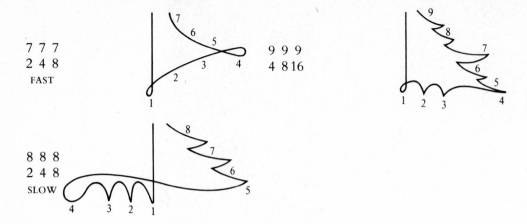

7 7 7
2 4 8
FAST

9 9 9
4 8 16

8 8 8
2 4 8
SLOW

ACCENTS

Accents are one means of providing for rhythmic vitality. They should be used with great discretion in the performance of music. A thorough knowledge of composer, style, period, and performance practice are essential to the appropriate interpretation of accents. There are three main types of accents, which a composer may utilize separately or in combination:

Agogic accent
Tonic accent
Dynamic accent

AGOGIC ACCENT

An *agogic accent* (Gk. *agogos,* leading or drawing forth) results from a longer duration of a note.

Example 56

A combination of these accents, in very obvious form, is illustrated in Example 57.

Example 57

TONIC ACCENT

Tonic accent simply refers to a rising pitch. The X notes in Example 57, by their placement and context, are more exposed and noticeable than the other tones in the fragment.

Example 58

Appropriate:
Inappropriate:

DYNAMIC ACCENT

Dynamic accents include the signs and symbols:

$$sf \quad > \quad - \quad \wedge$$

It is understood that, in most music, these signs are within the context of the general dynamic level.

Example 59

SYNCOPATION

Syncopation is the term that denotes the interruption of normal (i.e., expected) rhythm, accent, or meter. Its use, or equivalency, is first found in the music of the French Ars Nova in the fourteenth century and has been observed in all Western music since that time.

A common change in rhythm is shown in Example 60:

Example 60

Similarly, a change in accent is "unexpected" (Example 61):

Example 61

Example 61 illustrates an actual duple meter within the confines of a ternary meter. (Compare to Example 62.)

Example 62

A change of meter is another possibility of disturbing the normal pulse (Example 63):

Example 63

HEMIOLA

Hemiola (Gk. *hemi-*, half), when referring to time values, denotes the relationship of 3:2. It is the shift from three units of measure to two, or the reverse. Two common successive examples are shown in Example 64:

Example 64

a.   **b.**

The term is also used, less accurately, to describe a vertical (simultaneous) combination of three against two (Example 65):*

*The preferred term for a vertical two against three (Example 65) is *sesquialtera.*

Example 65

POLYRHYTHM

Polyrhythm denotes the simultaneous use of two or more different (and contrasting) rhythmic schemes (Example 66). Polyrhythms were prominent in the music of the fourteenth and early fifteenth centuries and again are a striking feature of twentieth-century rhythmic organization.

Example 66

POLYMETRIC

The term *polymetric* should be used to describe compositions which are notated in more than one meter simultaneously (Example 67):

Example 67

ISORHYTHM

Isorhythm is a term used to describe a constructive device frequently observed in fourteenth-century compositions. Briefly, isorhythm provides for a consistent (or frequent) reiteration of a rhythmic pattern, as in Example 68.

Example 68

MESSE DE NOTRE DAME (excerpt)

Guillaume de Machaut (1300-1377)

The bracketed measures in the tenor illustrate a *talea*. This pattern of: 𝅗𝅥. | 𝅘𝅥 𝅘𝅥 | 𝅘𝅥𝄾𝄾| 𝅗𝅥. |𝅘𝅥 | 𝅘𝅥𝅘𝅥 |𝅘𝅥𝄾𝄾 | is presented three complete times, with one free measure at the final cadence of the *Christe* section of the *Kyrie*.

Although the principle shares the same unifying rhythmic role as the *ground bass* of the seventeenth and eighteenth centuries and the *ostinato* of the nineteenth and twentieth centuries, the term is restricted in usage specifically to the fourteenth century.

"MOTOR" RHYTHM

A recently coined term that describes constant motion in one or several parts is *motor rhythm* (Example 69):

Example 69

QUARTET, OP. 76, NO. 3 (excerpt)

Final measures of first movement

Franz Joseph Haydn (1732-1809)

W. Ph. V. 344

RHYTHMIC CONTROLS

The control of rhythm on the part of the composer is as challenging as the control of other elements—melody, harmony, and color. After establishing a rate or tempo, the rhythmic requirements should include both *predictability* and *surprise*. Observe the following examples:

Example 70

WELL-TEMPERED CLAVIER, Vol. I

From Fugue 2

Johann Sebastian Bach (1685-1750)

a. Neutral
b. Neutral or predictable
c. Surprise

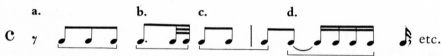

a. Neutral
b. Surprise
c. Predictable
d. Surprise

a. Neutral
b. Surprise
c. Predictable; the extra beat is surprise
d. Predictable
e. $\frac{4}{4}$ is predictable; the tie is surprise
f. Predictable
g. X has, or should have, real suspense. Will the measure be $\frac{2}{4}$, $\frac{3}{4}$, $\frac{5}{4}$, $\frac{3}{8}$ or entirely different?

ACCELERATION AND REPOSE

The rhythmic gesture may include a notated acceleration (*accelerando*):

Example 71

or a notated retard (*ritardando*):

Example 72

VITAL AND STATIC

If the rhythm is essentially unpredictable, or is marked by syncopation and accents, the effect is one of vitality (Example 73):

Example 73

Conversely, an intentionally static composition, or section thereof, may be achieved by even and quite predictable rhythms (Example 74):

Example 74

THRUST AND STABILITY

Obviously, a rhythmic pattern may begin on a strong beat or a weak beat, or with an *upbeat*. Each of these will have a pronounced effect on the expressive quality of the music (Example 75):

Example 75

provides for stability—appropriate for a march

provides for thrust or movement toward a point of repose

has a similar effect of achieving thrust by the use of an upbeat, called *anacrusis*. The initial value of the anacrusis is subtracted from the final measure.

RUBATO

Rubato, a performance practice appropriate for certain periods and styles, is the antithesis of rhythmic precision. The term is used to describe the gradual quickening or slowing down within a phrase or section. A typical *rubato* might approximate the renotated version shown in Example 76:

Example 76

Original:

Renotated as:

MELODIC RHYTHM
COMPOSITE RHYTHM
HARMONIC RHYTHM
"MACRO" RHYTHM
STRUCTURAL RHYTHM

Since all temporal functions of music relate in some way to rhythm, in its smallest or largest dimension, an explanation of a few additional concepts will, perhaps, help illustrate and clarify the important role this element contributes in the unfolding of a musical composition.

---

*The apostrophe (') is called an *atem* and is used by vocalists and instrumentalists as a breathing point in lieu of a notated rest.

MELODIC RHYTHM

Melodic rhythm refers to the actual durations and rests of any given single line in its horizontal movement.

Example 77

LES BERCEAUX (THE CRADLES) (excerpt)

Gabriel Fauré (1845-1924)

COMPOSITE RHYTHM

Composite rhythm is a term describing all *vertical* durational activity of two or more voices. Example 78 illustrates. A more complete example of fifteenth- and sixteenth-century practice is provided in Chapter 11, pp. 150-152

Example 78

HERODES HOSTIS IMPIE (excerpt)

Eustachio Romano (Sixteenth century)

The simplest rhythmic pattern is the alternation of stress and release, or of strong and weak beats. Such a pattern defines *duple* meter (Example 79):

Example 79

It is again emphasized that this discussion refers to theoretical organization and patterns in time; it is *not* to be construed as a performance ideal. Obviously, the following passage (Example 80) would *not* sound as illustrated—unless specifically so indicated by the composer.

Example 80

A pattern consisting of one strong beat followed by two weaker beats is termed *ternary meter* (Example 81).

Example 81

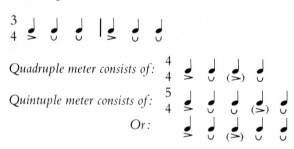

The terms *simple* and *compound* meters refer to the division of the beats. Any simple rhythm multiplied by three is termed compound.

Example 82

A subdivision that relates to another meter is called a *borrowed division* (Example 83):

Example 83

The three eighth notes in the time of two are called a *triplet.* Similar terminology follows in Example 84:

Example 84

4 is a *quadruplet*

5 is a *quintuplet*

6 is a *sextelet*

Frequently used meters with their descriptive names are given below:

Simple duple:	$\frac{2}{2}$ $\frac{2}{4}$ $\frac{2}{8}$ $\frac{2}{16}$
Simple triple:	$\frac{3}{1}$ $\frac{3}{2}$ $\frac{3}{4}$ $\frac{3}{8}$ $\frac{3}{16}$
Simple quadruple:	$\frac{4}{2}$ $\frac{4}{4}$ $\frac{4}{8}$ $\frac{4}{16}$
Simple quintuple:	$\frac{5}{2}$ $\frac{5}{4}$ $\frac{5}{8}$ $\frac{5}{16}$
Compound duple:	$\frac{6}{2}$ $\frac{6}{4}$ $\frac{6}{8}$
Compound triple:	$\frac{9}{2}$ $\frac{9}{4}$ $\frac{9}{8}$
Compound quadruple:	$\frac{12}{4}$ $\frac{12}{8}$ $\frac{12}{16}$

HARMONIC RHYTHM

Harmonic rhythm is a term used to describe the frequency of chord change in a composition. Example 85 shows the same melody harmonized in three different ways:

Example 85

a. A *slow* harmonic rhythm indicates infrequent chord changes, as this extreme example shows.

b. A *moderate* harmonic rhythm is achieved by chord changes on some—but not all—of the given melodic notes.

c. A *fast* harmonic rhythm involves a chord change for each note (or nearly so) of the melody.

DETERMINATION OF TEMPO

Most Renaissance and Baroque scores have been inherited without tempo indications. Performance practice of this music depends, then, on tradition—if one exists —and on the musicologists' investigations of the period. Often harmonic rhythm, together with the medium (voices, keyboard, an instrumental ensemble), give the best musical clues in determining an appropriate tempo.

Although personal taste is both inevitable and desirable, common agreement would probably establish the following general tempi, as applied to Example 85:

a. Allegro
b. Moderato
c. Andante to Adagio

Arbitrarily, Example 85c could be marked *Presto,* of course, but the effect, particularly if intended for voices, would be curious and quite detrimental to its natural implications. Any determination of tempo must consider: clarity of the lines and sonorities in performance, and the ability of the sounds to project acoustically. In vocal music, a foremost factor is the character of the text; in instrumental music the performer must rely on consensus or reason—or ideally, both.

MACRORHYTHM

The Introduction to the Symphony No. 7 of Beethoven is a striking example of rhythmic organization underscored by accents, dynamic punctuations, and contrasts of orchestral color. Because of the placement of the *tutti* chords (*f* or *ff*) and the internal *sforzato* dynamics, a macro- (Gk., large, long, great) rhythm is both seen and heard. Compare the following diagram to the piano reduction of the symphony.

Example 86

POCO SOSTENUTO, SYMPHONY NO. 7

First movement, measures 1-16

Ludwig van Beethoven (1770-1827)

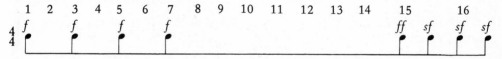

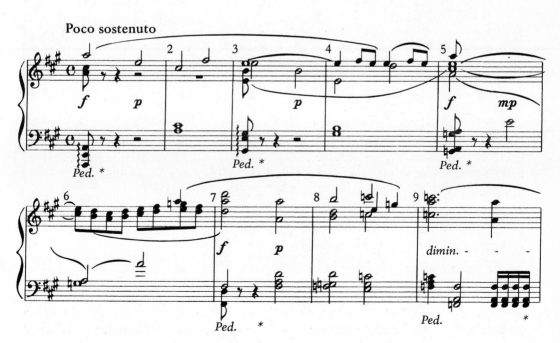

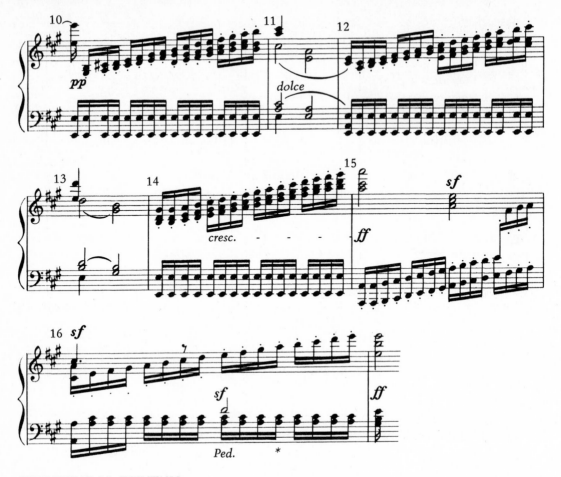

STRUCTURAL RHYTHM

Analysis of the entire Introduction of the Seventh Symphony reveals the following structure:

measures:	7	7	7	12	7	12	10
dynamic:	*f*	*p*	*ff*	*pp cresc.*	*ff*	*p*	*ff > p*
		└─ 21 ─┘		└──── 19 ────┘		└──── 22 ────┘	

To a large extent the structure or form of these 62 measures is determined by the macrorhythm rather than by contrasting thematic ideas.

PROPORTIONAL RATIOS IN MUSIC

Numerous writers have commented on the common goals of the artist and the mathematician—that is, "to seek and to create unity in his universe." The relationship of musical proportions to known mathematical ratios is extraordinary, revealing, and provocative. Phythagoras seems to have had knowledge of a special ratio known currently as the "golden ratio," the "divine proportion," or simply the "golden mean." If one considers a pentagonal face and constructs two diagonals, the point of intersection divides each diagonal in the golden ratio.

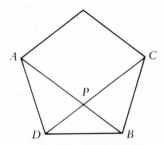

The point of intersection, *P*, divides the diagonal line *AB* in the golden ratio. This ratio has a numerical value of approximately 1:618 and is often designated by the Greek symbol ϕ (phi).

Similarly, in a triangle:

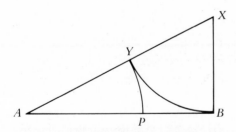

with *AB* being twice the length of *XB*.
Using *X* as center, draw arc radius *XB* so that it cuts *AX* at point *Y*. Using *A* as center, draw arc radius *AY* so that it cuts *AB* at *P*. *P* is the "golden cut" of line *AB*.

One more example will suffice for purposes of illustration. The golden rectangle is defined as one whose ratio of length to breadth is ϕ.

This means that if the length equals 1 (one unit), then the breadth will equal .618 of that particular length.

The significance of the golden mean lies not, of course, in its abstract mathematical value or in the extraordinary properties of the number ϕ per se, but in the aesthetic appeal and recurrent manifestation of this particular ratio in art and nature —from the proportions of the Parthenon to the design of Mondrian's paintings, from the placement of sunflower petals to the structure of the shell of the nautilus.

In music, proportion or golden-mean proportion is rarely identified. Observation of master composers' sense of balance, high point, and climax of dramatic shape in terms of the golden ratio yields a tabulation that is nothing less than amazing. For example, the Introduction to the Symphony No. 7 of Beethoven consists of 62 measures (all in the same $\frac{4}{4}$ meter). 62 x .618 = 38.316. Therefore the 38th through the 39th measures represent the area of the golden mean. This point in time is, indeed, the climax of this section of the composition. Countless analyses of movements or of entire compositions have revealed an extraordinary correlation of golden mean to climax, special dynamic, the only fermata, and so forth, in an entire work.

The golden ratio perhaps represents "rhythm in its ultimate sense":

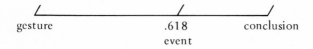

gesture   .618   conclusion
          event

CHAPTER SUMMARY

The elements of music refer to the broad components of organized sound: rhythm, melody, harmony, and color. Texture and form may be designated as compounds of one or more of the simple elements.

Rhythm denotes the organization of time and duration. All aspects of temporality relate to one or more of the general classifications of rhythm: metrical rhythm, measured rhythm, and free rhythm. Rhythmic modes established the consistent repetition of simple patterns in ternary meter (c. 1200). Mensural notation provided both accuracy of duration, and division and subdivision of larger units of time.

Terms and concepts relating to rhythmic organization include: syncopation, hemiola, polyrhythm, polymeter, isorhythm, and "motor" rhythm.

Melodic rhythm refers to the actual durations and rests of any given single line in its horizontal movement; *composite rhythm* is a term describing all vertical durational activity of two or more voices; *harmonic rhythm* is a term used to describe the frequency of chord change in a composition.

The relationship of musical proportions to known mathematical ratios is frequently observed. The "golden ratio," or "golden mean" (1:618) is of particular analytical interest.

SUGGESTED STUDIES

1. Learn the rhythmic terminology in current use.
2. Study and practice conducting patterns.
3. Sing and study musical examples that contain varied accents, syncopations, hemiola, isorhythm, or polyrhythms.
4. Invent a short rhythmic composition (without pitches) that illustrates predictability and surprise, acceleration and repose, thrust and stability.

Chapter 6

ELEMENTS OF MUSIC
Melody

MELODY

Successive notes of varying pitch and duration produce *melody*. Western melody—including Gregorian chant, folk songs, and composed melodies in all media—evidences certain common principles of motion. These common principles are discussed on pages 73-77.

CONTOUR

Melodic *contour* refers to shape and to the physical placement of pitches. By superimposing graphic or geometric designs over a staff, without the benefit of pitches and duration, one can create a basic outline that clearly illustrates the concept of melodic contour. Experimentations such as those in Example 87, including a subsequent filling-in of pitches, may not produce memorable and profound melody; yet the idea of contour and of the *visual* appearance of melody will have been realized.

Example 87

The number of possible melodic contours is infinite, since shape is the essence of creative imagination. The five examples that follow illustrate contour and gesture:

Example 88

a. Gregorian sequence

b. *THE SILVER SWAN* (excerpt)

Orlando Gibbons (1583-1625)

Observe the solution of balance, symmetry, and proportion in these 7 measures by Gibbons.

c. *DIDO AND AENEAS* (excerpt)

Ground bass

Henry Purcell (c. 1659-1695)

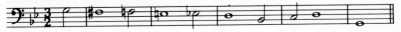

d. STRING QUARTET, OP. 3, NO. 5 (excerpt)

Haydn

e. *PRELUDE TO THE AFTERNOON OF A FAUN* (excerpt)

Claude Debussy (1862-1918)

DRAMATIC SHAPE

Examples 88d and e illustrate one of the most common melodic shapes in Western music, a series of gradually rising pitches that reach a primary high point at approximately two-thirds or three-quarters of the total time span. This contour, as well as any of the others quoted or observed, may also be applied to a composition as a whole. In that case the resultant contour is often referred to as the *dramatic shape* of music. Not infrequently, particular contours and dramatic shapes become part of a composer's identity. As an example, several of the melodies of Richard Strauss might be graphically shown as follows:

Example 89

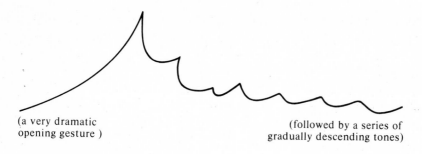

(a very dramatic
opening gesture)

(followed by a series of
gradually descending tones)

EIN HELDENLEBEN, OP. 40 (excerpt)

Richard Strauss (1864-1949)

By permission of Associated Music Publishers, Inc.

DON JUAN, OP. 20 (excerpt)

Strauss

Used by permission.

Similarly, Ernst Toch diagramed the whole of the *Meistersinger Prelude* of Richard Wagner (1813-1883) in the following fashion (Example 90):

Example 90

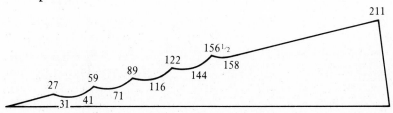

From Ernst Toch, *Shaping Forces in Music,* © 1948 Criterion Music Corp. Used by permission.

Melodic contour, as established by conjunct and disjunct motion, ascending and descending motion, "gravity," thrust and momentum, and high-low turning points, is infinite in its variety, behavior, and ability to fascinate.

CONJUNCT AND DISJUNCT MOTION

Melody of all periods and by all composers shows an interchange between *conjunct* (stepwise) and *disjunct* (by leap) motion. Example 91 illustrates:

Example 91

a. Gregorian plainsong

Ky - ri - e   e - le - i - son (ij)

Ky - ri - e   e - le - i - son

b. *L'HOMME ARMÉ*

Fifteenth-century folk song

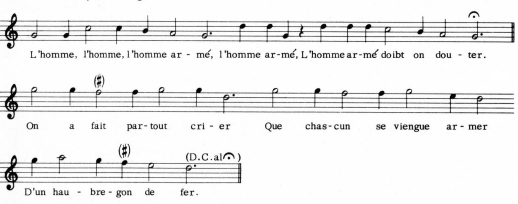

L'homme, l'homme, l'homme ar - mé, l'homme ar - mé, L'homme ar-mé doibt on dou - ter.

On   a   fait par-tout cri - er   Que chas-cun se viengue ar - mer

D'un hau - bre - gon de   fer.

The armed man is to be feared; everywhere it has been proclaimed that everyone should arm him-self with an iron coat of mail.

c. SYMPHONY NO. 104

First movement, eighteenth-century symphonic theme

Haydn

d. Nineteenth-century operatic motive (piano reduction)

Richard Wagner (1813-1883)

e. STRING QUARTET IN G MINOR

First movement, turn-of-the-century instrumental theme

Debussy

Permission for reprint granted by Durand & Cie, Paris, France, copyright owners; Elkan-Vogel Co., Philadelphia, Pa., agents.

f. *MUSIC FOR STRINGS, PERCUSSION, AND CELESTA*

Twentieth-century orchestral subject

Bartók

Copyright 1937 by Universal Edition. Copyright assigned to Boosey & Hawkes, Inc. Reprinted by permission.

Compare these examples with two invented fragments that do not balance conjunct and disjunct motion. In Example 92, the pitches become predictable *in kind.* Psychologically, one stops listening after a short period of time. Similarly, the constant disjunct motion of Example 93, while not exactly boring, does lack balance. Obviously there are occasions when a composer deliberately utilizes these types of consistent motion for reasons of predictability and variety within the total fabric of a composition.

Example 92

Example 93

ASCENDING AND DESCENDING MOTION

It is apparent that melody is also a balance of *ascending* and *descending* motion, as the previous examples illustrate. The movement in either direction can comprise short gestures, as in the Bartók subject, or encompass a broad range as in the opening of *Don Juan* by Richard Strauss, Example 94.

Example 94

DON JUAN, OP. 20

Opening theme

Strauss

GRAVITY

Melodic motion, in its physical behavior, may be compared to *gravity,* in that opposing directions seek accommodation. Observe the two "gravitational pulls" in Example 95:

Example 95

DOPO IL CREDO

Ricercar

Girolamo Frescobaldi (1583-1643)

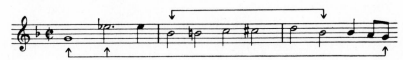

The above example might be compared to two objects thrown into the air: the one that achieves the greater distance—g^i eb^{ii} g^i—takes longer to descend than the one traveling a shorter distance—bb^i d^{ii} bb^i.

Countless physical analogies can be made to pitch gestures. One additional comparison (Example 96) will suffice for illustration:

Example 96

IMMER LEISER WIRD MEIN SCHLUMMER

Johannes Brahms (1833-1897)

The behavior is perhaps analogous to that of a *coil,* which gathers tension when compressed and springs back to its natural shape when released. Musically, tension occurs from X to Y; release is established at Z.

THRUST AND MOMENTUM

Thrust and momentum are difficult achievements without the dual components of pitch and duration sharing equally in tension and release.

Example 97

WELL-TEMPERED CLAVIER, Vol. I

Fugue 8 (excerpt)

J. S. Bach

In Example 97, thrust is effected at a, b, c, d, and e for a variety of reasons:

Disjunct motion followed by conjunct motion

Changes in direction

Tied rhythm

Increase in motion, accomplished by the introduction of smaller note values

The point of greatest tension in measures 1-3 is at *a;* secondary tension is at *b.* Initial and interceding beats are either neutral or have varying degrees of relaxation.

MELODIC CONSTRUCTION

The simplest yet most profound question one can ask when analyzing music is: How does the composer get from the first note to the last? The Bach fragment in Example 98 suggests several principles of *melodic construction.*

Control of high-low points

Control of contour (shape)

Control of tension and release

Implication of two voices from a single series

ANALYSIS OF BACH FRAGMENT

Example 98

OBSERVATIONS:

1. 1-13 constitute the pitch series for the *subject* of the *D♯ Minor Fugue.*
2. 3 is the primary high point (PHP).
3. 8 and 10 are secondary high points (SHP). Observe that these SHP's are not repeated consecutively.
4. 1 and 9 provide a tonic "anchor"; they are also primary low points (PLP).
5. 6 is a secondary low point (SLP); it is not repeated as a turning point.

FURTHER OBSERVATIONS:

1. Note the placement of 3, 8, 10 in time, which might be referred to as the "pacing of musical events."
2. Observe the spacing of relaxation (e.g., 4-7, 9, 11-13), which is nearly symmetrical after the first three pitches.
3. Note the placement of the secondary turning point (F♯ at 6), which occurs as the halfway point in terms of pitch, yet occurs at the beginning of measure 2 in terms of rhythmic organization. This conflict of placement is one of the many features that yield the physical and psychological bases of music.

The contour of the Bach fragment may be shown graphically as:

Example 99

Observe also that the high and low turning points begin to suggest that two ideas, or forces, are present in a single line:

Example 100

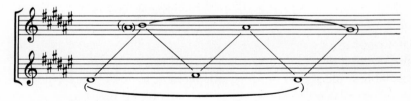

The basic musical gesture is probably the mainspring of composition. From this physical and psychological foundation, cells, motives, figures, subjects, themes, and so on can be fashioned in accordance with purely musical and expressive dictates.

CELL, FIGURE, MOTIVE

The terms *cell, figure,* and *motive* are seemingly used synonymously (and rather subjectively) to describe the smallest unit of musical measurement. Of the three, the *motive* appears to have the sharpest identity and the greatest tenacity within a musical framework. The length of a motive varies from 2 to 8 or 9 notes; typically, the pitches are related to an easily recognizable rhythmic pattern. One further characteristic might be that the motive is often a part of and contributes to a larger pitch series, such as a theme. The *figure*, without this latter quality, has a less sharp profile in general. *Cell* is a particularly useful term for describing the 2- or 3-note groupings, recognizable but elusive, that permeate so much of the music of the Middle Ages and the twentieth century.

SUBJECT, THEME

The term *subject*—used in the seventeenth and eighteenth centuries for all kinds of ideas—most typically refers to a short pitch series related to a contrapuntal composition such as invention, ricercar, or fugue. *Theme* is used to describe a longer pitch series, most often in connection with a homophonic movement such as sonata, rondo, or variations.

PHRASE, PERIOD

A *phrase* is an incomplete musical idea consisting of 6 to 8 notes in some examples of plainsong or chorales, or of 2 to 8 measures in traditional music. The *period* comprises 2 (or more) phrases, effecting a complete musical syntax. Much familiar music of the late eighteenth and nineteenth centuries, as well as an abundance of folk and popular music, contains a very orderly phrase-period organization:

Example 101

```
/_____period (often 8 measures)_____/
/_____phrase_____/   /_____phrase_____/
"incomplete" cadence                      "complete" cadence
        (progressive)                              (terminal)
```

In current usage, the terms *polyphonic* and *contrapuntal* are synonymous in meaning and denote the combination of two or more independent melodic lines. The term *counterpoint* (L. *punctus contra punctum*, point against point) may be accurately interpreted as melody against melody or *melodic combination.*

MELODIC COMBINATION

Even in the most linearly conceived compositions, the vertical aspects have always been considered. Fourteenth-century polyphony aspired to well-controlled intervals between the voices with a balance of perfect and imperfect consonant intervals; major and minor triads are the vertical resultants in sixteenth-century contrapuntal composition; eighteenth- and nineteenth-century polyphony was not infrequently derived from a specific harmonic progression. Since early in this century, contrapuntal works rarely fail to satisfy vertical logic. Polyphony differs from homophony in regard to rhythmic independence, interest between parts, and achieving of a meaningful melodic contour in each part.

Examples 102-105, drawn from the fifteenth century to the twentieth century, illustrate various principles of control:

Control of melodic contours
Control of rhythmic thrust
Control of the interval distance between voices
Control of consonance and dissonance

Example 102

MISSA SANCTI JACOBI (excerpt)

Fifteenth century

Guillaume Dufay (c. 1400-1474)

Example 103

AMOR CHE MI CONSIGLI? (excerpt)

Frottola

Constanzo Festa (c. 1490-1545)

Example 104

CHORALE PRELUDE (excerpt)

Samuel Scheidt (1587-1654)

Example 105

CHROMATIC INVENTION (excerpt)

Bartók

From *Mikroskosmos,* Vol. III, by Béla Bartók. © Copyright 1940, Boosey & Hawkes, Ltd., London. Used by permission.

SUBJECTIVE DESCRIPTION

Subjective descriptions of melody—as static, quiet, lively, or dramatic—are derived from the combination of several factors:

Tempo and dynamics
Conjunct or disjunct motion
Small or extended range

Even or jagged rhythms
Consistency or diverseness of ideas

Compare two examples:

Example 106

AGNUS DEI

From *Missa Sine Nomine*

Dufay

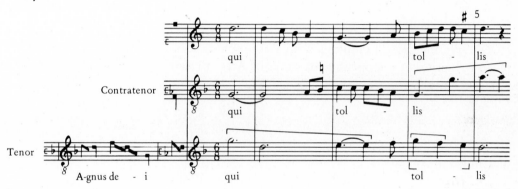

Example 107

MADAMA BUTTERFLY (excerpt)

Giacomo Puccini (1858-1924)

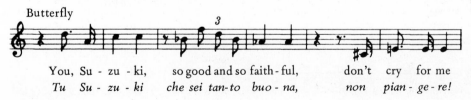

TYPES OF MOTION

Four types of melodic motion are associated with contrapuntal writing:

1. *Parallel:* in which the voices remain equidistant
2. *Similar:* in which the voices move in the same direction but change distance
3. *Oblique:* in which one voice remains stationary while the other(s) move
4. *Contrary:* in which the voices move in opposite directions

Example 108

a. Parallel   **b.** Similar

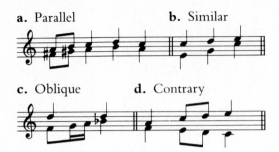

c. Oblique   **d.** Contrary

Observe the special employment of contrary motion in Example 109, which is a piano reduction of the opening measures of Arthur Honegger's *Symphony No. 5.*

Example 109

SYMPHONY NO. 5 (excerpt)

Piano reduction

Arthur Honegger (1892-1955)

Printed with authorization of Editions Salabert SA France, Copyright Editions Salabert, 1950. Piano reduction by Peter Hansen, *An Introduction to Twentieth Century Music,* Second Edition. © Copyright 1967 by Allyn and Bacon, Inc., Boston. Reprinted by permission of Allyn and Bacon, Inc.

CONTRAPUNTAL DEVICES

Contrapuntal devices refer to specific manipulations of pitches and their durations. A given melody, often called *cantus firmus* (L., fixed melody; pl. *cantus firmi*), is capable of appearing in several common forms:

Example 110

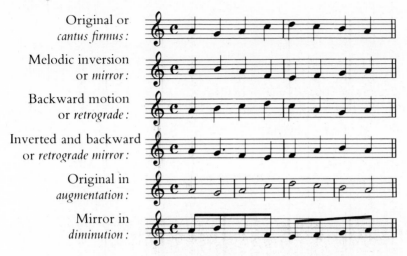

Original or *cantus firmus*:

Melodic inversion or *mirror*:

Backward motion or *retrograde*:

Inverted and backward or *retrograde mirror*:

Original in *augmentation*:

Mirror in *diminution*:

All these devices have been known and used by composers from at least the fourteenth century onward.

MELODIC SEQUENCE; IMITATION; CANON

Melodic sequence, imitation, and *canon* are compositional procedures that rely on the premise of *repetition.*

Melodic sequence is the repetition of a few notes or a short phrase at a different pitch level from the original. The repetition occurs *in the same voice.* Melodic sequence is observed in the music of all eras from the Medieval period to the present. The procedure provides for unity and continuity within a composition. Example 111 illustrates:

Example 111

BENEDICTUS (excerpt)

Monteverdi

ho-san - na in ex-cel - sis, in ex-cel - sis, in ex - cel - sis.

If several parts are repeated at a different pitch level, as is the case in the Monteverdi example, the procedure is typically called a *harmonic sequence.*

Imitation provides for a reiteration of a melodic idea in a *different voice*.

Example 112

DIES IRAE (excerpt)

Requiem Mass

Tomás Luis de Victoria (c. 1549-1611)

STIMMTAUSCH

Differentiation is made between the terms *imitation* and *voice exchange*. Exchange of notes between two parts without interval or octave modification is called *Stimmtausch* (Example 114).

Imitation probably dates from about the time of Perotin (c. 1225) and has been widely used ever since in both art and folk music. Imitation may be made of a few notes or of many. An entire composition in strict imitation is called a *canon* (Gk., law, rule).

CANON

Canon has an intriguing history, spanning more than 600 years. Of special interest to the music student are the riddle and mensural canons of the fifteenth and sixteenth centuries, the *Art of Fugue* and *Goldberg Variations* of Bach, and the canons of Webern and Dallapiccola in the twentieth century.

A canon in the Renaissance was any piece in which two (or more) people read differently from the same notation. The voices often began together but used different proportion signs and/or different clefs. For accurate performance, a directive was required. The directive was called *canon.*

Example 113

AGNUS DEI: EX UNA VOCE TRES

Mensuration canon

Josquin des Près (1450-1521)

Reprinted by permission of the publishers from Archibald T. Davidson and Willi Apel, HISTORICAL ANTHO-LOGY OF MUSIC, vol. 1, Cambridge, Mass.: Harvard University Press, Copyright 1949, by the President and Fellows of Harvard College.

Early names for compositions involving canonic procedure include *rota, rondellus,* or *round,* of which "Sumer is icumen in," dating from about 1300, is an example:

Example 114

SUMER IS ICUMEN IN

Haydn's three-voice canon can be sung forward or backward, either right side up or upside down. From these modest 6 measures an amazing number of possibilities can be projected if all versions and verses are sung.

Example 115

THE TEN COMMANDMENTS

Haydn

3 parts
Canon cancrizans (Crab canon)*

© 1966 by C. F. Peters Corporation, New York. Reprint permission granted by the publishers.

Igor Stravinsky's eloquent *In Memoriam Dylan Thomas* attests to the compositional vitality of canonic writing. The entire work is in three parts and was inspired by the poet's famous opening line "Do not go gentle into that good night." The composer utilizes a five-tone "set" that is subjected to the devices of inversion, retrograde, and retrograde-inversion. Example 116 illustrates.

*Haydn's text on receiving an honorary doctorate from Oxford University.

Example 116

IN MEMORIAM DYLAN THOMAS (excerpt)

Prelude

Igor Stravinsky (1882-1971)

Copyright 1954 by Boosey & Hawkes, Inc. Reprinted by permission.

RICERCAR, FUGUE, INVENTION

Ricercar (It. *ricercare*, to seek out), *fugue* (L. *fuga*, flight), and *invention* (L. *inventio*) are polyphonic compositions employing imitative counterpoint. There is no set "form" for any of these compositions, although a few general observations regarding procedure can be made.

IMITATIVE RICERCAR:

1. As the instrumental counterpart to the sixteenth-century vocal motet, the ricercar usually has four or five independent voices.
2. Often, but not always, the ricercar is polythematic.
3. The ricercar is generally considered to have been the predecessor of the seventeenth- and eighteenth-century fugue.
4. Some examples are to be found in the twentieth century, among them, two in Stravinsky's *Cantata* (1951).

Example 117

ARIADNE MUSICA (excerpt)

Fugue

Johann Kaspar Ferdinand Fischer (c. 1665-1746)

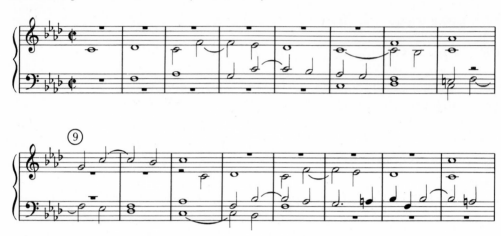

Johann Kaspar Ferdinand Fischer's *Ariadne Musica* represents an important collection of preludes and fugues preceding the 48 preludes and fugues of J. S. Bach. Several of Fischer's fugues suggest a transition from the ricercar type to the highly developed fugues of Bach and Handel.

FUGUE:

1. Each fugue is written in a set number of voices; two-voice to five-voice are commonly found, with three or four parts being the norm.
2. Each voice is independent and participates in presenting the principal melodic material (subject).
3. The repetition of the subject, usually at the fifth above or the fourth below, is called an *answer*.
4. In the highly developed fugues of the eighteenth century, there is usually a *minimum* tonal scheme of at least three parts (e.g., tonic-dominant-tonic).
5. There are numerous fugues to be found in twentieth-century music literature; *Ludus Tonalis,* by Paul Hindemith, contains excellent examples.

INVENTION:

1. Bach used the title "Inventiones" for fifteen two-part contrapuntal studies.
2. In this collection, each voice is of equal importance and participates in presenting, developing, and summarizing the musical ideas.
3. Some of the Bach *Inventions* illustrate specific constructive techniques, such as:
   a. motivic development: C major, e minor
   b. strict canon and invertible counterpoint (exchange of voices): c minor
   c. mirrors: E major
4. Imitation is usually at the octave, rather than at the fifth.
5. Several twentieth-century composers have written sets of inventions; the scenes of Act III of Alban Berg's opera *Wozzeck* are entitled "Inventions."

CHAPTER SUMMARY

Successive notes of varying pitch and duration produce melody. The term *contour* refers to the shape of melody. Although the possibilities are infinite, the contours of many Western melodies contain a balance of conjunct and disjunct motion and a careful control of ascending and descending motion, as well as a balance of tension and release. Cell, figure, motive, subject, theme, phrase, and period are units of musical measurement that may apply to melodic organization.

Two or more independent lines, sounding simultaneously, effect a polyphonic or contrapuntal texture. Four types of melodic motion are associated with contrapuntal writing: parallel, similar, oblique, and contrary. Contrapuntal devices refer to specific manipulations of pitches and their durations. These include: melodic inversion, retrograde motion, combined retrograde and inversion, augmentation and diminution.

Melodic sequence, imitation, and canon are compositional procedures that rely on the premise of repetition. Ricercar, fugue, and invention are polyphonic compositions employing imitative counterpoint.

SUGGESTED STUDIES

1. Examine melodies from diverse eras for observation of conjunct-disjunct balance; for constructive techniques of cell, figure, and motive; and for the graphic and dramatic shapes they present.
2. Examine melodies which utilize the devices of inversion, retrograde, and diminution.
3. Subject a melody of your choice to the devices of inversion, retrograde, and augmentation.
4. Write an original short canon; musical style should not be a consideration.
5. Analyze Bach's *Invention 1* (Example 118) for melodic contours, treatment of subject, derivation of other musical ideas, and the overall design of the piece.

Example 118

INVENTION 1

Bach

Chapter 7

ELEMENTS OF MUSIC
Color

Timbre denotes the quality, or "color," of a tone, which, as previously stated, is determined by the relative intensity of the overtones.

COLOR

Color is a term most typically used to describe instrumental combinations. "Dark" and "bright" are in common usage and, although subjective, do have a physical basis, provided by a conflict (or lack thereof) of multiple overtone series. In *highly exaggerated* dynamics, two chords with their partials are illustrated (each sounding note is in itself a fundamental):

Example 119

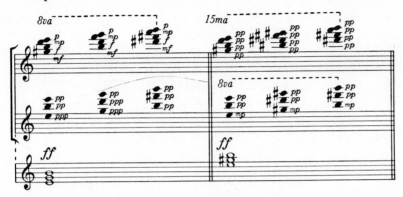

a. Three oboes   **b.** Three flutes

The fourth and fifth harmonics on the oboe are prominent, which not only accounts for its so-called nasal quality but also presents strong conflicts among the overtones when the three oboes are scored chordally (Example 119). (Observe the "rub" of the G♯-G♮'s; of the D♮-D♯'s.) For the flutes, however (Example 119), the most prominent overtone is the second partial, establishing a "clearer" basic tone and presenting fewer conflicts when used vertically. The major third is also a significant reason for the brighter sound.

INSTRUMENTATION

THE ORCHESTRAL PAGE

Initial observations concerning an orchestral page include:

1. The order of instruments from top to bottom is: woodwinds; brasses; percussion; harp (also piano; solo, if any; voices, if any); and strings (Example 122).
2. In most instances, the instruments within each section are placed from high-sounding to low-sounding. The principal exception is that horns, which relate to both woodwinds and brass, are placed above trumpets on the page.
3. The tempo indication is placed above the woodwinds and often above the strings.
4. Dynamics are placed below the notes for instruments, and above the notes for voices.
5. The variety of key signatures is caused by the fact that some instruments are *transposing* instruments (i.e., sound at a different interval than written).

TRANSPOSITION

Standard orchestral instruments that *transpose* are the English horn, clarinet, French horn, and trumpet. The piccolo sounds an octave higher than written, while the double bass and contrabassoon sound an octave lower. Transpositions are named according to the note that sounds when a written C is played. In all cases, it is a matter of exact compensation. For example, any instrument sounding a major second lower must be written a major second higher than the desired concert pitch. Common transpositions are illustrated in Example 120.

Key signatures often correspond to the transposition interval. Therefore, for a composition in C major, the signatures will correspond to those illustrated in Example 121.

Twentieth-century compositions without key signatures will typically have no signatures for the orchestral instruments, although the usual transpositions will be in effect.

In current practice, one also observes scores that are written at concert pitch. The composer usually mentions this fact on the title or instruction page. In such cases, transpositions must be made for the performers' parts (i.e., one does not expect the performer to transpose at sight or to write out the transposition).

Example 120

All *written* notes to sound c^1:

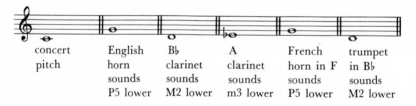

| concert pitch | English horn sounds P5 lower | B♭ clarinet sounds M2 lower | A clarinet sounds m3 lower | French horn in F sounds P5 lower | trumpet in B♭ sounds M2 lower |

The trumpet in F sounds a perfect fourth higher than written.

Example 121

| concert | English horn, French horn in F | trumpet, clarinet in B♭ | clarinet in A |

INSTRUMENTS

A knowledge of instrumental ranges, transpositions, relative dynamic strength in each register, the individual sound in combination with other instruments, and special effects is essential for an inquiring musician. Possible and practical ranges, together with transpositions, are listed below.

Example 122

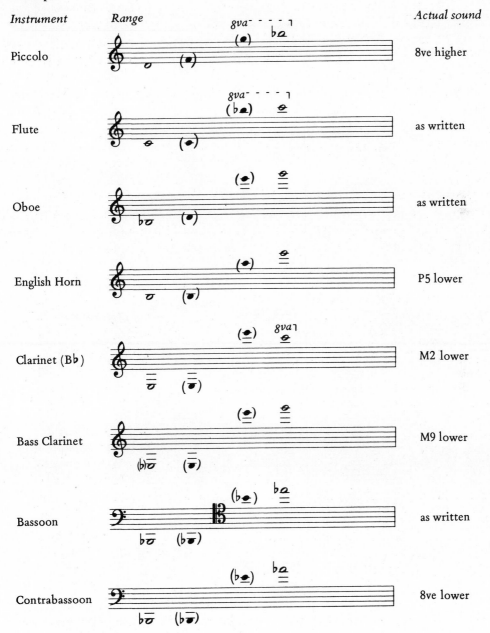

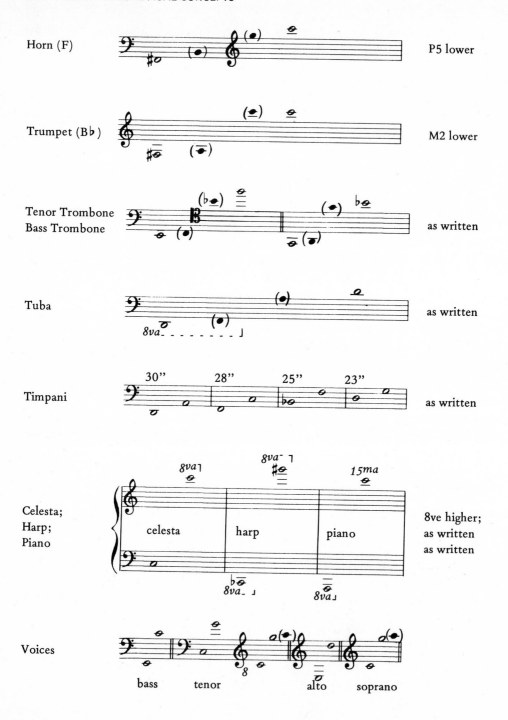

Horn (F)   P5 lower

Trumpet (Bb)   M2 lower

Tenor Trombone
Bass Trombone   as written

Tuba   as written

Timpani   as written

Celesta;   8ve higher;
Harp;   as written
Piano   as written

Voices

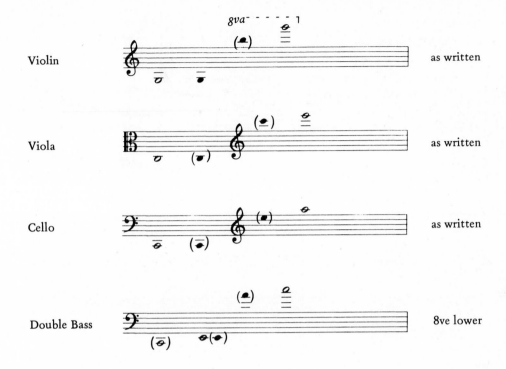

It is suggested that, if possible, each instrument be demonstrated in the classroom.

The excerpt from *Romeo and Juliet* (Example 123) reveals several principles of traditional scoring.

OBSERVATIONS:

Measure 1. The string sonorities are balanced in terms of weight and dynamics.
The harp adds color—observe the dynamic specification.
A low pedal is provided by the bassoon.
Punctuation comes from the plucked double bass.

Measure 2. Flutes and oboes, staggered in their entries, provide motion.

Measure 3. The melodic line is high and bright and is capable of penetrating through the orchestral mass.
The remaining woodwinds effect a harmonic background.
A single horn carries a countermotive—observe the high tessitura.
The violins and violas have a textural function—observe dynamic.
Cellos and double basses punctuate.

Example 123

ROMEO AND JULIET (excerpt)

Peter Ilyich Tschaikovsky (1840-1893)

The twentieth century has elicited new attitudes from most composers regarding orchestral scoring. Example 124 illustrates a few techniques of more recent vintage: disposition in opposition to the overtone series, multiple pedals, *Klangfarben* (see p. 407) procedures, and improvisation:

Example 124

CHAPTER SUMMARY

Timbre denotes the quality, or "color," of a tone; this quality is determined by the relative intensity of the overtones.

Instruments of diverse timbres, ranges, and special capabilities are combined to form a standard modern orchestra. In scoring for the orchestra, the notated page has a set order of instruments from top to bottom: woodwinds, brasses, percussion, and strings. Additional instruments, such as harp, piano, voices, and so on, are placed above the strings.

Transposing instruments include the English horn, clarinets, French horn, and trumpet. The piccolo sounds an octave higher than written, while the double bass and contrabassoon sound an octave lower.

*Clarinet and horns are written at concert pitch.

SUGGESTED STUDIES

1. Transcribe about 16 measures of the vocal line of a Schubert (or similar) song for a clarinet in B♭.
2. Learn the range and transposition (if any) for each of the orchestral instruments that have been listed.
3. Compose an imitative duo for two single-line instruments of about 18 measures. Consideration of the following points is recommended:

   a. Careful control of melodic lines—conjunct-disjunct balance, good rhythmic flow.
   b. Control of consonance-dissonance.
   c. *Consistency* of pitch materials: modal, tonal, or nontonal are all acceptable possibilities. But use only *one* category.
   d. Use instruments in their sonorous ranges—avoiding excessively high or low ranges in woodwinds and brasses.
   e. Manuscript should be neat and clearly legible, with large, black notes (and rests).
   f. The project should be performed in class.

Chapter 8

COMBINATION OF ELEMENTS
Texture
Musical Synthesis
(Form in Music)

TEXTURE

Texture is a term that is applied to a number of phenomena in music. The common descriptions of texture—monophonic, polyphonic, homophonic, and heterophonic—identify density and function.

Monophony and polyphony emphasize the horizontal dimension of music; homophony underscores the vertical dimension; heterophony is a combination of these two dimensions.

Example 125

Monophony (single-line melody, unaccompanied): Gregorian Chant

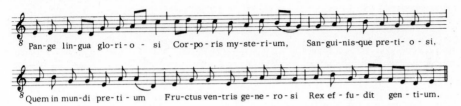

Polyphony is two or more simultaneous melodic lines. Actually, *polyphonic* meant *written* as several parts. "Familiar polyphony" was chordal (note for note) as of c. 1470. Today, chordal passages are typically referred to as *homophonic*.

Example 126

Polyphony:*KYRIE* (excerpt)

From *Missa Sine Nomine*

Dufay

Homophony is three or more tones sounding simultaneously with essentially the same rhythm in each voice. It embraces many different kinds of music—for example, hymns, Bach's settings of chorales, Chopin's waltzes, and Brahms' Intermezzi, as well as examples similar to the Mozart fragment in Example 127.

---

*Brackets are sometimes used in modern transcription to show the original ligatures.

Example 127

Homophony *THE MAGIC FLUTE* (excerpt)

Wolfgang Amadeus Mozart (1756-1791)

Heterophony is the elaboration, in time, of one melody or harmony.

Example 128

THE SHROVE-TIDE FAIR

First tableau from *Petrushka*

Stravinsky

Texture plays a far more important role in music than is often understood. A dense, low-register passage probably suggests a different mood and set of connotations for the listener than a texture that is produced from two or three lines in the middle or high registers. Three examples are presented below that may evoke such subjective descriptions as "light," "heavy," "thick," and so forth.

Example 129

DA CAPO ARIA

From *Alarico*

Agostino Steffani (1654-1728)

Example 130

ADAGIO, SYMPHONY NO. 6, OP. 74 (excerpt)

Piano reduction

Tschaikovsky

Example 131

KLAVIERSTUECK, OP. 33a (excerpt)

Arnold Schoenberg (1874-1951)

With the development of idiomatic instrumental music, commencing about 1600, texture per se gradually assumed equal status and prominence with the other primary elements. Harmonic oscillations, inner pedals, and "accompaniment figurations" are methods of providing a backdrop for a musical action in the foreground. Stravinsky's *Petrushka,* Example 128, is a superb illustration. Other excellent examples would include Vivaldi's concerti, the late symphonies of Mozart, the Beethoven symphonies, the large orchestral works of Debussy and Ravel, the early ballets of Stravinsky, Opus 16 of Schoenberg, *Threnody* of Penderecki, *Atmosphères* of Ligeti. All of these works contain extended passages that are essentially nonthematic. In such instances, textures establish a continuity of sound and even suggest a third dimension of music.

ACCOMPANIMENT FIGURATIONS

Accompaniment figurations are significant not only for orchestral textures; they often provide as well the "harmony in motion" that supports a melodic idea in a substantial amount of eighteenth- and nineteenth-century keyboard music. Four examples illustrate common usage.

ALBERTI BASS

Named after Domenico Alberti (1710-1740?), the *Alberti bass* consists of broken-chord figurations, useful as middle-range accompanimental texture. Although overused and maligned, the Alberti bass offers rhythmic viability in an otherwise static harmonic situation (see Example 132).

Example 132

PIANO SONATA, K. 545 (excerpt)

From the first movement

Mozart

Classical accompanimental configurations are modified in the nineteenth and twentieth centuries to accommodate style. Their musical function, however, remains the same—to provide motion.

Example 133

PRELUDE, OP. 28, NO. 1 (excerpt)

Frédéric Chopin (1809-1849)

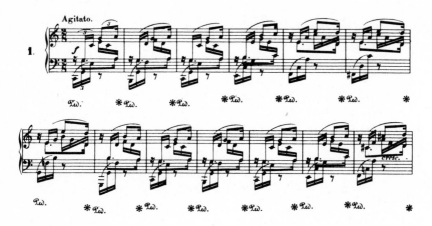

Example 134

PRELUDE Op. 28, NO. 24 (excerpt)

Chopin

In Example 135 we see a twentieth-century solution, similar to that of Stravinsky or Bartók (see *Petrushka* or Bartók's *Third Piano Concerto*).

Example 135

Seventeen measures, excerpted from Mozart's *Concerto for Piano and Orchestra*, K. 595 (Example 136), illustrate the function and importance of texture in this late Classical composition.

Example 136

PIANO CONCERTO, K. 595 (excerpt)

Mozart

OBSERVATIONS:

1. Superimposed on the piano solo are light woodwind textures that "breathe" (measures 2-7).
2. The woodwind background changes from detached to sustained (measures 2-7 versus 8-10),
3. The strings add a new color and dynamic (measure 10).
4. The strings of measure 10 *generate* the solo of measure 11.
5. The strings in measures 14-16 relate to the solo of measures 1-7.

Two additional examples of orchestral texture attest to the significance of this parameter, Examples 137 and 138.

Example 137

DAPHNIS ET CHLOÉ

Maurice Ravel (1875-1937)

Example 138
CONCERTO FOR ORCHESTRA (1943)
First movement
Bartók

I
(INTRODUZIONE)

SPATIAL ORGANIZATION (A third dimension)

Although music is usually referred to as being two-dimensional, a third dimension is both seen and heard, especially in orchestral music. Example 139 charts a hypothetical orchestral passage:

Example 139

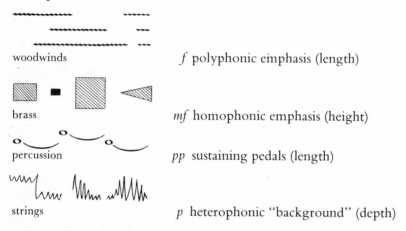

woodwinds   *f* polyphonic emphasis (length)

brass   *mf* homophonic emphasis (height)

percussion   *pp* sustaining pedals (length)

strings   *p* heterophonic "background" (depth)

These differing functions and dynamics provide for "layers of sound," not dissimilar to a third dimension. Gabrieli's polychoral works, the Berlioz and Benjamin Britten *Requiems,* Varèse's *Poème Électronique,* are all compositions that insist on a spatial organization of sound sources (i.e., wide separation of the different instrumental, vocal, or electronic "choirs"). Such arrangements tend to emphasize the dimension of depth.

MUSICAL SYNTHESIS

Synthesis is the combination of separate substances, elements, or subordinate parts into a new construction or composition. The term might well be used, especially in initial studies, as a replacement for "form," which has variable meanings as well as implied limitations.

FORM IN MUSIC

A musical composition is the combination of pitches, durations, timbres, and, in most music, simultaneities of sound. Any such combination, placed in time, will create shape, design—or, in current musical parlance, *form*. In broadest terms, a composition is a sequence of musical events. Another definition, attributed to Pierre Boulez, is that of "a counterpoint of sound and silence." These definitions are, of course, entirely quantitative. Yet any group of sounds that "puncture" silence—no matter how seemingly disparate, illogical, or mutually incompatible—do produce shape. In short, nothing exists in time or space without *shape*.

One of the most succinct yet meaningful and accurate definitions of form states: "Form is the sum of those qualities in a piece of music that bind together its parts and animate the whole."[1]

In discussing musical form, the phrase "form *in* music" is often applied. This is a broad phrase possibly implying a predetermined *design* of some kind. Its use is preferable, however, to use of "forms *of* music," for in that phrase lies the persistent connotation of a mold into which the composer pours the musical elements and a few performance instructions.

There is no one fugal *form* nor, indeed, one sonata *form* or rondo *form;* it is the very diversity of these procedures and general designs that, in part, renders them worthy of aural and intellectual consideration. Investigation of Western music from all periods seems to suggest, instead, *principles of organization* that apply, in varying degrees, to broad categories of musical design.

Organization requires control. From among the numerous factors of control considered by the composer, a few of the most essential are cited:

CONTROL FACTORS

1. Control of dynamic and static gestures
2. Control of repetition and variation principles
3. Control of internal arrival points
4. Control of phrasing and cadencing
5. Control of tonal orientations or implications
6. Control of texture and color
7. Control of the pacing of musical events, assisted by tempo and dynamics
8. Control of the relationships between the subparts and the whole (i.e., microform-macroform correlations)

LOGIC AND COHERENCE

No single set of axioms guarantees a satisfying design; yet these control factors can, in the best of circumstances, achieve the ultimate goals of musical design, which are *logic* and *coherence*.

---

[1]Wallace Berry, *Form in Music* (Englewood Cliffs, N. J.: Prentice-Hall, 1966), Preface, unnumbered.

PRINCIPLES OF ORGANIZATION

The following five principles may assist in the understanding of musical organization:

1. *Principle of contrast:*
   (I, of musical ideas):

a	b		binary (bipartite)
a	b	a	ternary (tripartite), aria

2. *Principle of contrast:*
   (II, of tonal schemes):

first tonal area	second tonal area	varied tonal areas	first tonal area

   sonata (single movement)

3. *Principle of repetition:*

   a   a   a   a   etc., or   strophic
   ab ab ab ab etc.

   a   b   a   c   a   d   a...   rondeau, ritornello
   A B A(') C A(')   small rondo
   A B A(') C A('') B(') A(''')   large rondo

4. *Principle of variation:*
   a. An idea subjected to a changing environment, or

   cantus firmus mass
   ricercar
   fugue
   passacaglia
   chaconne

   b. A musical idea constantly modified

   Baroque, Classic, Romantic variations

5. *Principle of contiguity:*
   A constantly evolving matrix of sound. The German term *durchkomponiert* (through-composed) has similar implications

   through-composed songs
   most canons
   "continual" variations

It is immediately apparent that most compositions combine two or more of these organizing principles. Perhaps the greatest obstacle to a musical understanding of new or unfamiliar music is the elusiveness of the design or one's lack of comprehension of it. It is essential that one should learn, through listening and analyzing, to grasp the architectural and dramatic shapes of music and the relationship of the parts to the totality. Since no two pieces are identical, it is reasonable to suggest that each composition be accepted (or rejected) on, and in, its own terms.

CHAPTER SUMMARY

Texture is a term that applies to a number of phenomena in music. Common descriptions are: monophonic, polyphonic, homophonic, and heterophonic. Monophony and polyphony emphasize the horizontal dimension of music; homophony underscores the vertical dimension; heterophony is a combination of these two dimensions.

Accompaniment figurations are significant not only for orchestral textures; they often provide as well the "harmony in motion" that supports a melodic idea in a substantial amount of eighteenth- and nineteenth-century keyboard music. One such figuration is called an Alberti bass.

Musical synthesis is the combination of separate substances, elements, or subordinate parts into a new construction or composition. Synthesis refers to form in music. "Form is the sum of those qualities in a piece of music that bind together its parts and animate the whole."

Principles of organization include:

Principle of contrast:
    I, of musical ideas
    II, of tonal schemes
Principle of repetition
Principle of variation
Principle of contiguity

Most compositions combine two or more of these organizing principles.

SUGGESTED EXPERIMENT

Spatial organization may be realized by playing a different instrument, pitch, and dynamic from each corner of a classroom. Under such conditions, an ordinary e minor triad will suddenly have new life and potential.

Example 140

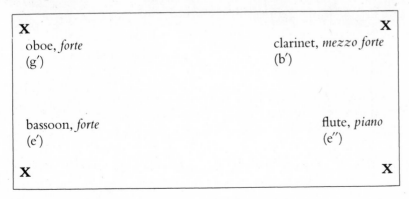

X	**X**
oboe, *forte* (g′)	clarinet, *mezzo forte* (b′)
bassoon, *forte* (e′)	flute, *piano* (e″)
X	**X**

SUGGESTED STUDIES

1. It is suggested that readings be undertaken on the procedures and forms cited on the preceding pages. Possible sources: *Harvard Dictionary; Groves' Dictionary of Music and Musicians.*
2. Aural analysis, observing the principles of organization, is recommended.
3. Basic study of phrase and period structure, as well as of simple binary and ternary principles, should be made.
4. Sing, perform, and analyze the following example. Be prepared to discuss repetition, contrast, and contiguity. The remaining parts of this second movement consist of four variations on the given 20 measures.

Example 141

STRING QUARTET, OP. 76, NO. 3

Second movement

Haydn

PART II

THE TRIADIC BASIS

"Everything is in flux."

—Heraclitus, c. 500 B.C.

Chapter 9

ARS ANTIQUA AND ARS NOVA

HARMONIC EVOLUTION

The tertian system evolved over a span of several hundred years—its emergence, development, and supercession generally relating to the broad period 1450 to 1950.*
The term *tertian* (L. *tertianus,* third) simply refers to the calculation and organization of pitches in series of thirds: C E G B D F A C.

Certainly numerous influences contrived to effect the orderly and sophisticated tertian system. Initial investigation should consider both sacred and secular musical composition; melody and harmony as separate, interrelated, and combined evolutions; and the countless X-factors of insatiable curiosity and experimentation on the part of musicians.

ARS ANTIQUA

In several respects, the origins of the tertian system can be traced to the twelfth and thirteenth centuries. That period is referred to as the *Ars Antiqua* (Old Art) by modern writers, to differentiate it from the fourteenth century, called the *Ars Nova* (New

---

*Willi Apel gives these dates as 1450-1900.

Art). For nearly 150 years the Ars Antiqua was dominated by French composers, particularly by Léonin (mid-twelfth century) and Pérotin (late twelfth and early thirteenth centuries), both of whom composed and taught at Notre Dame in Paris.

Rhythm in the Ars Antiqua relied chiefly on the rhythmic modes (review the table on p. 48). In some forms—for example, the *polyphonic conductus*—the parts have essentially the same rhythm. In other forms, however—for example, the *Paris Motet*— the lower voice (the tenor) typically uses a slower-moving rhythm than the two upper voices:

Example 142

AUCUN–LONC TANS–ANNUNTIANTES

Motet*

Petrus de Cruce (d. c. 1300)

*Motet: (Fr. *mot,* word)

X = vertical instances of thirds or sixths. Clearly, these sonorities are rhythmically *weak;* perfect octaves and fifths are rhythmically *strong.*

Important legacies from the period are the rhythmic independence of the voices in polyphonic music as well as the natural rhythm of secular monophonic compositions written and performed by *trouvères, troubadours,* and *Minnesinger.* Triple time (*tempus perfectum*) prevailed, but one also frequently observes duple time with perfect prolation ($\frac{6}{8}$ ♪♪♪ ♪♪♪). Melodic shape was curvilinear (Example of Petrus de Cruce), with considerable conjunct motion interrupted by occasional leaps of thirds, fourths, and fifths. However, in melodic combination (two or more voices simultaneously) all intervals are used in various combinations. Although octaves, unisons, and perfect fifths are preeminent, thirds and sixths gain substantial acceptance.

An extraordinarily beautiful example of twelfth-century music is the Latin *Hymn to St. Magnus,* which comes from England rather than from the Paris schools. The example illustrates an organum in thirds—a decidedly unique deviation from continental practices, which still favored organum in perfect fourths or perfect fifths. The English practice of singing in consecutive thirds is called *gymel* (from L. *cantus gemelus,* twin song).

Example 143

HYMN TO ST. MAGNUS

Twelfth century

Et tu - tor lau - da - bi - lis, tu - os sub - di - tos

Ser - va car - nis fra - gi - lis mo - le po - si - tos.

Organum in various styles continued to be composed, as well as the principal forms of the Ars Antiqua. These included:

Clausula—The tenor was derived from a short fragment or melisma from the Alleluia. To this cantus firmus one or two upper voices were added in faster-moving note values (see Example 152).

Motet—(See Example 142) Originally the upper voices were set to religious texts in Latin. During the late thirteenth century French texts were introduced, first for the upper voices and subsequently for all three voices.

Rondel (or rondellus)—The rondel is a polyphonic form using the principle of exchange. Different phrases or motives were exchanged among the three voices, for example:

upper voice	a	b	c
middle voice	b	c	a
lower voice	c	a	b
(tenor)			

The principle is very significant because it contributed to the development of imitation and canon.

Rondeau—(Example 144) The rondeau is a form built on the principle of repetition—for example, A B a A a b A B. The rondeau uses a text in the vernacular.

Example 144
TANT CON JE VIVRAI
Rondeau
Adam de la Halle (c. 1230-1287)

1. 4. 7. Tant con je vi- vrai 2. 8. N'a- me- rai au- trui que mi.
3. Jà n'en par- ti- rai 6. Loi- au- ment mis
5. Ains vous ser- vi- rai vous tous.

Conductus—A form freely composed on an original tenor. Of special interest to the development of Western music is the fact that all the voices move in essentially uniform rhythm, possibly foreshadowing the "familiar style" of the fifteenth and sixteenth centuries (see Example 145), the chorale style of the seventeenth and eighteenth centuries, and perhaps homophonic texture in general.

Example 145

HAC IN ANNI JANUA

Three-voice conductus, early thirteenth century

Although the Conductus (Example 145) was probably composed by a method referred to as *successive counterpoint*—that is, each of the upper voices is calculated intervalically from the tenor—the simultaneity of these three voices produces sonorities of both beauty and interest. The invervals between the voices of the Conductus are shown for the first four measures.

upper two voices

5 3 2 1 3 5 7 8 | 3 3 5 5 3 | 3 1 3 3 5 4 3 3 | 6 4 3 1 3

lower two voices

8 6 5 3 1 2 3 4 | 3 1 3 5 3 (2) | 5 3 1 3 3 5 | 5 3 1 3 (2)

Tabulation reveals the following:

Unisons	7
Seconds	4
Thirds	22
Fourths	3
Fifths	10
Sixths	1
Sevenths	1
Octaves	2

Further, a reduction in the first 4 measures of just the strong beats suggests the origins of the tertian system.

Example 146

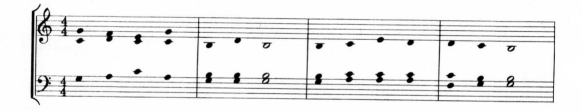

The simultaneities show a kind of embellishment of GB or GBD in a manner not too dissimilar to that found in some twentieth-century works—for example, *Farben*, by Schoenberg (Example 368) or Terry Riley's *In C*. If the upper voices are performed by two instruments of different colors, the resultant colors and textures are at once static yet variegated, simple but complex.

SECULAR MONOPHONIC SONG

Aside from its poignant beauty, the Minnesinger *May-Song* provides abundant insight into the art of *secular* monophonic song of the early thirteenth century.

Example 147

MINNESINGER *MAY-SONG*

Neidhart von Reuental (c. 1180-1240)

Transcribed by Edith Borroff. Used by permission.

OBSERVATIONS:

1. The composition suggests motivic construction; the rhythmic figure ♩ ♪♩. is a modal pattern, and numerous repetitions occur throughout the course of the song.

2. The phrases are defined by the text, by contrast and repetition, and by tonal orientations.
3. The first two lines of the *May-Song* form a *period,* comprising two phrases.
4. The seven phrases effect a *closed form:*

   A (ab)   A (ab)   B (c)   A (ab)
   period   period   phrase (?)   period

   A fascinating feature of this design is the functioning of *phrase c* as a complete period (*B*).
5. Regular rhythmic groupings occur throughout (a compound duple meter is suggested).
6. The line is curvilinear with considerable disjunct motion.
7. The tonal orientation, within the octave d^i a^i d^{ii}—with the final d^i—is Dorian in character; the sixth degree is nearly avoided; an emphasis on g^i occurs in phrase 5, suggesting an early equivalent to modulation.
8. Tertian orientation is clearly suggested—to the extent that the *May-Song* becomes a study in thirds; substructure notes of phrases 1 and 2 establish two triads:

   a^i d^{ii} a^i f^i d^i f^i a^i (g^i) d^i (circled notes)

ARS NOVA

The fourteenth century witnessed extraordinary developments in literature, painting, and music. Italy, France, and England all produced prolific and masterful composers.

Rhythm in the Ars Nova became freer, abandoning strict adherence to the rhythmic modes. Late fourteenth-century French secular music embraces a degree of rhythmic complexity not again observed until the twentieth century; the triple division of the pulse is still predominant, but the duple division of the pulse gained acceptance, and was used equally by the mid- to late fourteenth century.

Three rhythmic devices are commonly identified with the period:

Hocket is a device that interrupts by rests the normal flow of the line (Example 148, upper voice measure 10, measure 22).

Syncopation is a device of temporal suspense and contributes to a kind of *rubato* in the texture (Example 148, measures 8, 20, 23).

Isorhythm provides for the reiteration of rhythmic patterns two to many measures in length (Example 148, tenor, measures 1-4). The rhythmic pattern is called *talea.* There is also a repetition of melodic segments, called *color,* which normally does not coincide with the talea.

As a result of the rhythmic freedom, melody quite naturally becomes more florid than in the Ars Antiqua. Although a preponderance of melodic intervals are seconds and thirds, one observes also the upward leap of a major sixth (Example 148, measures 21-22), or even the upward leap of a major seventh (Example 148, measure 17).

One of the most remarkable single musical compositions of the fourteenth century is the *Messe de Notre Dame* of Guillaume de Machaut (1300-1377).

Example 148

KYRIE IV

The Gregorian Chant; cantus firmus for the tenor

Ky -ri - e   e - - -   le - i - son *(3 times)*

KYRIE

From *Messe de Notre Dame*

Guillaume de Machaut (1300-1377)

The Mass is a unique work for several reasons: it is the first complete polyphonic setting of the ordinary of the mass by a single composer; unlike previous models it is a unified whole rather than a collection of settings; its four-voice texture anticipates common acceptance of this number of voices by nearly a hundred years; nearly one-half of the "vertical coincidences"—that is, chords—are complete triads containing what today we call a root, third, and fifth (marked X). Although a majority of these sonorities have the root of the triad in the lowest-sounding voice, occasionally the third of the triad is the lowest pitch (marked Y).

Example 149
KYRIE I
From *Messe de Notre Dame*
Guillaume de Machaut

The cadence in measures 26-27 is of particular interest in its vii-i movement and the double leading tones: C♯ to D and G♯ to A.

Example 150

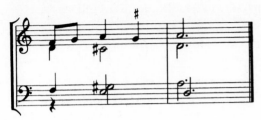

CHAPTER SUMMARY

The tertian system evolved over a span of several hundred years from c. 1450 to c. 1950. The term refers to calculation and organization of pitches in series of thirds: C E G B D F A C.

In several respects, the origins of the tertian system can be traced to the twelfth and thirteenth centuries. These centuries are referred to as the *Ars Antiqua*. Rhythm in the Ars Antiqua relied chiefly on the rhythmic modes; the intervals of pitch employed were principally octaves, unisons, and perfect fifths, although thirds and sixths gained substantial acceptance.

Several forms emerged, which included: clausula, motet, rondel, rondeau, and conductus. Secular monophonic song was abundantly composed and offers great insight into the musical art of the thirteenth century.

The fourteenth century is referred to as the *Ars Nova*. During this century extraordinary developments took place in literature, painting, and music.

Rhythm in the Ars Nova became freer and eventually very complex. Three rhythmic devices are commonly identified with the period: hocket, syncopation, and isorhythm.

Melody becomes more florid than that of previous centuries. Three-voice texture is predominant, although Machaut's setting of the Ordinary of the Mass is in four voices.

SUGGESTED STUDIES

1. Sing and analyze the following *Trouvère Ballade:*

Example 151

TROUVÈRE BALLADE

Colin Muset (after 1234)

Transcribed by Edith Borroff. Used by permission.

Be able to discuss the following points:

a. The types of melodic construction: cells, motives, and so on.
b. The internal organization: by phrases, periods, or other groupings
c. The overall design
d. The rhythmic groupings; the implied meters
e. The modal characteristics; the tonal orientation
f. Cadence practice

2.

Example 152

CLAUSULA (excerpt)

For *Hec Dies;* early thirteenth century, in the style of Perotin

Be able to discuss the following points:

a. The source and purpose of "clausulae"
b. The rhythmic features of the example, paying particular attention to the lower voice
c. The vertical or "harmonic" intervals between the two voices
d. Internal organization: by means of repetition, contrast, and variation

3.

Example 153

BALLATA

Francesco Landini (1325-1397)

3 (2) Non trovando all' affanno
   Rimedio alcun, tanto sono in martire

4 (1) Et assai mi raggiri
   Che ne' pensier mi paia aver fallato.
   Ma pur s' i' sono errato
   Piacciati farne chiara la mie mente.

5 (1) De'! sospirar . . .

a. Diagram the musical and poetical form of the *Ballata.*

b. Mark all vertical intervals. Be able to discuss the proportion of perfect-consonant
    to imperfect-consonant intervals.

c. Be able to discuss the kinds of motion used: contrary, oblique, similar, and parallel.

Chapter 10

THE FIFTEENTH CENTURY
Precursors of Modern Music

In the history and theory of music, the fifteenth century has two principal divisions: the first half is dominated by English and Burgundian composers, and the second part is preempted by Flemish composers.

Both parts are of extraordinary importance in the development of Western music. The first half of the century produced several notable composers, foremost of whom are John Dunstable (c. 1370-1453) and Guillaume Dufay (c. 1400-1474). Their innovative contributions as well as the quality of their scores might well nominate them as "precursors of modern music."

BURGUNDIAN AND ENGLISH MUSIC (c. 1400-1450)

In the music of Dunstable, Dufay, and their contemporaries, the parameters of rhythm, melody, "harmony," and color effect a cohesive whole; the parts are both logical and consistent, the sum is at once coherent and expressive.

Numerous rhythmic figures from this era are both vital and remarkably durable:

Example 154

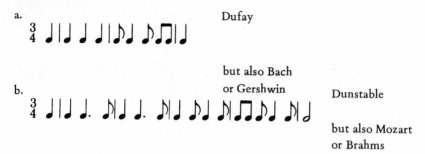

Further, the rhythm of this period has a natural quality and elasticity that one commonly associates with folk music. Rests frequently clarify a phrase structure that is balanced yet agreeably asymmetrical—for example, 3 measures plus 4 measures (see final measures of Example 162, *Iste Confessor*, Dufay).

Example 155

AVE MARIS STELLA

Dunstable (c. 1370-1453)

Ga-bri - e - lis o - - re, fun - - - - da

nos in pa - - - ce mu - tans E-ve no - men.

In the melodic writing, the interval of a third is characteristic and prominent. Incomplete triads (without thirds) are found principally at the beginnings and endings of phrases, while within the phrase there is frequent use of complete triads in root position, 1-3-5, as well as of chords in first inversion, 1-3-6, with the third of the chord in the lowest voice (chord of the sixth).

Example 156

Dunstable
x Chords of the fifth
triads in root position

Dufay
x Chords of the sixth
triads in first inversion

Three-voice polyphony is the normal texture of the period, employed for hymns, movements of the mass, motets, and chansons.

Dunstable's *Ave Maris Stella* illustrates several important musical concepts that composers continued to employ for the next 450 years. Complete triads, 1-3-5, resulting from the polyphonic fabric are marked X. Modal cadences with double leading tones—that is, C# to D and G# to A—stem from earlier Medieval concepts but also anticipate a later V-I and vii°-I cadence practice.

Example 157

There are numerous variants of this cadence, which are shown with the following graphs:[1]

Example 158

Common cadences before 1600 (1 = Final, in tenor)

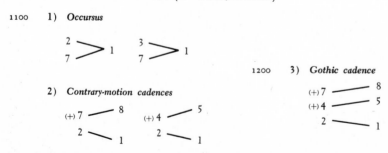

[1]Edith Borroff, *Music in Europe and the United States: A History.* (Englewood Cliffs, N. J.: Prentice-Hall, p. 720). Used by permission.

1300   4) 7–6–8 *(Landini) convention*

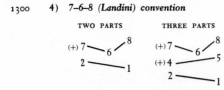

1500   6) *5–1 Cadence with suspended leading tone*

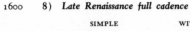

1400   5) *5–5 Crossover cadences*

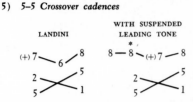

7) *Two-part Renaissance cadence*

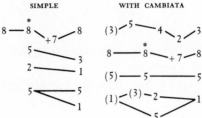

1600   8) *Late Renaissance full cadence*

(+)   sometimes raised to form leading tone
+   raised to form leading tone
*   suspension (see below)

Control of dissonance-consonance is frequently derived from a particular melodic figure in which a consonant note becomes a dissonance and then resolves to a consonance.

Example 159

The dissonant seventh resolves to the imperfect consonance (major sixth). The delayed note is commonly called a *suspension*.

Measure 5 of *Ave Maris Stella* also contains an expressive figure important as a melodic-rhythmic embellishment.

Example 160

The dissonant note B leaps back to the perfect octave after providing a pungent dissonance. The basic melodic progression is as follows:

P5   P8

The intervening embellishment is called an *échappée,* or *escape tone.* Embellishment figures of various kinds have an important role in linear decoration throughout the fifteenth and sixteenth centuries.

Chords of the sixth, 1-3-6, derived not only from polyphonic considerations of consonant intervals within a plainsong but also from improvisational practices of the fourteenth and early fifteenth centuries. Writers are not totally agreed as to the origins and subsequent developments of two kinds of improvisations, although the aural resultants yield remarkable similarities. The two improvisations are:

1. *English discant*

Example 161

WORCESTER SCHOOL (excerpt)

Fourteenth century

(Blessed is the womb of the Virgin Mary.)

Quoted in *The New Oxford History of Music* (London: Oxford University Press, 1954), vol. 2, p. 351.

In English discant the cantus firmus (plainsong) is in the tenor (lowest-sounding voice). To this cantus firmus a treble voice and a middle voice improvised two modified melodies, effecting a series of parallel sixth chords. The first and last sonorities of a discant passage are typically perfect consonances, 1-5-8. Measure 2 in the above example also shows a slight deviation from parallel motion.

2. *Fauxbourdon* is a term applied to a Burgundian practice (fifteenth century) in which the two outer voices were notated. The upper voice sang the plainsong while the lower voice moved in essentially parallel sixths below; the middle voice improvised a perfect fourth below the plainsong.

The introduction of "sixth-chord style" contributed an important landmark in the evolution of harmony.[2] Discant and fauxbourdon also provide some of the most arresting and eloquent passages of music ever written, as Dufay's *Iste Confessor* confirms.

Example 162

ISTE CONFESSOR

Fauxbourdon Hymn

Dufay

[2]Willi Apel, *Harvard Dictionary of Music* (Cambridge, Mass.: Harvard University Press, 1944), p. 259.

FLEMISH MUSIC (c. 1450-1550)

The second half of the fifteenth century and first part of the sixteenth century were dominated by an impressive roster of Flemish composers that included Jean Ockeghem (d. 1495), Jacob Obrecht (d. 1505), Heinrich Isaac (c. 1450-1517), and Josquin des Près (d. 1521). The style as well as the specifics of craft of these and other Flemish composers were widely imitated in all parts of Europe and effected, in the sixteenth century, not only a "golden age" of polyphony but also one of the great and transcendent periods of musical art.

Of special significance in this period is the emergence of four-voice texture. Earlier polyphonic procedures continued, with notable interest in imitative counterpoint and the employment of contrapuntal devices such as augmentation, inversion, and retrograde motion. Four-voice texture also involved a new chordal style, commonly termed "familiar style." Josquin's eloquent motet *Tu Pauperum Refugium* illustrates the new style and points clearly to the element of harmony as a third parameter of music.

Example 163

TU PAUPERUM REFUGIUM

Motet

des Près

OBSERVATIONS:

1. Complete triads are the norm, with two roots frequently present: 1-3-5-8. Root-position chords are somewhat more abundant than chords of the sixth (first inversion).

2. Roots of chords occasionally are a perfect fifth or perfect fourth apart, foreshadowing a specific harmonic system of approximately 100 years later.

3. Although modal cadences persist, the new V-i (measures 10, 19, 45) cadence is both evident and tenacious.

4. Textures vary from block chords to florid counterpoint; similarly, four-voice texture is juxtaposed with two-voice sonorities.

5. The modal succession of chords is oriented to two primary notes of repose: E and A.

CHAPTER SUMMARY

In the history and theory of music, the fifteenth century has two principal divisions: the first half is dominated by the composers John Dunstable and Guillaume Dufay; the second half of the century produced such illustrious composers as Jacob Obrecht, Heinrich Isaac, Jean Ockeghem, and Josquin des Près.

In the music of Dunstable, Dufay, and their contemporaries, the parameters of rhythm, melody, "harmony," and color effect a cohesive whole; the parts are both logical and consistent, and the sum is coherent and expressive. Rhythm in this period has a natural quality and elasticity that one commonly associates with folk music; in melodic writing, the interval of a third is characteristic and prominent. Triads in root position and in first inversion are commonly employed. Three-voice polyphony is the normal texture of the period, employed for hymns, movements of the mass, motets, and chansons. Cadences of diverse types become musically and theoretically significant. Two kinds of improvisations enjoyed wide popularity: the English discant and the continental fauxbourdon.

Of special significance during the Flemish period (c. 1450-1550) is the emergence of four-voice texture. Four-voice texture also involved a new chordal style, commonly termed "familiar style."

SUGGESTED STUDIES

1. Analyze Example 156 in terms of intervals between voices, rhythmic features of each line, the contour of each line, and the cadences employed.
2. Using two to four staves, notate the cadences from the chart on pp. 142-143 , Example 158. Use the notes "d or d^i" as *finals*.
3. Compose a short piece of about 12 measures that illustrates either English discant or fauxbourdon. Use Examples 161 and 162 as models.
4. Be able to discuss or write about Josquin's motet *Tu pauperum refugium* in the following terms:

    a. rhythmic and textural features
    b. cadence practice
    c. types of vertical sonorities used
    d. unity and variety of the whole

Chapter 11

MUSIC OF THE SIXTEENTH CENTURY

Music of the sixteenth century may be considered the summation of trends, techniques, and craft of preceding eras from as far back as the Ars Nova. The perfection achieved by numerous composers suggests that the ingredients for a "high art" include a common practice and general philosophical agreement as to the purpose, function, and aesthetics of music. Music literature of this century is both abundant and abundantly beautiful; the euphonious harmony, counterpoint, and texture are worthy of serious study. Mastery of the contrapuntal and harmonic style of this period will provide profound insights into the craft of composition of Western music.

RHYTHMIC CONTROL

A feature of some polyphonic music of the fifteenth and sixteenth centuries is its continual rhythmic flow. As a reminder—music of this period was notated without bar lines; therefore the phrase structure of each line was determined by the text or by a clearly defined point of repose. Two concepts are observed, both of which retain their validity to the present time:

150

1. *Composite rhythm:* this results from the vertical combination of the several lines.
2. *Overlapping phrases:* these effect a rhythmic control devoid of stoppage and angularity, and were a major feature of style.

Example 164

Example 165

MADRIGAL (excerpt)

Luca Marenzio (c. 1560-1599)

An entirely different concept of rhythm prevailed in the familiar style. There, each voice moves essentially in the same rhythm (similar to thirteenth-century conductus style) with occasional rhythmic embellishments from one or two voices. This rhythmic style is appropriate for congregational singing of psalms and chorales as well as for other forms in which the text is intended to be heard clearly (see Example 176).

MELODIC WRITING

Examples 166-169 serve to illustrate several common characteristics of melodic writing in the fifteenth and sixteenth centuries. The excerpts, both vocal and instrumental, contain a variety of musical gestures, yet similar controls of pitch and duration are evident:

1. Phrases often begin with long note values, rhythmically modulate to shorter values, and, of course, arrive at a point of repose. What one observes here is a fundamental axiom of music and life that insists that every living organism be endowed with a beginning, a middle, and an end.
2. Each phrase contains a balance of conjunct and disjunct motion.
3. Intervals of a fourth or larger typically change direction after the leap. (Observe the arrows of Examples 166-168.) Similarly, a scalar passage which encompasses a perfect fourth, fifth, or octave will point back to the generating note.
4. Usually a phrase has only one high point, dramatically placed to achieve vitality and a musical *event* within the line.

Stylistic differences among composers of this era tended to be minimized—resulting in a kind of universal vocabulary. Nonetheless, the selective processes of individual composers have obviously always differed.

Example 166
MILLE REGRETZ (excerpt)
des Près

Example 167

KYRIE ELEISON (excerpt)

Tomás Luis de Victoria

Ky - ri - e e - - lei - son Ky-rie___ e - - - lei - son

Example 168

MISSA PAPAE MARCELLI (excerpt)

Giovanni Pierluigi da Palestrina (1524-1594)

Ag - - nus De - - - - - - - i

Example 169

RICERCARE DEL 12 TONO (excerpt)

Andrea Gabrieli (1510-1586)

Music of the late fifteenth and the sixteenth centuries provides the first real indication of the emergence of *harmony* as an equal entity to the other parameters. As previously described, the chordal style developed from modal polyphony, and in sixteenth-century music chordal and fugal passages are frequently found in the same composition. The complete triad is the basis of harmony, and although a diatonic modality still prevails, there are at the same time clear indications of the emergence of major and minor tonalities. Some composers—for example, Gesualdo and Lasso— effected highly chromatic passages, yet the main pitch framework of the sixteenth century is essentially diatonic.

In a discussion of harmony, certain concepts require an initial explanation. These include determination of roots, the triadic structure, and root movement.

DETERMINATION OF ROOTS

In tertian harmony chords are spelled in thirds; the *root* is the starting note and no note must be extraneous, although notes may be omitted. In the composite D E G B, the root is E and the total chord spells as: E G B D. Four examples further illustrate:

Example 170

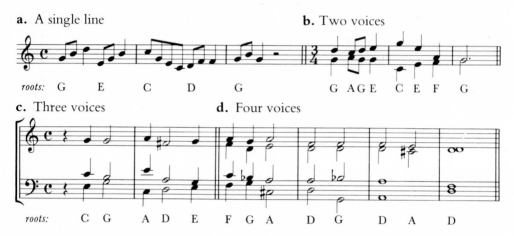

Two observations are pertinent to the above examples:

1. Not all tones of a triad need be present for a clear determination of the root.
2. The root does not always appear in the bass; rather, it may be given to any voice.

TRIAD

The *triad,* a tertian sonority of three different pitches, is described by the bass note:

Bass note	Description	Name
root of chord	root position	chord of the fifth
third of chord	first inversion	chord of the sixth
fifth of chord	second inversion	six-four chord

ROOT MOVEMENT

Root movement is a term used to describe the scale distance between vertical sonorities:

Example 171

by seconds   by thirds   by fourths   by fifths

Often the style of a particular era or of an individual composer will reveal a marked preference for certain kinds of root movement. As a general observation, not to be interpreted too literally, composers in the Renaissance often favored root movement by seconds and thirds, except at cadence points, where movement by fourths and fifths is predominant; the emphasized movement in the Baroque and Classical periods is that of fourths and fifths; while the relationship of thirds was an important feature of the early Romantic period. Since that time, all possibilities have been rather freely employed—determined by the selective processes of the composer.

FOUR-VOICE TEXTURE

Early development of polyphony and harmony in Western music witnessed an extension in the number of parts used in a given composition: from monophonic to two-voice, typical in the eleventh and twelfth centuries; to three-voice, common from the thirteenth century on. Harmonic studies are usually centered on a four-voice texture. There are at least three explanations for this practice:

1. Music in four parts is abundant from the fifteenth century to the present.
2. Four parts offer equal representation of each voice type by range (soprano, alto, tenor, bass) from about 1550 onward.
3. Most of the mechanical problems that require investigation and technique in writing are in evidence in a four-voice texture.

Sixteenth- and seventeenth-century choral music was often written for five, six, or eight voices. Thomas Tallis's *Spem in alium nunquam habui,* an attempt at forty independent lines, is one of music literature's most exciting textures.

In the manipulation of four voices, one needs to keep in mind the connective processes in music. Although spelling, structuring, and doubling are crucial items of information, the triad has little significance without a context and an environment that provide for the connections of sound in time. There are two immediate problems, both of which require a comprehensive understanding. These are:

1. Doubling (note repetition in a vertical sense)
2. Four-voice structure (chord spacing)

DOUBLING

Obviously, the utilization of a triad (three tones) in a four-voice setting necessitates the repetition or *doubling* of one of the notes. Despite disagreement among theorists, the student is advised to consider the following premise:

> For major and minor triads in root position, DOUBLE THE ROOT.

Quite rightly, this premise is subject to modifications: for reasons of voice leading; when the root is an *altered* scale degree (this, in turn, may be modified depending upon context and function); or because of the preference of a composer for a particular kind of sonority and disposition—such as two roots, two thirds, and omission of the fifth.

The following are common exceptions to regular doubling:

1. Tripled root and one third—common in cadences of all periods (Example 172a)
2. One root, doubled third, one fifth—common in certain progressions, particularly V, VI in a minor key (Example 172b)
3. One root, one third, doubled fifth—for reasons of voice-leading and when chords are repeated (Example 172c).

Example 172

STRUCTURE (spacing)

In a homophonic four-voice texture there are two principal types of structure, commonly denoted as *open* and *close*.

Example 173

a. Open　　　　　　　　　　　　**b.** Close

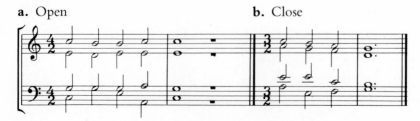

The *disposition* of the UPPER THREE VOICES determines the structure. Despite the musical importance of the bass, it is not a factor in structural disposition.

IN OPEN STRUCTURE:
1. The distance between the soprano and tenor is *greater* than an octave.
2. The order, from the top down, is chord tone, omission, chord tone, omission, chord tone (Example 173a).

IN CLOSE STRUCTURE:
1. The distance between the soprano and tenor is *less* than an octave.
2. The upper three chord tones are immediately adjacent (Example 173b).

Example 174

When employing root-position chords, the student is advised to maintain the *same* structure within the phrase. By so doing, voice-leading is smoother, the general sound is consistent, and mechanical errors such as parallel perfect fifths or octaves are typically avoided.

Example 175

ADOREMUS IN AETERNUM (excerpt)

Gregorio Allegri (1560-1652)

OBSERVATIONS:
1. The root movement in Example 175 is that of a third, fourth, second, and fifth.
2. From 1 to 2 (third), the *common tones* are retained; the bass moves in *oblique* motion to the soprano.
3. From 2 to 3 (fourth), the common tone is retained, and again *oblique* motion results between the outer voices.
4. From 3 to 4 (second), no common tones exist; therefore the bass and soprano

move in *contrary* motion, while the inner voices move to the immediately adjacent chord tones.

5. From 4 to 5 (fifth), the bass moves *obliquely* to the held common tone in the soprano. The alto moves directly to the nearest chord tone c_i, while the tenor line contains a decoration and delay in its resolution to the half note a. The circled notes illustrate a suspension with an ornamental resolution.

Oblique and contrary motion effect a smooth, contiguous sound. For both aesthetic and mechanical reasons, contrary motion is often preferred. Oblique motion is common where roots are a third apart. Similar motion is frequently found where roots are a fourth or fifth apart, but here caution is necessary to avoid parallel perfect fifths and octaves.

OBSERVATIONS:

1. The entire example is in *close* structure.
2. The five major and minor sonorities each contain:

> Two roots
> One third
> One fifth

Example 176

PSALM 1: *QUI AU CONSEIL*

Louis Bourgeois (c. 1510-1561)

Louis Bourgeois's *Psalm 1* is exemplary for harmonic study, for it clearly illustrates several important principles of part writing while providing an arresting example of sixteenth-century familiar style.

OBSERVATIONS:

1. The phrase structure is particularly sophisticated:

measures: 5 + 4½ + 4½   (14)
4 + 5   + 6   (15)

2. Each phrase begins with the same kind of triad (F major), but the cadences achieve great variety:

measure   5   F ⌉
10   C ⌉
14   d
18   g
23   C ⌋
28   F ⌋

Symmetry and balance are shown by the brackets.

3. Almost all triads are in root position, yet there is no monotony in any single line or in the totality of the *Psalm.*

4. Measures 7-9, among others, contain crossed voices (tenor above the alto). This is a common sixteenth-century procedure; as a result, variety in texture and color are achieved.

5. The melodic rhythm and, in this instance, the harmonic rhythm, frequently accelerate as a cadence is approached. This practice is often observed in music from the sixteenth through the nineteenth centuries.

6. Measures 10-18 illustrate impeccable principles of part writing—warming the heart of any pedant! These principles are discussed below.

Example 177

PSALM 1: *QUI AU CONSEIL*

Measures 10-18

Bourgeois

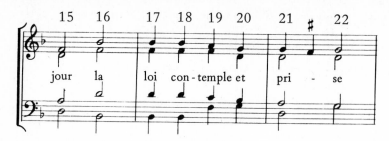

OBSERVATIONS:

1. All triads are in root position and each contains

> 2 roots
> 1 third
> 1 fifth (except final chord)

2. Triads are built on the tonic (I), supertonic (ii), subdominant (IV), dominant (V), and submediant (vi). Scale degrees 1, 2, 4, and 5 are frequently described as *tonal* degrees, while 3 and 6 are designated as *modal* degrees. Since, in this composition, modality and tonality "coexist," a tabulation is revealing:

> I   8 (including repetitions)
> ii   5
> IV   3
> V   1
> vi   5

Other than the tonic chord, the *Psalm* seems to emphasize the supertonic and submediant triads (ii and vi).

3. Root movement includes:

	chord number
by second	2 to 3
by third	5 to 6
	15 to 16
by fourth	3 to 4
implied fifth	21 to 22

4. In a change of harmony, the upper three voices move as *conjunctly* as possible to the next adjacent chord tones.

5. In root movement by thirds (chord 5 to 6) the common tones are retained from chord to chord or (chord 15 to 16) the upper three voices move contrary to the bass to the next adjacent chord tones.

HARMONIC TEXTURES IN THREE, FIVE, AND SIX VOICES

THREE-VOICE TEXTURE

Although initial harmonic studies tend to emphasize the manipulation of four voices, an examination and use of other textures should be considered an important part of the student's musical experience. Each line of these five measures (Example 178) contributes a melodic and rhythmic dimension. Harmonically, this chorus is effected from six different triads, all in root position. Each sonority contains one root, third, and fifth, with the exception of those chords marked X.

Example 178

ST. JOHN PASSION (excerpt)

William Byrd (1543-1623)

OMISSION OF FIFTH

In these instances, the fifth of the chord is typically omitted. Byrd's example would indicate that a majority of the chords without fifths contain two roots and one third. Occasionally, a sonority contains one root and two thirds (marked $\frac{X}{X}$)— probably for reasons of voice-leading. The fifth of a triad, while contributing to the fullness of sound, is obviously the least essential member of a chord and may therefore be omitted if part writing or control of line so necessitate.

FIVE-VOICE TEXTURE

The effect of the chord fifth in a five- or six-voice texture is quite unobtrusive. Example 179 contains ten instances of a doubled fifth—two roots, one third, two fifths. All other sonorities contain a triple root; in this example a doubled third occurs only once.

Example 179

MY BONNY LASS (excerpt)

Ballett

Thomas Morley (1557-1602)

SIX-VOICE TEXTURE

Example 180 is an extraction of accented sonorities within a polyphonic texture, as observed in the Agnus Dei I of Palestrina's *Pope Marcellus Mass.* A majority of sonorities contain three roots; thirds and fifths are rather equally distributed. It is important to observe, however, that the chord third, functioning as a leading tone (f♯i in measure 1), remains undoubled.

Example 180

HARMONIC CADENCES

During the Renaissance, several harmonic cadences emerged, all of which possessed an extraordinary longevity in music literature. Six of the most commonly employed cadences are cited below, Example 181.

Example 181

a. *Perfect authentic:* V to I. Both the bass and soprano of the tonic have the chord root.

b. *Imperfect authentic:* V to I. Tonic-chord soprano note is chord third or fifth.

c. *Half* or *semi:* to V. (Normally the dominant is preceded by ii or IV.)

d. *Plagal:* IV to I. This is the familiar "Amen" cadence.

e. *Deceptive:* V to VI is the most typical progression.

f. *Phrygian:* iv₆ to V in a minor key. It is called Phrygian because of the half-step motion in the bass. Its most typical uses are as an internal cadence or at the conclusion of an inner slow movement of a multimovement composition.

CHAPTER SUMMARY

Music of the sixteenth-century may be considered the summation of trends, techniques, and craft of preceding eras from as far back as the Ars Nova (fourteenth century). A feature of some polyphonic music was its continual rhythmic flow. In such examples, two concepts are observed: composite rhythm and overlapping phrases. An entirely different concept of rhythm prevails in the familiar style, in which each voice moves essentially in the same rhythm. Melodic writing exhibits several common characteristics: longer note values at the beginning of the phrase, a balance of conjunct and disjunct motion, careful control of turning points after larger intervals, and dramatic placement of the primary high point within the phrase.

In a discussion of harmony, certain concepts must be fully understood. These include: determination of chord roots, triadic structure (spacing of a chord), doubling, and root movement. Grasp of these concepts provides the basis of proficient part writing for the student.

Examination of harmonic textures in three, five, and six voices shows rather specific adherence to certain principles of doubling. During the Renaissance, several harmonic cadences emerged, all of which possess an extraordinary longevity in music literature.

SUGGESTED STUDIES

1. Transpose Example 177 to the key of D major. Compose an additional 8 measures using the same vocabulary, doublings, spacings, and general part-writing procedures observed in the example.
2. In four voices, correctly notate the following harmonic cadences in the keys indicated:

   a. *Perfect authentic* in B♭ major
   b. *Imperfect authentic* in A major
   c. *Half* (or semi) in E♭ major
   d. *Plagal* in D major
   e. *Deceptive* in C minor (use harmonic minor)
   f. *Phrygian* in B minor (use harmonic minor)

Chapter 12

BASIC PART WRITING IN FOUR VOICES

CHANGE OF STRUCTURE

Four different sonorities—tonic, dominant, subdominant, and submediant—are utilized in Example 182. Within this restricted vocabulary, the composer balances repetition and variation and provides for a symmetrical period in essentially parallel construction. The fragment is the essence of harmonic simplicity.

Example 182

AVE MARIA (excerpt)

Attributed to Jacob Arcadelt (c. 1514-1575)

Bracketed chords in Example 182 show two common ways of accomplishing *change of structure* within the phrase:

1. Between repeated chords; any chord repetition permits the change of structure from close to open, or the reverse, open to close.
2. Between two chords whose roots are a fifth apart; typically, but not invariably, the third of one chord moves to the third of the next chord *in the same voice*. After the new structure has been established, normal doubling procedures apply.

NONCHORD TONES

The circled notes (X, Y) in measure 7 of Example 182 are extraneous to the harmony but of paramount significance to the musical fabric. Their function is that of melodic *connection* between two different chords—in this instance, from bb^i to f^i.

PASSING TONES

Typically these tones bridge a distance of a third or fourth; they are commonly called *passing tones*. The note marked X occurs on the weak part of the beat and is therefore *unaccented*; note Y appears on the strong part of the beat and is frequently denoted as *accented*. In this latter case (of an accented passing tone), a distinction is made by several writers who would refer to this note as an *appoggiatura* (It. *appoggiare*, to lean) (see p. 175). Of the several categories of nonchord tones—each with varied, and on occasion confusing, nomenclature—passing tones have been the most widely used by composers of all periods. Passing tones achieve a conjunct melodic motion between the essential chord tones of the basic sonorities.

Passing tones may function as connections in several different ways:

1. They may appear on a weak beat or a strong beat (Example 183c).
2. They may ascend or descend in direction (Example 183a, b).
3. They may appear in more than one voice simultaneously (Example 183b, c).

Example 183

SUSPENSIONS (DELAYED NONCHORD TONES)

A nonchord tone that is momentarily delayed in its normal movement or resolution is called a *suspension*.

The total suspension figure comprises:

1. *Preparation:* the note is prepared as a harmonic tone in the same voice. The rhythmic value of the preparation is usually equal to or greater than the suspension itself.
2. *Suspension:* the note becomes a dissonance on the accented part of the beat.
3. *Resolution:* the note resolves, usually stepwise down, on the unaccented part of the beat. Sometimes a distinction is made for the upward resolution of a suspension by calling it a *retardation*.

There are four common appearances of the suspension in parts above the bass: 2-1, 4-3, 7-6, and 9-8. The behavior of the 6-5 melodic figuration is closely related but contains no actual dissonance.

All suspensions in Example 186 are marked S. Additional illustrations are shown in Example 184.

Example 184

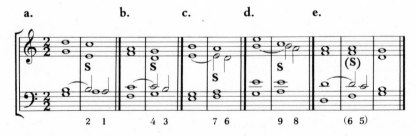

A majority of the above examples of suspension will be found in an ornamented and decorated version in the Palestrina composition of Example 200.

IRREGULAR DOUBLING

The asterisked (*) chords in Example 182 are instances of *irregular doubling*. In both cases they appear to be caused by the composer's desire to avoid parallel perfect fifths and octaves, which would suddenly reduce four independent voices to one voice accompanied by three "shadows" (see Example 185b).

The considerations of independence of line and consistency of texture seem to be logical explanations for the rather consistent avoidance of these parallel perfect consonants. Certainly there is no acoustical problem, nor are these parallels aesthetically unpleasant. Parallel perfect fourths are freely used in a texture of three or more voices, in all periods.

Example 185

a. Arcadelt **b.** Invented with regular doubling

Josquin's eloquent 17 measures (Example 186) masterfully control both horizontal and vertical dimensions of sound.

Example 186

AGNUS DEI

From *Missa Pange Lingua* (excerpt)

des Près

OBSERVATIONS:

1. The 17 measures suggest a grouping of three 5-measure phrases (*a, b, c*) with the third phrase containing a 2-measure extension.
2. The organizing principles are those of contiguity and repetition.
3. Motivic construction is implied by the constant interplay, and imitative use, of two short musical ideas, marked X and Y.
4. Root movement indicates a preference for seconds (12) and fifths (14), followed by fourths (8) and thirds (1).
5. The outside voices frequently complement each other with contrary motion; similar and oblique motion provide variety; the occasional omission of the upper voice achieves subtle changes in texture and color.

All chords in Example 186 are in root position with the exception of those marked Z. These instances illustrate Josquin's use of the chord of the sixth.

FIRST INVERSION (CHORD OF THE SIXTH)

A *chord of the sixth* (i.e., a chord in *first inversion)* is a triad in which the chord third is in the bass. Chords of the sixth have been freely utilized by all composers of the tertian period. In addition to their particular sonority, which enriches the harmonic resources of tertian music, sixth chords have a pronounced effect on the contour of the bass line. By the simple alternation of root-position and first-inversion triads, the bass can become an entirely conjunct and contiguous line. Two observations are pertinent concerning the chord of the sixth:

---

1. In a major or minor triad in first inversion, the soprano (upper voice) is often *doubled.*
2. Following a first-inversion chord, a *change of structure* from open to close, or reverse, may be made.

Common four-voice vocal dispositions are shown in Example 187. All first-inversion chords are marked by the number *6.**

Example 187

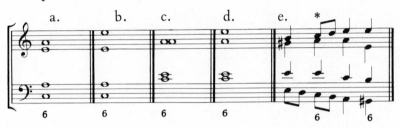

Example 187e illustrates a chord of the sixth (*) with the third in both the bass and soprano; this disposition is a convenient and effective use of the sonority as a passing chord. At this same point, the structure has changed from close to open; the measure itself is constituted of mixed structure.

The antecedents of first-inversion chords include *fauxbourdon* and its counterpart, the *English discant,* which were procedures for improvisation with a *cantus firmus.*

One of literature's most famous polyphonic songs is Heinrich Isaac's *Isbruck, ich muss dich lassen* (Example 188). In the quoted fragment, each line is independently contoured, yet the vertical situations are clearly defined. The example illustrates the use of the *diminished triad* and additional nonchord tones not previously discussed. At the same time, the Isaac song prompts a consideration of the ways in which harmonic resources may be increased through *altered chords, modulation, interchangeability of modes* (bimodality), and *secondary function.*

---

*Chords of first inversion were called chords of the sixth—that is, 1-3-6—intervals of a third and a sixth above the lowest note, during the Renaissance. After 1600, a system emerged called *figured bass,* which is discussed on pp. 200-202. In the figured-bass system a chord of first inversion is designated as $\frac{6}{3}$ or simply as 6.

Example 188

ISBRUCK, ICH MUSS DICH LASSEN (excerpt)

Heinrich Isaac (1450-1517)

Isbruck, ich muss dich lassen,
ich far dahin mein strassen in fremde Land dahin.
Mein freud ist mir genommen,
die ich nit weiss bekummen,
wo ich im elend bin,
wo ich im elend bin.

Innsbruck, I must leave you,
Traveling long roads away
Into a strange land.
My joy is taken away
That I knew not how to enjoy,
And now I am in misery.

From Edith Borroff, *Music in Europe and the United States: A History,* © 1971, Prentice-Hall, Inc., p. 189.

Example 189

EXCERPT, *ISBRUCK, ICH MUSS DICH LASSEN* (time values doubled)

Isaac

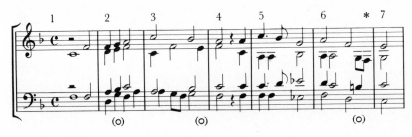

Isaac's concern for line and color seems to account for the reordering of the spacing in measures 5-7, where the tenor sings consistently above the alto. This procedure, which may apply to any or all voices, is called *crossed voices.*

   It is recalled that pitch resources of the fifteenth and sixteenth centuries emanated from the Church modes; therefore the Isaac progression would be typically denoted as *modal succession.* The modal characteristics are Ionian, transposed to F.

There is an indication, however, that most of the chords relate specifically to a central, or tonic, triad. These relationships, when systematically employed, create what is termed *functional harmony* (tonal progression). Usually, this descriptive term is reserved for progressions derived from a major or minor tonality or key.

DIMINISHED TRIADS

The Isaac excerpt comprises major and minor sonorities and, at three points, *diminished triads*, marked (o). Built of two consecutive minor thirds, the diminished triad occurs as a result of scale formations on the seventh degree in major and minor keys (vii°) and on the second degree in a minor key (ii°). Cadential use of the diminished sound predates the tertian period, while its utilization in the late Renaissance is for the purpose of lending occasional color. The diminished chord is found in root position and in second inversion, but the most frequent usage of any diminished triad is as a chord of first inversion.

Chord root and fifth have strong tendencies to resolve to a third, for example, B-F to C-E; the inner tone of the triad remains neutral, free to move in either direction, by step or by leap. For acoustical reasons, it is advisable to *double the third of the chord*. In practice it is observed, however, that the fifth is frequently doubled. This facilitates part writing, while accomplishing the resolution of the tritone. The chord root, often the leading tone of a scale, is the least preferred doubling.

Example 190

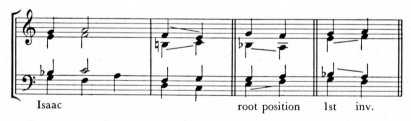

Isaac   root position   1st   inv.

The innovative practices of secular music were of particular importance to harmonic syntax. Noteworthy is a large repertory for voice and lute, in which an essentially chordal accompaniment supports a solo melody. Compiled in 1574, *The Bottegari Lutebook* is one of the most rewarding collections of the late Renaissance. The 132 compositions, by several leading composers, would indicate that "singing to the lute" formed an important genre of court entertainment and musical media.

Example 191

ARIA DA STANZA

No. 54

Cosimo Bottegari (1554-1620)

From *The Bottegari Lutebook* (Wellesley Edition No. 8, 1965), ed. Carol MacClintock. Used by permission.

OBSERVATIONS:

1. The slightly asymmetrical phrase structure (5 + 3) of this *Aria* is musically satisfying.
2. Both phrases conclude with authentic cadences: in measure 5 to A♭ major; in measure 8 to f minor.
3. The usual avoidance of parallel perfect fifths and octaves is relaxed in favor of characteristic lute chordal dispositions.
4. The nonagreement of key signature with the actual tonal orientation is quite typical of this collection and of the practice of this era.

EMBELLISHING TONES

An entire category of nonchord tones has a musical function which is primarily that of decoration and embellishment. These include the *cambiata, changing tones, neighboring* (or auxiliary) *tones, escape tone,* and *appoggiatura.*

CAMBIATA

The cambiata (It. *cambiare,* to change or exchange) is an ornamental figuration used with great frequency in the sixteenth century. The *nota cambiata* moves by leap in the same direction as the basic harmonic progression; characteristically, it moves too far and must retreat stepwise in the opposite direction for its resolution (Example 192):

Example 192

CHANGING TONES

Changing tones may be considered as a possible development of the same figuration. The chord tone is embellished by the notes immediately above and below (or the reverse order) in a step-leap-step pattern. Changing tones may be accompanied by a new chord at the point of resolution; they may be diatonic or chromatic, according to the considerations of style (Example 193):

Example 193

NEIGHBORING TONES

Of less complexity, neighboring tones (neighbor tones, auxiliary tones, auxiliaries) are closely related to changing tones. In any given voice, a chord tone is embellished—above or below—by a single nonharmonic note. A neighboring tone may be diatonic or chromatic, although it is not common practice to inflect the third of the chord (Example 194):

Example 194

ESCAPE TONE

The escape tone, or *échappée,* is the reverse of the cambiata; that is, it is approached by step in the direction opposite to that of the basic progression, then turns and resolves by leap (Example 195):

Example 195

APPOGGIATURA

A final, and somewhat controversial, embellishing tone, is the appoggiatura (It. *appoggiare,* to lean). One of the few areas of agreement among writers concerning the appoggiatura is that it is rhythmically strong; the dissonance is on the strong part of the beat. Two principal interpretations of the term are listed below:

1. A nonharmonic tone on the rhythmically strong part of the beat resolves stepwise to a chord tone on the weak part of the beat (Example 196a, b).
2. A nonharmonic tone approached by leap and resolving, typically, stepwise down (Example 196c, d).

Example 196

OBSERVATIONS:

1. The appoggiatura may occur in any voice, although it is perhaps most striking when used in an exposed upper voice.
2. *Appoggiature* are observed in all eras. In the eighteenth and nineteenth centuries simultaneous *appoggiature* form what is commonly referred to as an *appoggiatura chord.*

It is typical that embellishing tones of all varieties, with the exception of the appoggiatura, are *rhythmically weak.*

THE SIX-FOUR CHORD

The passage from Morley's *Agnus Dei* (Example 197) is an exciting combination of the modal and tonal systems. The linear emphasis does not preclude harmonic clarity; viable rhythms do not impede the quiet and consistent motion; predictability and surprise are coequals.

Morley's example also serves to introduce chords of *second inversion.*

A triad whose *fifth* is in the bass is denoted as a *six-four chord:* $\substack{6 \\ 4}$ (see measures 2 and 8).

Example 197

AGNUS DEI

Final 9 measures

Morley

Morley's excerpt contains two such sonorities, each employed in a precise manner. Unlike the unrestricted employment of root-position and first-inversion chords, the use of the six-four chord has been specific and selective. Four of the most common uses are cited in Example 198.

Example 198

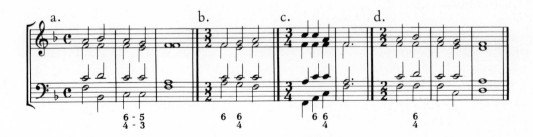

a. *Cadential six-four:* As its name implies, this usage is most often found at points of cadence; the usual behavior is for 6 to move to 5 in the same voice while 4 moves to 3, also in the same voice.

b. *Passing six-four:* Often observed in a rhythmically weak position in the measure, the passing six-four is primarily melodic in function; it is particularly appropriate when the outside voices move in conjunct contrary motion.

c. *Arpeggiated (or chordal) six-four:* Appropriate for keyboard or instrumental music, the arpeggiated six-four is simply a chord outline, melodically deployed.

d. *Stationary six-four:* Derived from the melodic motion of two upper neighboring tones.

DOUBLING

> With few exceptions, practice of composers has consistently doubled the *bass* note, the fifth of the triad.

FUNCTION AND RESTRICTED USE

A triad in second inversion is apt to change or negate its basic function. For example, the *function* of all of measure 2, Example 198a, is dominant, with the upper voices a^i f^i behaving as nonchord tones to g^i e^i. In Examples 198b, c, d, the six-four chords are decidedly weak, approaching a kind of nonfunction. More than any other triadic formation, the six-four sonority poses serious musical problems. Its utilization, in initial studies, should be severely restricted.

THE AUGMENTED TRIAD

The five-voice texture of the Tomkins anthem (Example 199) provides for a rich contrapuntal fabric. Imitation (measures 4-6) and a tenor pedal (measures 4-7) are compositional devices that assist in the unfolding of musical content. In two instances, marked +, harmonic tension is heightened by the use of *augmented triads* in an otherwise major-minor environment.

Of the four kinds of triads, the augmented triad (+) has been the least frequently utilized. It is not formed from any of the modes, and its solitary natural occurrence is on the third degree of the harmonic minor scale, III+. Even in this possible context it is primarily a melodic, not a harmonic, phenomenon.

Example 199

O LORD, I HAVE LOVED

Final 7 measures

Thomas Tomkins (1572-1656)

CHAPTER SUMMARY

A change in chord structure (spacing) may occur within the phrase under the following conditions: between repeated chords and between two chords whose roots are a perfect fifth apart.

Nonchord tones are of paramount significance to the musical fabric of homophony. Passing tones and suspensions are types of nonchord tones frequently used. Passing tones may function as connections between the notes of intervals larger than a second. Suspensions provide for rhythmically strong dissonances that resolve to chord tones on a weaker pulse.

A first-inversion chord is a triad in which the chord third is in the bass (lowest-sounding voice). In a major or minor triad in first inversion, the soprano (upper voice) is often doubled. Following a first-inversion chord, a change of structure from open to close, or the reverse, may be made.

Chords of first inversion were called chords of the sixth—that is, 1-3-6—intervals of a third and a sixth above the lowest note, during the Renaissance. After 1600, a system emerged, called *figured bass,* in which first-inversion chords are designated as $\frac{6}{3}$ or simply as 6.

A diminished triad is built of two consecutive minor thirds; it occurs as a result of scale formations on the seventh degree in major and minor keys (vii°) and on the second degree in a minor key (ii°).

The musical function of an entire category of nonchord tones is primarily to decorate and embellish. These include the cambiata, changing tones, neighboring (or auxiliary) tones, escape tone, and appoggiatura.

A triad whose chord fifth is in the bass (lowest voice) is denoted as a six-four chord $\frac{6}{4}$. Unlike the unrestricted employment of root-position and first-inversion chords, the use of the six-four chord has been specific and selective. Four of the most common uses are cited: 1. cadential six-four; 2. passing six-four; 3. arpeggiated (or chordal) six-four; and 4. stationary six-four. With few exceptions, practice of composers has consistently doubled the *bass* note, the fifth of the triad.

Augmented triads (two major thirds) were initially used for harmonic tensions. Of the four kinds of triads, the augmented triad has been the least frequently utilized. It is not formed from any of the modes, and its solitary natural occurrence is on the third degree of the harmonic minor scale, III⁺. Even in this possible context, it is primarily a melodic, not a harmonic, phenomenon.

SUGGESTED STUDIES

1. Analyze the following example in terms of:

    Root movement
    Melodic motion

Structure of chords; changes in structure
Doublings
Nonharmonic tones: passing tones and suspensions
Sixth chords

Example 200

O BONE JESU

Attributed to Giovanni Pierluigi da Palestrina

2. Complete Example 201 to four voices, except where rests are indicated. Include a harmonic analysis.

Example 201
Christopher Tye (c. 1500–c. 1572)

3. In Example 202, complete the figured bass to four parts. Use close structure and regular doublings. Include a harmonic analysis.

Example 202

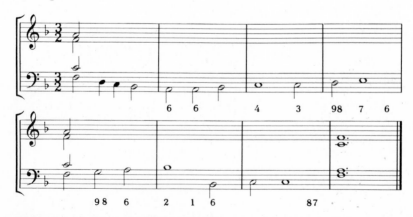

All chords marked 6 are chords of first inversion.
All other sets of numbers (9-8, 7-6, 4-3, and 2-1) are *suspensions* above the bass note.

4. Analyze Example 203 in the following terms:

The rhythmic-melodic factors of organization
The root movement of chords
The relationship of each chord to the tonal axes G and B♭
The identification of all nonchord tones
The musical organization as a whole in terms of unification and diversity

Example 203

AVE VERUM CORPUS

Measures 1-18
Byrd

5. Composition and invention:

a. Using Example 204, invent two inner voices to the given soprano and figured bass.

Example 204

From John Dowland (1562-1626)

b. Invent inner voices for the given soprano and bass in Example 205. Provide a harmonic analysis and identify all cadences.

Example 205

Adapted from Guillaume Costeley (1531-1606)

c. In Example 206, add three lower voices to the given soprano and numerals. (All notes marked + are to be treated as nonchord tones.)

Example 206

From Michael Praetorius (1571-1621)

d. In G major (*allegro*, duple meter), invent a four-voice piece from the given Roman numerals:

I   IV₆   V   I₆   ii₆   V   vi   IV   V

V/vi   vi   V₆   I   IV   ii   V   I

IV₆   V₄₃   I ‖

e. Compose a short original composition (about 14 measures) using the concepts and vocabulary that have been introduced in Chapter 12.

6. Prepare an analysis of *D'une Coline* (Example 207) in the following terms:

The meaning of *vers mesuré;* the special metric-rhythmic features of this work
A comparison of three- and five-part texture to four-part writing
The design of the composition

The extent and type of repetition
The shape of each line; the kinds of motion between the outside voices
The root movement
Identification of nonharmonic tones
The relationship of this analysis to performance

Example 207

D'UNE COLINE

Claude le Jeune (1528-1600)

Reprise à 5
Dessus

Cinquiesme

Haut Contre
Taille

Basse Contre

Et la main j'y tens, Mais las c'est en vain.

Je la voy de loin, Et je l'ai-me fort, Je la veu cueil-lir,

Et la main j'y tens, Mais las c'est en vain.

7. Compose an accompaniment (keyboard, lute, or guitar) for the following solo line (Example 208). Use Example 207 as a model.

Example 208

ARIA DA STANZA

No. 53

Cosimo Bottegari

From *The Bottegari Lutebook* (Wellesley Edition No. 8, 1965), ed. Carol MacClintock. Used by permission.

8. Sing and analyze the following Jacob Handl *Motet*. Be prepared to cite three or four points on each of the following:

   a. melodic rhythm
   b. melodic contours
   c. harmonic part writing
   d. texture and color
   e. principles of repetition and contrast.

Example 209

ECCE QUOMODO

Motet

Jacob Handl (1550-1591)

Chapter 13

SACRED POLYPHONY OF THE LATE SIXTEENTH CENTURY

In the late sixteenth century several composers demonstrated both their religious fervor and their consummate creative talents by the composing of sacred polyphony. Most notable of these composers are Orlando di Lasso (c. 1532-1594, Flemish), Ludovico da Victoria (c. 1540-1611, Spanish), and Giovanni Pierluigi da Palestrina (c. 1526-1594, Italian). Their sacred compositions reflected a general statement of the Catholic Church following the Council of Trent (1545-1563), which concluded "that everything 'impure and lascivious' must be avoided in order 'that the House of God may rightly be called a house of prayer.'"[1]

Such sentiments are reflected in the music by the nearly "constant flow of consonance." Dissonance is severely limited and carefully controlled. The analysis and imitation of sixteenth-century sacred polyphony is frequently the basis of a long and exacting study of *modal counterpoint*[2] and is beyond the scope of this text. A few observations are pertinent, however, for the beginning student who wishes to explore this great literature.

---

[1]Donald Grout, *A History of Western Music,* shorter rev. ed., p. 181.

[2]See G. F. Soderlund, *Direct Approach to Counterpoint in the 16th Century Style* (New York: Appleton-Century-Crofts, 1947), p. 24.

Example 210

OCULUS NON VIDIT

Motet from *Cantiones Duarum Vocum*

Orlando di Lasso (1532-1594)

Lasso's two-voice motet produces an eloquent flow of consonance aided by a masterful control of rhythm. The work is highly imitative, but it is not a strict canon. Imitation is at

the P 5th below:	ms. 1-5	the P unison mirror:	ms. 16-17
the P 8ve below:	ms. 5-7	the P 8ve below:	ms. 21-22
the m 7th below:	ms. 9-11	the P 5th above:	ms. 25-26
the P 5th below:	ms. 13-14	the P unison mirror:	ms. 27-28

After each point of imitation, a freely conceived counterpoint moves to a point of repose. The cadences, however, are always "covered"—that is, both voices do not contain rests at the same time. It is a counterpoint of perfect and imperfect consonances; dissonances are approached and quitted in conjunct motion. The following observations of the Lasso motet constitute a paraphrase of principles of sixteenth-century contrapuntal writing.[3]

OBSERVATIONS:

1. Unisons are used only at the beginning and at the end; they are approached and left by contrary motion. (In *Oculus non vidit* there are no unisons.)
2. Fifths are approached by contrary and oblique motion; more rarely by step in the upper and skip in the lower part.
3. Octaves are approached by contrary motion (also by oblique motion).
4. Parallel thirds and sixths are essentially limited to three in succession.
5. The two voices are usually an octave or less apart (close position); compound intervals do occur for variety in texture and sonority.

Lauda Sion, a four-voice motet by Palestrina, is quoted in its entirety.

Example 211

LAUDA SION
Motet for four voices
Giovanni Pierluigi da Palestrina

[3]Willi Apel, *Harvard Dictionary of Music* (Cambridge, Mass.: Harvard University Press, 1944), p. 465.

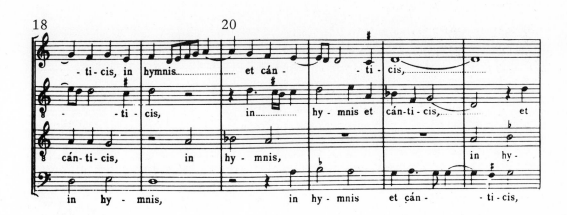

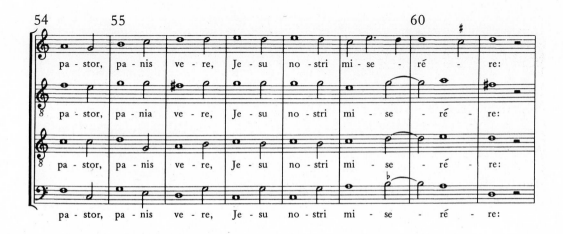

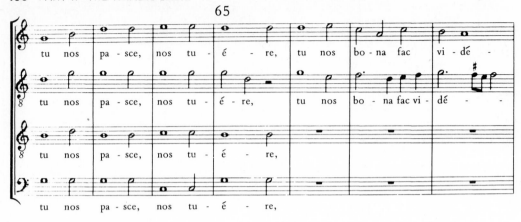

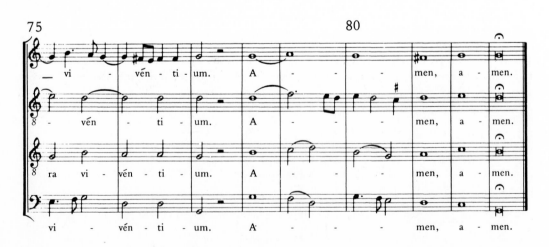

Example 212

LAUDA SION

Analysis of soprano-alto, ms. 1-12

Palestrina

OBSERVATIONS:

1. Perhaps the most intriguing observation of Palestrina's motet is the fact that the upper two voices (or lower two voices) can be detached from the whole and still retain a perfect solution to interval control.

2. The style is one that emphasizes consonances: perfect octaves, perfect fifths, perfect unisons, major and minor thirds, major and minor sixths.

3. The two instances of fourths in the above example are as follows:

   m. 5   P 4th: behavior is that of a dissonance, suggesting a 4-3 suspension.

   m. 6   A 4th: the tritone is the strongest dissonance of the excerpt and resolves by step in each voice out to a minor sixth.

4. All measures except m. 11 have perfect or imperfect consonances on the first beat, marked *.

The entire motet is tonally oriented to G, with internal fluctuations between Mixolydian and transposed Aeolian modes as well as G major. As previously stated, a *modal-tonal* vocabulary is quite commonly employed by sixteenth-century composers.

The student will have observed numerous instances of accidentals placed *above the note.* These accidentals are missing in the original manuscripts but are suggested by modern editors since, in the performance of the music during the composer's lifetime, the accidentals would certainly have been played by the performers. This tradition—of intending an F♯ or C♯ but not indicating it—will seem strange to a twentieth-century musician, who is so accustomed to specificity. Nevertheless, the tradition persisted from the tenth through the sixteenth centuries. The performance-practice tradition is commonly called *musica ficta.* In the thirteenth century the term was *musica falsa.*

Philippe de Vitry, commenting on the already long and somewhat bizarre tradition, stated around 1325 that the system was "non falsa, sed vera et necessaria"—not false, but true and necessary.[4] Although many writers have discussed the *musica ficta* system in numerous treatises, this enigmatic notation remains puzzling for most students of music.

CHAPTER SUMMARY

Late-sixteenth-century sacred polyphony is notable for its nearly "constant flow of consonance." Dissonance is severly limited and carefully controlled. The analysis and imitation of sixteenth-century sacred polyphony is frequently the basis of an exacting study of modal counterpoint.

Melodic imitation is a principal compositional device: 7-6 and 4-3 suspensions are frequently used for momentary tension-release; cadences are often "overlapped" to effect the smooth rhythm flow; textural variety is achieved by occasional omission of one or two voices (four-voice texture) and by alternation of polyphonic rhythm with block rhythm.

SUGGESTED STUDIES

1. Sing and analyze in detail the complete Palestrina motet, *Lauda Sion,* Example 211. Be able to comment on the following points: intervals between voices, types of imitation, types of cadences, melodic/rhythmic figures or motives employed, metric changes. Provide a harmonic analysis of measures 52-83.
2. Using Example 210 (two-voice motet by Lasso) as a model, compose about 12 measures using imitative modal counterpoint. Try for thirds, sixths, and tenths on strong beats; resolve all dissonances; avoid extensive disjunct motion; imitate Lasso's final cadence.

---

[4] Willi Apel, *Harvard Dictionary of Music* (Cambridge, Mass.: Harvard University Press, 1944), p. 465.

Chapter 14

THEORETICAL CONCEPTS AND PRACTICES OF THE BAROQUE ERA (c. 1600-1750)

The Ars Nova of the fourteenth century, the Nuove Musiche of the seventeenth century, and the twentieth century's "new music" all represent substantial or even radical departures from the conventions and mannerisms of the immediately preceding eras. It is observed that as a common musical practice reaches a peak of development and begins a decline, a new, regenerative force gradually—or suddenly—vies with older traditions.

In 1602 the composer Giulio Caccini published a collection of accompanied solo songs entitled *Nuove Musiche* (new music). The title was prophetic. Not only did a new dramatic, declamatory, and instrumental style emerge, but from these innovations of Nuove Musiche developed the grandiloquent era known as the Baroque period. Reaction to the previous polyphonic era prompted a remarkable reexamination of all the parameters of music.

In the area of rhythm, one of the most radical innovations was the use of dramatic declamation in music. This declamation is called *recitative* and follows the free rhythm of a prose text. Obviously, the principle of prolongation, particularly of vowels, is applied. One normally does not sing at the tempo of conversational speech: to do so would give many accompanied songs a compression bordering on either the comical or the absurd. Rhythms in the Baroque era are at once vital and natural. Rhythm energizes and propels motion in time to an extent not previously achieved. The long note values persist in the early seventeenth century but are gradually reduced in the later Baroque to smaller values. For example, a major portion of J. S. Bach's works consists of running eighth notes or even sixteenth notes. The notational appearance and the musical effect are decidedly different from late-sixteenth-century *longas* and *breves.*

Melodic lines reflect the rhythmic innovations. Vocal lines become, on occasion, very florid or even virtuosic. At the same time, the emergence of an equal and independent instrumental idiom expands the range and type of lines. The range of almost any instrument is greater than any single vocal range; further, string and keyboard instruments do not have to breathe in the normal physiological sense, nor must they enunciate a text. All of these factors were decisive in molding the melodic writing style of Baroque composers.

Harmony, within a modal, major-minor framework, accommodated both function and system. Modal succession was replaced by *tonal progression.* The tenets of the system are discussed more fully in Chapter 15 under "chord classification."

Texture and color contributed significantly to the Baroque ideal of contrasts. Music of the high Baroque reflects its name (originally used to describe pearls of uneven surface, seemingly from a Portuguese word meaning "irregular"); it is a resplendent musical style, rich in contrasts of light and dark, full and transparent—as are the contemporaneous paintings of Rembrandt and El Greco.

Form and genera expanded with the spirit of the times. Opera, oratorio, cantata are not infrequently of grand proportion. The instrumental suite, the concerto grosso, and instrumental sonatas, suites, and partitas, although of lesser dimensions, are substantial and stand as complete musical statements. In most Baroque compositions, contrasts of tempi between sections or movements are common.

One of the most significant innovations of the early Baroque period is a notational practice called *figured bass.*

FIGURED BASS

Figured bass, or *thorough-bass,* is a system of musical shorthand that provides for a bass line and a set of numbers and symbols. The system evolved from the improvisational practices of the sixteenth century and was initially employed by Viadana, Croce, and others in the late sixteenth century; its use was nearly universal in the period 1600-1750. After 1750 figured bass was used for analysis and part writing.

Example 213

AMARILLI MIA BELLA (excerpt)

Continuo madrigal

Giulio Caccini (c. 1548-1618)

Amarillis my beautiful, do you not believe, oh my heart's sweet desire, that you are my love.

The numbers and symbols of the figured bass system indicate pitches to be sounded above the bass:

1. A triad in root position is usually without any figure—with the understanding in performance practice that the third and fifth above the bass are added as appropriate.
2. A triad in first inversion has the figures ⅜ and is commonly abbreviated as 6.
3. An isolated accidental below the bass will always refer to the third (tenth, seventeenth) above the indicated note.
4. Any chromatic alteration must be shown; the placing of a sharp, natural, or flat immediately before the figure is the most common practice—although editorial procedures vary; the diagonal slash (/) or straight slash (–) through a figure indicates a sharping of that particular note.
5. Figures for compound intervals observed in Example 213, measure 9: 11 ♯10 14, were modified in a later period of history to their simpler forms: 4 ♯3 7. In all periods, however, the performer probably took certain liberties regarding the placement of the specific pitches; for example, g f♯ might also be g^i f♯^{i}.

Example 214 illustrates possible realizations of a given figured bass:

Example 214

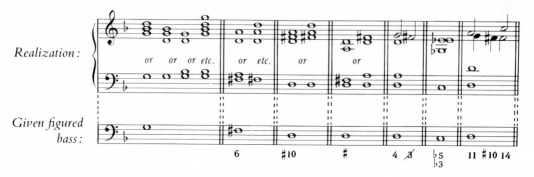

Realization:

Given figured bass:

SECONDARY FUNCTION

One of the most important concepts in theory—one crucial to the understanding and analysis of chordal relationship—is that of *secondary function*. The concept provides for the momentary borrowing of resources that relate to scale degrees other than the tonic.

From its inception and earliest practice, the preponderance of secondary function has been directed to the dominant level: V of V, or vii° of V. Example 215 lists the most common relationships involving secondary function:

Example 215

Tonality and musical continuity are in no way destroyed by the use of secondary function. The concept establishes an accurate description of musical function; its use allows for a momentary emphasis of a diatonic chord other than the tonic and secures additional resources within any given tonality. The augmented resources are illustrated in Example 216:

Example 216

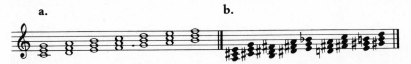

a. Original resources from C major

b. New resources from *secondary dominants* and from *secondary leading tones*

Chromatic inflections frequently relate to secondary function or bimodal interchange, or a combination of both.

Dowland's *Ayre,* Example 217, is a model of structural balance (8 + 8 + 6 + 8), harmonic clarity, textural variety, and rhythmic interest. The composer's setting of "come, come, come" (measures 15-16 and 19-20) effects a change in texture, illustrates his "delight" in text setting, and produces a kind of conversational and immediate quality within the Ayre. Harmonic variety is achieved by employing secondary dominants and leading-tone triads, which are marked on the score. The cadence in measure 8 as well as the final cadence in measure 22 (marked *) are instances of Picardy thirds, explained briefly on page 204.

Example 217

WHAT IF I NEVER SPEED

Ayre (choral)

John Dowland (1563-1626)

V of G

* = Picardy third

V of D; V of G; V of C

BIMODALITY

The practice of employing chords from the parallel relationship (Example 218) is commonly observed. Two terms are used synonymously for this concept: *interchangeability of modes,* and *bimodality.* In some eras, and with certain composers, the bimodal relationships are prominent. The increase in harmonic resources is shown in Example 218.

Example 218

a. Original resources from C major
b. New resources from *harmonic minor,* parallel relation

Related to the bimodal concept is the mannerism of substituting a major tonic triad at cadence points within a minor-key framework. This device, Example 219, is referred to as a *Picardy third:*

Example 219

In the creation of new and viable sound, composers have devised several concepts that expand the diatonic resources of the modal and tonal systems:

ALTERED CHORDS

Sonorities that utilize one or more tones foreign to a given scale are frequently referred to as *altered chords.* In the Renaissance and Baroque periods, with the exception of a few composers who experimented with chromaticism, altered chords are not an especially common phenomenon; rather, a tone that requires an accidental more often denotes one of the following:

A change of tonality
A change from major to minor (or the reverse)
A change in the function of the chord

A modulation may augment the original harmonic resources by as much as a hundred percent, depending on the choice of the new key. Example 218 illustrates four relationships, from a possible total of twenty-two.

Example 220

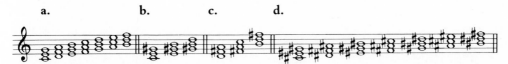

a. Original resources in C major
b. Added resources from A harmonic minor (submediant relationship)
c. Added resources from G major (dominant relationship)
d. New resources from C♯ major (chromatic relationship)

NOTE: Chromatic and enharmonic modulation will be discussed in a subsequent chapter.

MODULATION

Modulation is a process that achieves a change of tonality. The change may be effected by melodic or harmonic factors. Depending upon its behavior, the modulation is called *transient* or *permanent.*

Modulations are also categorized according to the kind of change that is used to relate one tonal area to another; according to this categorization, they are usually called diatonic, chromatic, or enharmonic modulations. Example 221 illustrates a *diatonic,* or *common chord,* modulation. The simple prerequisite for a diatonic modulation is one triad that is found, unaltered, in both the old and new keys. As an example, the triads CEG, DFA, FAC, ACE, and BDF are *common* to the diatonic scale resources of C major and A harmonic minor.

Example 221

Normally, a distinction is made between a change in tonal center and a change from major to minor, or vice versa, using parallel relationships. The former is a true modulation (Example 221), while the latter is simply a *change of mode* (Example 222):

Example 222

Example 223

LAMENTO D'OLIMPIA (excerpt)

Monteverdi

Monteverdi's *Lament* for solo voice and basso continuo (Example 223) ideally illustrates a declamatory style of the early Baroque period. (The text, omitted here, describes moments of personal tragedy.)

OBSERVATIONS:

1. The metric and rhythmic freedoms provide for nonpredictability; at the same time the reiteration of certain pitches effects irregular groupings in time.
2. The structure of the two phrases is asymmetrical, distributed at a ratio of 10 half notes to 22 half notes. Balance and unity are achieved, however, by a repetition (with variant) of the most poignant melodic figure. (Compare measure 2 to measure 6.)

In reduction to its essential pitches, the melodic motion of these measures may be represented as follows:

Example 224

Observe that the melodic contour and the placement of primary and secondary high points and low points is carefully controlled. The motion is often disjunct, achieving definition and accent for specific notes and words. There are two *tonal axes:* D (measures 1-2 and 5-6) and A (measure 3). Measure 4, which is central in terms of time span, is transient in C and accomplishes the return to D.

CHORDS OF THE SEVENTH

Slow-moving triadic harmonies are enriched, in four instances, by the addition of *chordal sevenths* (marked X and Y in Example 223). The presence of the seventh in

Western music was typically a result of linearity up to the time of Monteverdi; thereafter, the chord gradually emerges as an independent, clearly defined harmonic entity.

An additional third may be added to any triad, forming a seventh with the root (Example 225).

Example 225

Seven chords of different *color* or *quality* are derived from the major and harmonic minor scales. Although terminology varies, a logical nomenclature identifies first the triad quality (major, minor, diminished, augmented), and second, the distance from the chord root to the seventh (major, minor, diminished, augmented).

DOMINANT SEVENTH

Throughout the seventeenth and eighteenth centuries, certain qualities of seventh chords were more frequently employed than others. The triad with seventh, built on the fifth scale degree, common to both major and minor modes, is typically the most prominent. A general hierarchy of usage would perhaps have the following order:

1. Major-Minor
2. Diminished-Minor
3. Minor-Minor
4. Diminished-Diminished
5. Major-Major

Example 226

Obviously, these seventh chords, which result from the diatonic scales, are the most frequently used. Others are observed especially in the nineteenth century, both in practice and in theory:

Example 227

Observe in Example 227 that, although c^i and $b\sharp^i$ are octave equivalents, in equal temperament, their functions differ.

PREPARATION AND RESOLUTION

Since the initial use of sevenths resulted from linearity, it is reasonable to observe that the *preparation* and *resolution* of chordal sevenths are based upon melodic considerations. The terminology used to describe these procedures unfortunately borrows from nonchord-tone nomenclature.

Preparation: as passing-tone figure
as upper-auxiliary figure
as suspension figure
as appoggiatura figure

Example 228

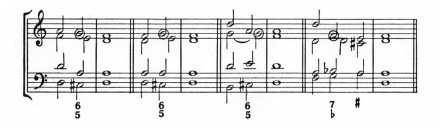

Resolution: the usual resolution of any minor seventh, irrespective of inversion, is *stepwise down.*

In practice there are, fortunately, nonconformists. "Irregular" (more accurately, "less usual") resolutions are illustrated in the following examples from the works of two rather successful composers (Example 229):

Example 229

a. Monteverdi. Resolutions made for reasons of linearity and mode.

b. J. S. Bach. The melodic figure in the bass takes precedence over typical resolution.

DISSOLUTION

A common behavior pattern for the seventh is that of common-tone absorption into the subsequent harmony. A distinction is sometimes made by referring to this behavior as *dissolution* (Example 230).

Example 230

THIRD INVERSION

The *third inversion* ($\frac{4}{2}$) of any seventh chord may be approached, employed, and resolved in the ways illustrated in Example 230. However, there are two very frequent and additional uses, which are illustrated below (Example 231).

Example 231

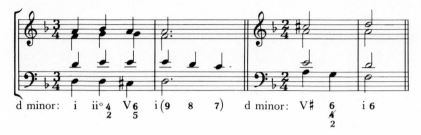

d minor: i   ii°$^4_2$ V$^6_5$ i(9 8 7)   d minor: V♯ $^6_{♯4}_2$ i 6

CONVERGENCE OF THIRDS

In Example 232 the organizational feature, in terms of harmony, is the *convergence of two sets of thirds*—yielding in the approach to cadence. Doublings, resolution of chord sevenths, and perhaps even the resolution of melodic dissonances are all of secondary consideration. As a result, melodic and harmonic independence is achieved, producing a passage of singular beauty. This compositional procedure is again rather frequently encountered in the works of certain twentieth-century composers.

Example 232

SALMO A 4 VOCI ED ORGANO (excerpt)

Monteverdi

To the tonal
orientation
of D: III   iv III$^+$ VI^7 (ii°6)   VI   ii°6 (iv^7) ii°6 iv V^7 i $^6_4$ V4 $\cancel{8}$ I♯
             (as V) $^4_3$

*Accidentals appearing above the notes are not contained in the original manuscript but are suggested by most editors. In this instance, however, their inclusion would detract from the premise of convergence of major triads. Further, the two suggested B♭'s in the tenor line (measures 2, 4) create melodically an augmented second and an unresolved augmented fourth, respectively.

DOMINANT SEVENTH AS SECONDARY FUNCTION

Since the addition of the seventh does not alter the triad function, seventh chords are frequently employed as secondary function.

Example 233

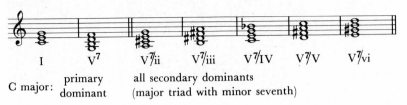

I   V⁷   V⁷/ii   V⁷/iii   V⁷/IV   V⁷/V   V⁷/vi

C major: primary   all secondary dominants
       dominant   (major triad with minor seventh)

Example 234

i   V⁷   V⁷/III   V⁷/iv   V⁷/V   V⁷/VI

c minor: (as a major
          triad)

MAJOR-MINOR SEVENTH FROM ALTERATION

An additional occurrence of this sonority is found on the fourth scale degree of the minor mode. Its introduction was prompted, perhaps, by consideration of scale (melodic minor), or by mechanical reasons—the avoidance of the melodic interval of an augmented second (Example 235).

Example 235

c minor: i   IV 6/5   V 6/5   i 9 8   —   6/5   6/5

Figured-bass symbols for all seventh chords are illustrated below:

Example 236

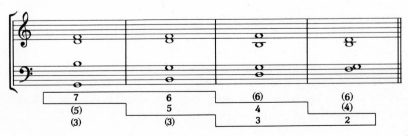

The pattern 7-$^6_5$-$^4_3$-2 is a convenient memory guide. (In place of the 2, some theorists prefer to use $^4_2$, which distinguishes this inversion more clearly from a 2-1 suspension figure.)

AUGMENTED SECOND

As previously stated, in vocal music of all periods prior to the nineteenth century, the melodic interval of an *augmented second* is typically avoided.

Example 237

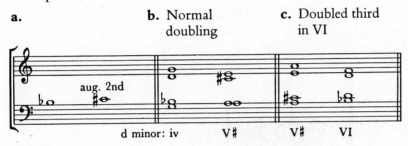

a. **b.** Normal doubling **c.** Doubled third in VI

d minor: iv V♯ V♯ VI

THE TRITONE (Augmented fourth, diminished fifth)

By way of review, the melodic and harmonic employment of the *tritone* is shown below.

Example 238

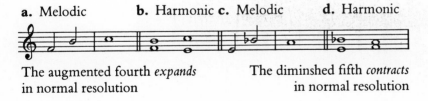

a. Melodic **b.** Harmonic **c.** Melodic **d.** Harmonic

The augmented fourth *expands* in normal resolution

The diminished fifth *contracts* in normal resolution

CHAPTER SUMMARY

In 1602, the composer Giulio Caccini published a collection of accompanied solo songs entitled *Nuove Musiche* (new music). The title was prophetic. Not only did a new dramatic, declamatory, and instrumental style emerge, but from these innovations of *Nuove Musiche* developed the grandiloquent era known as the Baroque period.

One of the most radical innovations was the use of dramatic declamation in music, called *recitative*. It follows the free rhythm of a prose text. Melodic lines reflect the rhythmic innovations. Vocal lines become, on occasion, very florid or even virtuosic. At the same time, the emergence of an equal and independent instrumental idiom expands the range and type of lines. Harmony, within a modal, major-minor framework, accommodated both function and system. Modal succession was replaced by tonal progression. Texture and color contributed significantly to the Baroque ideal of contrasts; forms and genera expanded with the spirit of the times.

One of the most significant innovations of the early Baroque period was a notational practice called *figured bass*. Figured bass is a system of musical shorthand that provides for a bass line and a set of numbers and symbols.

One of the most important analytical concepts in theory is that of secondary function. The concept provides for the momentary borrowing of resources that relate to scale degrees other than the tonic. Modulation, on the other hand, is a process that achieves a change in tonality.

Seventh chords result from the addition of a third to a triad—for example, c e g *b*. Seventh chords have a precise terminology that describes the color or quality of the triad and of the chordal seventh from the chord root. The major-minor seventh (dominant seventh) is probably the most widely employed seventh-chord sonority during the Baroque and Classical periods.

SUGGESTED STUDIES

1. Complete Example 239 to five parts (close structure). Comment briefly on each of the following items:

The phrase structure
The types of cadences
The implied tonal orientation (level) at each cadence
The kinds of root movement

Example 239

EXULTENT CAELI

Monteverdi

*Sharp added to signature, note values halved.

2. Continue the realization of the given figured bass in Example 240 with three or four voices.

Example 240

ORFEO (excerpt)

Solo recitative

Monteverdi

3. Analyze and be able to discuss the given passage from *Orfeo* of Monteverdi (Example 241) in the following terms:

The kinds of root movement
The kinds of nonharmonicism
The extent and kind of repetition
The kinds of compositional devices

Example 241

ORFEO (excerpt)

Monteverdi

Chapter 15

THE MAJOR-MINOR SYSTEM OF TONAL MUSIC

The major-minor system became firmly established in the first half of the seventeenth century. Tonal progression supplanted modal succession; harmonic function became synonymous with musical organization; nonharmonicism and modulation, in the modern meaning of these terms, were employed consistently and with a full knowledge of their theoretical and musical significance.

Observation of Baroque harmonic practice reveals a system that is governed principally by root movement by perfect fifth. Implied in the system are the specific relationships of all diatonic triads to a central tonic chord.

Example 242

CHORD CLASSIFICATIONS

Example 242 illustrates a series of relationships, or *chord classifications,* to a given tonic:

First relationship (classification): the dominant and leading-tone triads are the most closely related to the tonic—in terms of *function* (effected by the presence of the raised seventh degree of the scale and, in the case of the dominant, a root whose distance from the tonic is a perfect fifth)
Second relationship: ii (ii°) and IV (iv)
Third relationship: vi (VI)
Fourth relationship: iii (III or III⁺)

In progressing from the most distantly related sonority to the tonic, one may establish a root-movement chain of perfect fifths.

Example 243

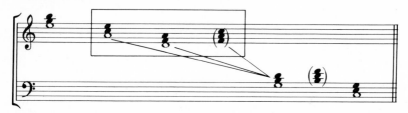

II, IV, VI often have a common function—that of dominant prefix or "approach chord." Baroque composers certainly did not indulge in an endless series of iii, vi, ii, V, I progressions—although analyses of the substructure of compositions of this period indicate a strong reliance on set relationships. Modifications in the chain of fifths were fortunately numerous, and include:

1. Omission of a relationship, e.g.
       I   vi——V   I, or
       I   iii——IV——I
2. Alteration of a chord or the use of secondary function
3. Tonal variation achieved by modulation
4. Use of only one or two relationships—common throughout the Baroque and Classical periods—
       I   V   I   V   I, or
       I   IV   V   I   ii   V   I
   as well as use of the infinite combinations that are a part of invention.

Example 244 illustrates the basic system as well as the modifications. In this famous recitative and lament, other important Baroque concepts and compositional procedures may be observed. The recitative is supported by a keyboard part in which the performer makes certain decisions regarding position and deployment or chords, but within the harmonic confines indicates by the composer. Observe that the essential shape of the line is downward from cⁱⁱ to dⁱ and accomplishes a modulation from c minor to g minor.

Example 244

DIDO AND AENEAS (excerpt)

Purcell

mem-ber me, but ah!_____ for-get my_ fate. Re-mem-ber me,

re-mem-ber me, But ah!_____ for-get my fate, Re-

mem-ber me, but ah!_____ for-get my_ fate.

GROUND BASS

The lament is constructed on a *ground bass*. Purcell's 5-measure series (measures 1-5, Example 245) is an example of the bass patterns used in the Baroque period as a foundation and unification for through-composed variations—specifically, the *chaconne* and *passacaglia*. The pattern, Example 245, has an interesting division into two parts: three consecutive pairs of descending semitones, followed by a counterthrust in the opposite direction. The corresponding change in rhythm (marked XX) provides an element of nonpredictability.

Example 245

The relationship of the ground bass to the vocal line is subtle; the descending semitones are somewhat concealed by rhythmic shift:

Example 246

Observe the poignant word-painting by the use of the tritone for "trouble" in measure 11 of Example 244. Example 244 illustrates three different versions, or treatments, of the ground bass:

Without harmonization, marked X
First harmonization, marked Y
Second or altered harmonization, marked Z

These harmonic variants are very important as a musical consideration, for the procedure effects a change of musical environment for the constant reiteration of the bass pattern. The first harmonization illustrates two forms of dominant (measure 6) and two forms of subdominant (measure 7).

CADENTIAL FORMULA

The cadence in measures 9-10 (ii⁶₅ i⁶₄ V i) is a cadential formula of unusual durability—used quite consistently by composers for nearly two hundred years.

Example 247

a. Purcell   b. Common four-voice   c.
                dispositions

AUGMENTED SIXTH CHORDS

The final measure of Purcell's recitative employs a sonority of unusual quality, which includes the melodic interval of an *augmented sixth:*

Example 248

Augmented sixth sonorities have an extended and interesting history, observed from about the time of Gesualdo in the sixteenth century. In the Baroque and Classical periods, augmented sixths were used sparingly at points of musical tension and decidedly in a linear context; usage in the Romantic period became frequent to the point where entire compositions were built around this focal sonority. Conversely, its absence from most twentieth-century scores is conspicuous.

    Three most common formations of augmented sixth chords are shown below. Other, less frequently used forms are shown at a later point in the text.

Example 249

a. Italian   b. German   c. French

These three forms share common properties:

1. All are typically found in a minor key.
2. All employ the *raised fourth degree* of the scale.
3. All have the same harmonic function, either as iv (Italian and German) or ii (French).
4. All contain unclassified triads (i.e., spellings other than major, minor, augmented, or diminished); for example: C♯ E♭ G or A C♯ E♭ G.
5. The resolution of the augmented sixth interval typically expands to the octave.

Example 250

The German sixth chord (IV⁶⁄₅) typically resolves to a tonic ⁶⁄₄ to avoid parallel perfect fifths.

During the Classical and Romantic periods, modification of the behavior of augmented-sixth chords is noticeable:

Example 251

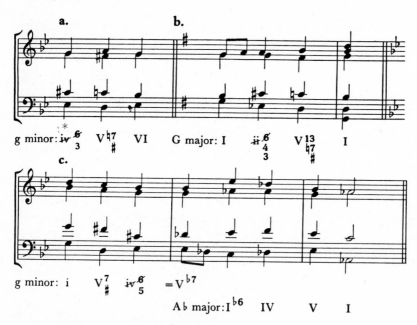

a. "Irregular" (less-usual) resolutions
b. Appearance in a major key
c. Enharmonic spellings used for modulation to distant key

*To indicate that an augmented sixth chord is not major, minor, diminished, or augmented in its *triadic quality,* the author uses hereafter the symbols: *iv̶* and *ii̶.*

NOTE: The raised fourth degree may be employed for other chords—that is, nonaugmented sixth chords—expecially vii°⁷ of V. For example, in g minor: C♯ E♮ G B♭ = vii°⁷/V.

CONCERTO GROSSO

One of the most important legacies of Baroque instrumental music is the concerto grosso, which developed over a hundred-year period from about 1650 to 1750. In addition to the contrasting concertino and ripieno instrumentation, the concerto grosso prominently displays the era's interest in instrumental idiom; in texture per se, including heterophony; and in the aspects of harmonic rhythm and pacing. Occasional fast movements have, for example, an exceedingly slow harmonic rhythm. The number of movements varies from three (Vivaldi) to five or more (Corelli)—depending upon the composer and the stage of development. Bach's six *Brandenburg Concertos* (1721) and Handel's *Grand Concertos,* Op. 6 (1740) are superb examples of this genre—as are Corelli's twelve masterful concertos, constituting his Opus 6.

KEYBOARD REALIZATIONS

Corelli's *Concerto* (Example 252) is illustrative of the Baroque composer's interest in contrasts: the formal design of the entire concerto is a series of alternating slow and fast sections; the instrumental contrast is provided by a group of soloists (It. *concertino,* concerted) and a larger and reinforced group (It. *ripieno,* full), which engage each other in a constant dialogue.

An interesting feature of this concerto is that the *ripieno* parts may be omitted, leaving a perfectly formed *trio sonata* from the remaining concertino parts. In this modern edition, the cembalo (organ or harpsichord) has been realized from the figured bass of the concertino.

OBSERVATIONS:

1. A consistent three- to four-voice texture is maintained, with all notes of the chords strictly conforming to the composer's figured-bass instructions.
2. The actual placement (*disposition*) of the notes is at the discretion of the keyboard performer, who, in this example, uses a combination of
   a. doubling of string parts
   b. providing for filler between the two violins and the violoncello
3. The cembalo part has no real rhythmic independence and effects an unobtrusive supporting sound for the strings.

The realization of Corelli's *Concerto* may be taken as quite representative of current editions and performance practice today. One imagines, however, that at an actual eighteenth-century performance—in the hands of a virtuoso keyboard artist—

the figured-bass realization would have been far more independent, embellished, and elaborate in general.

Improvisation is one of several concerns or interests shared by the eighteenth- and twentieth-century composer. For a revealing insight into improvisatory performance practice, the student is asked to compare a popular-song chord chart with any recorded or live version. One questions whether the *intent* of improvisation has really changed substantially in the past two hundred years.

Example 252

CONCERTO V, OP. 6, NO. 5

Cembalo realization by Waldemar Woehl

Arcangelo Corelli (1653-1713)

Reprinted from Peters Edition Nr. 4485.

NEAPOLITAN SIXTH CHORD

Measure 12 of the Corelli example (Example 252) contains still another interesting sonority, involving an alteration of a diatonic scale degree. The *Neapolitan sixth chord* derives part of its name from the fact that its early appearance was almost exclusively as a chord of first inversion (6).

Observations concerning the Neapolitan sixth include:

1. Baroque and early Classical usages of the Neapolitan sixth are generally restricted to the minor key.

2. In the Baroque and Classical periods, the chord is usually employed in first inversion.

3. The sonority is derived from a *major* triad built on the *lowered second degree* of the scale; therefore II, with a subdominant function.

4. The chord third is normally doubled in four-voice texture.

5. The resolution is typically to V, V^7, or i$^6_4$.

6. The figured-bass symbols are ♭6, or ♮6 in a sharped key.

Example 253

During the Romantic era, the Neapolitan sixth is used in a major key. The sonority may be employed in root position; occasionally, a chordal seventh is added.

INSTRUMENTAL SUITE

The instrumental suite is similarly a significant form, derived from the pairing of dance movements. Typically, the suite is in one key and each movement is essentially monothematic in binary or rounded binary form—that is, A B or A B (A).

Although there is no set number of movements for the instrumental suite, an *allemande* (German), *courante* (running), *sarabande* (possibly from the Persian *serbend*, song), and *gigue* (jig) are commonly found. Optional additional movements include the air, bourrée, gavotte, loure, passepied, minuet, and other dances of the period. An easy memory guide to the suite order is A C S O (optional movements) G.

Example 254

FRENCH SUITE NO. 1 IN D MINOR (excerpts)

Bach

ALLEMANDE

(Andantino ♩ = 72)

CHAPTER SUMMARY

The major-minor system became firmly established in the first half of the seven-teenth century. Tonal progression supplanted modal succession; harmonic function became synonymous with musical organization; nonchord tones and modulation, in the modern meaning of these terms, were employed consistently and with a full knowledge of their theoretical and musical significance.

Chord classifications refer to relationships of diatonic chords to a central tonic. These are as follows: first relationship, V and VII; second relationship, II and IV; third relationship, VI; fourth relationship, III.

A ground bass is a melodic pattern, typically found in the lowest-sounding voice, that provides a foundation and unification for through-composed variations.

Chords containing an interval of an augmented sixth have become denoted as augmented sixth chords. In the Baroque period these chords were used sparingly at points of musical tension. The common varieties of augmented sixth chords are termed Italian, German, and French. They all share three common properties: all are typically found in a minor key; all employ the raised fourth degree of the scale; and all have the same harmonic function, either as iv (Italian and German) or ii (French).

The Neapolitan sixth chord derives part of its name from the fact that its early appearance was almost exclusively as a chord of first inversion (6). It is a major triad built on the lowered second degree of the scale, therefore II_6, with a subdominant function. The chord third is normally doubled; its typical resolution is to V, V^7, or to i_4^6.

SUGGESTED STUDIES

1. Perform in class the Corelli *Largo* (Example 252), then discuss:

> After the first reading:
> > Appropriate instruments
> > The meaning of *Largo,* tempo, dynamics, phrasing
> After the second reading:
> > Articulation, ornamentation (trills)
> After the third reading (concertato only):
> > Concertato parts as a musical form
> After the fourth reading:
> > Structural, tonal, harmonic, and cadential analysis

2. In four parts, realize the following figured bass lines (Example 255 a and b). Identify and label all augmented sixth and Neapolitan sixth chords. Provide a harmonic analysis.

3. Invent a complementary period to the aria with figured bass given in Example 256. Realize the figured bass in manner and style appropriate for performance as an accompaniment.

Example 255

Example 256

Purcell

SUGGESTED MAJOR PROJECT

The project presents no new materials. Rather, the student is advised to apply the information, technique, skills, and knowledge of style and performance practice garnered from historical and theoretical studies. History and theory should be put to work, so to speak—not for the purpose of earning a grade or passing a required course but for the purpose of learning to apply information and skills in a practical and meaningful manner. It is desirable that the project suggested in this chapter not be construed as "just another theory assignment."

Many excellent compositions from the Baroque era for instruments and/or voices with a figured-bass line—that is, with *basso continuo*—have yet to be transcribed as modern performance editions. Numerous other compositions, existing in realizations made at the end of the nineteenth century, are seriously flawed by nonstylistic additions and omissions as well as by a glaringly deficient part writing. Both of these categories afford the contemporary music student an excellent opportunity to contribute personally to the quality of music editions by producing appropriate and technically perfect realizations from a figured bass. Specific project suggestions are cited below.

An additional area that has much potential both as a project and as a contribution is that of transcription of a composition from the original instrument to a different one. This suggestion may be controversial, yet it is worthy of serious consideration. Baroque literature for voice, flute, oboe, violin, and cello is abundant. Solo works with keyboard accompaniment for other brass, woodwinds, and strings is either rare or nonexistent. Succinctly stated, Purcell, Handel, and Bach did not compose suites or sonatas for clarinet or tuba, nor for a long list of other versatile orchestral instruments. Since all students need repertoire and performance practice experience with Baroque literature, transcription—even if one questions it in principle —may be rationalized as a minor transgression.

SUGGESTED PROJECT

Realize from a figured-bass line an appropriate keyboard accompaniment for a solo voice or instrument. A complete work with four short movements would be ideal for instrumentalists. Singers should prepare an edition of similar length and difficulty.

As an example, Handel's Sonata, Op. 1, No. 2 for flute and basso continuo might be transcribed for B♭ clarinet and piano. A few measures illustrate:

Example 257

ADAGIO, OP. 1, NO. 2

George Frederick Handel (1685-1759)

SUGGESTED COMPOSERS:

Arcangelo Corelli (1653-1713)
George Frederick Handel (1685-1759)
Benedetto Marcello (1685-1739)
Jean-Marie Leclair (1697-1764)

Example 258

SONATA DA CHIESA, OP. 3, NO. 7

Corelli

PART III

THE COMPLETED MAJOR-MINOR SYSTEM

"Mortal men live by mutual exchange."
—Lucretius

Chapter 16

CHORALE STYLE

DEFINITION

The 371 chorale harmonizations of J. S. Bach offer significant insight into the harmonic and contrapuntal writing of the high Baroque. Chorale melodies were invented by Reformation and later Protestant composers, or they were borrowed from existing liturgical and popular sources. Bach's chorales, except for about ten, were harmonizations of existing melodies and were used as portions of larger choral compositions—particularly of the cantatas and passions.

Chorales are short compositions varying from about 12 to 50 measures. The phrase lengths correspond to the text, where typically six to eight syllables define the phrase. Although the chorales are essentially through-composed (principle of contiguity), one often observes a musical repetition of the first two phrases, resulting in a generalized AAB, or *bar, form*.

Bach's musical process is observed on several levels:

1. Tonal clarity, particularly in the initial and final phrases, with tonal variety as an internal feature
2. Bass lines of unusual strength and sense of direction

3. Varied internal arriving points (cadences), often implying a circular design
4. Harmonic variety within an ordered system with typically strong root-movement progressions at points of cadence

Vor Deinen Thron Tret Ich Heimet (Example 259) is a version of the familiar *Old Hundredth*, derived from a *Pseaume* of Louis Bourgeois (1551). The four phrases of equal length are firmly anchored in D major without any real modulation. Harmonic progression stems from a sweeping bass line, which approaches an instrumental character (Example 260).

Example 259

VOR DEINEN THRON TRET ICH HEIMET

Bach

Example 260

Arrival points are varied. Psychologically, these cadences are of crucial importance in providing for direction, variety, and a valid musical experience. When played consecutively, the cadences form a logical harmonic progression (Example 261):

Example 261

A comparison of progression by fifths with Bach's actual practice is of interest:

First phrase:

Progression by fifths	{	I	III	VI	II(IV)		V	I	VI	II	V	I
Bach's harmonization	{	I	VI	III	IV	—	I	VI	II	V	I	

Last phrase:

Progression by fifths	{	V	I	VI	II	V	I	II	V	I
Bach's harmonization	{	V	I	VI	—	V	I	II	V	I

Hypothesis and practice would seem to have the greatest correlation at points of cadence. Cadences are typically strong, although in the 371 chorales there are obviously numerous exceptions. *Vor Deinen Thron* (Example 259) is ideal for initial study:

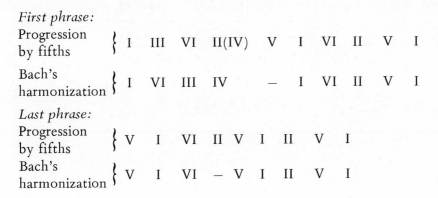

1st phrase cadence: II_5^6 V   I

2nd phrase cadence: I I_6 V

3rd phrase cadence: II_5^6 V♯   VI

            VI

4th phrase cadence: II_6 V_7 I

Without exception in this chorale, all cadence dominant and tonic chords are in *root position*.

Example 262

O HAUPT VOLL BLUT UND WUNDEN

Bach

Hassler's melody of 1601, set by Bach in *O Haupt voll Blut und Wunden* (Example 262), suggests the Phrygian mode and may account for the rather unusual final cadence, with a chord third in the soprano voice. The harmonization by Bach is, of course, in D major—with modulations to b minor, e minor, and A major.

MODULATION

It is recalled that there are three principal categories of modulation:

Diatonic (common chord)
Chromatic
Enharmonic

Of these three, diatonic modulation is the most frequently used in the Baroque and Classical periods.

An illustration of common sonorities of the four tonal levels of this chorale is found in Example 263:

Example 263

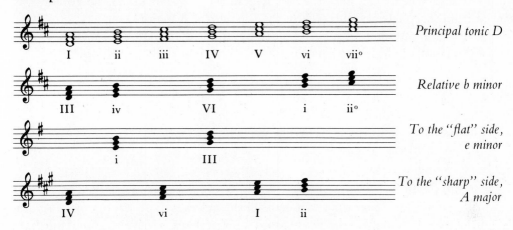

Well into the nineteenth century, most composers were content to utilize key relationships that were closely related to the principal key—that is, to one or two sharps or flats on either side of the tonic, as shown in Example 263. It should be observed that although C and C♯ are immediately adjacent in terms of sound, their key relationship is seven degrees removed.

MODULATORY PROCEDURE

The boxed chords in Example 262 are points of modulation and, for the purpose of emphasis, are shown below in Example 264:

Example 264

a D V $\boxed{\begin{matrix} I = \\ III \end{matrix}}$ VII$_6$ i
    b

b b $\boxed{\begin{matrix} I = \\ VI \end{matrix}}$ VII$_6$(II) I$_6$
    D

c D $\boxed{\begin{matrix} IV = \\ III \end{matrix}}$ VII^7 I^9
    e

d A $\boxed{\begin{matrix} IV = \\ I \end{matrix}}$ II (VII$_6$) I$_6$
    D

In Example 262, X (measure 8) marks a chromatic area. The dominant of e minor is an altered supertonic in the key of A major; the anticipated e minor chord becomes, rather, e^i g$\sharp$ b and d^{ii}. Chromatic modulation requires the alteration of one or more tones in the direction of the new key. In the above example, the note d^{ii} was changed from sharp to natural to affirm the tonality of A major.

Enharmonic modulation may be basically either diatonic or chromatic, but involves a respelling of chord tones in the direction of the new key (Example 265).

Example 265

A major I   iii   =   altered iv   V   I in A♭ major

In diatonic modulation (Example 266), a common chord—called the *pivot chord*—has a function other than dominant in the new key (i.e., III, VI, or I). Avoidance of the new dominant as the pivot chord does perhaps achieve a more immediate functional clarity for the new phrase. Exceptions are found, however, especially the formula observed in Example 266e. Additional modulatory schemes are included below:

Example 266

e.

G: V —— $^4_2$ I$_6$ V$^6_4$ I   IV   I

ANALYTICAL SYSTEMS

Du Friedefürst, Herr Jesu Christ (Example 267) is quoted with two analytical versions—a chordal analysis (I) and a structural harmonic analysis (II) derived from the theoretical contributions of Heinrich Schenker (1869-1935). The ability to perceive the basic harmonic structure of a composition is a highly relevant skill for the performer, composer, and music historian. However, it should be understood that any analytical system will contain aspects susceptible to subjective application and that any composition, irrespective of style, fortunately may be viewed from several perspectives.

Schenker refers to the following levels of harmonic activity:

Foreground: actual progression; treble line is called *Urlinie*
Middle ground: an intervening functional level (first phase of reduction)
Background: the harmonic structure at its most basic level (*Ursatz*)

Example 267

DU FRIEDEFURST, HERR JESU CHRIST

Bach

II

Analysis of first two phrases from *Structural Hearing,* by Felix Salzer, Dover Publications, Inc., New York, 1952, Vol. II, p. 49. Reprinted through permission of the publisher.

(The author of this text refers to these levels of activity as "harmonic dimensions" and uses "substructure" synonymously with Schenker's "background.")

It is possible that analyses I and II may both omit important considerations. Analysis I perhaps appears simply as a series of related chords; Analysis II examines the harmonic resultants of linear activity at structurally significant points.

An additional analysis (III) suggests that the first 4 measures are concerned with an alternation of tonic and subdominant, while the final 4 bars balance the tonal axis with an emphasis on dominant and submediant.

Example 268

III

In summary:

First dimension:	I	IV	vii°₆	I	etc.			
Second dimension:	I	IV	(I)		V	VI	ii⁶₅	V	I
Third dimension	I				V			I
(substructure):								

NONCHORD TONES

Nun Danket Alle Gott, the familiar hymn of Thanksgiving (Example 269), is analyzed in terms of nonchord tones. The chorale is typical of Bach's usage:

13 PT = passing tone
3 S   = suspension
2 ET = escape tone (échappée)
2 OR = ornamental resolution
1 NT = neighboring tone (auxiliary tone)
1 APT = accented passing tone (appoggiatura)
1 A   = anticipation

OBSERVATIONS:

1. Harmonic connection of triads and seventh chords becomes an art with the assistance of judiciously used nonchord tones. The procedure effects a quasi-
   counterpoint—perhaps more implied than real—yet tension and release and
   rhythmic flow are accomplished essentially by embellishing and connecting
   tones.

Example 269

NUN DANKET ALLE GOTT

Bach

2. Passing tones have the highest frequency of use followed, at considerable distance, by suspensions. Measures 5 and 9 contain examples of suspensions where the resolution and movement in the bass are simultaneous (Example 270). In such instances the Arabic designation conforms to the actual distance between the bass and the resolving tones (Example 270).

Example 270

9 8 7 becomes 9 7 6   9 6   4 4 7 7   9 9

CADENTIAL DECORATION

The Renaissance cadential decoration is retained in Baroque practice. When involving a dissonance, the decorative figure is commonly referred to as an ornamental resolution (Example 271).

Example 271

4   3 2 3   8   7 6 7   7   6 5 6

Example 272

ACH GOTT, WIE MANCHES HERZELEID

Bach

O Lord! How man - y ; mis - er - ies   As - sault and

MELODIC BASS, ROOT BASS

The chorale setting of *Ach Gott, Wie Manches Herzeleid* (Example 272) illustrates again the importance of a melodic bass line—achieved in part by the employment of chord inversions for both horizontal and vertical factors. Compare Bach's actual bass with the *root bass*.

FURTHER OBSERVATIONS:

1. The cadence plan for the entire chorale is V/V (measure 4) V (measure 8) V (measure 12) I (measure 16), which again provides a logical progression for the arrival points.

2. Of the total 36 chords in the harmonization, observe the preponderance of dominant function:

$$
\begin{array}{rl}
\textit{Tonic function:} & \text{I (11)} \\
& \text{vi (2)} \\
\textit{Dominant function:} & \text{V (9)} \\
& \text{vii}^\circ \text{ (2)}
\end{array}
$$

Secondary dominant function:	V/V (5)
	V/vi (2)
	V/ii (1)
Subdominant function:	IV (2)
	ii (2)
Total tonic:	13
Total dominant:	19
Total subdominant:	4

CHORD DISPOSITION (spacing)

3. Although the harmonization contains only nine different sonorities, variety is achieved by the emphasis on (or in) the dominant in the second phrase; by the use of inversions; by the addition of chordal sevenths; and by chordal disposition (i.e., the specific arrangement of pitches for a given sonority). In the simple and direct chorale, Bach tenders considerable interest in the sonorous possibilities of the tonic chord (Example 273).

Example 273

The unusual disposition (spacing) of chords in measures 13-14 probably results from linear considerations; this compositional procedure provides for still another aspect of variety.

CHORALE RHYTHM

Rhythmic flow in the chorales is regulated by the alternation of long and short, ♩ and ♪, but occasionally, especially at cadences, is intensified by common figures of shorter value: ♩♪, ♪♪♪ , or less often ♪♪♪ , and seldom ♪♪♪ . Bach is typically careful to introduce in the first phrases all note values to be used subsequently in the chorale. Sudden rhythmic outbursts are not common to Bach's style, although Handel occasionally indulges in them for dramatic reasons.

Example 274

ES IST GENUG

Bach

Es Ist Genug (Example 274) is a chorale of singular beauty with considerable harmonic complexity. The analysis provided in Example 274 represents *one* perspective and should not be regarded as the only possible analysis. Particularly, measures 10 and 11 might well be analyzed at the level of E.

HARMONIC AREA (region)

The chordal analyses contained within brackets are points of unusual interest, representing a harmonic activity at a level other than the central tonic. The bracket extending from measure 1 to measure 3 could be considered an *area* or *region* (mediant, in this instance) of harmonic function. Observe that in this chorale setting, the dominant region (V) has the greatest emphasis, balanced by the mediant region in the beginning and the submediant region near the end. The substructure (background or *Ursatz*) for the entire chorale could probably be defined as: I V I.

FURTHER OBSERVATIONS:

1. The chorale melody has strong Lydian-mode vestiges, and the opening whole-tone movement is extraordinary. Melodic repetition is the primary principle of organization: compare measure 5 to measures 1 and 2; measures 6½-11 to 1-6½; 15-17 to 12-14; 20 to 18.

2. The inner force—or perhaps "propulsion"—comes from the nearly constant alternation of tension and repose:

> *Tension:* measure 1-2 (chromaticism and sonorities foreign to the central tonic; fast harmonic rhythm)
> *Repose:* measure 3-4 (diatonic; slow harmonic rhythm; weak cadence)

3. Cadence emphasis is on I and V—which act as "anchors" in a shifting harmonic scheme (observe the chromatic bass line in measures 15-16).

4. Tone painting is of a high order, achieved not only by the poignancy of vertical

tone structures but also by the nonsymmetrical phrase structure and deliberately imbalanced inner accents.

CHAPTER SUMMARY

The 371 chorale harmonizations of J. S. Bach offer significant insight into the harmonic and contrapuntal writing of the high Baroque. Bach's musical process is observed on several levels: tonal clarity, strong bass lines, varied cadences, and harmonic variety achieved through secondary function and modulation.

The three principal categories of modulation are called diatonic, chromatic, and enharmonic. Of these three, diatonic modulation is most frequently observed in the chorales.

Harmonic connection of triads and seventh chords becomes an art with the assistance of judiciously used nonchord tones: passing tones, suspensions, escape tones, auxiliary tones, and anticipations. The use of these nonchord tones effects a quasi-counterpoint in which each voice of the chorale has melodic and rhythmic interest.

Rhythmic flow in the chorales is regulated by the alternation of long and short durations that underscore the text. The phrase lengths correspond to the text, where typically six to eight syllables define the phrase.

SUGGESTED STUDIES

1. Harmonize the following chorale melodies in four parts. Analyze the melody, considering shape of line, possible modulation implications, cadence points, melodic rhythm, harmonic rhythm.

   Sketch a bass line that will provide a melodic fluency and logical eighteenth-century harmonic progressions.

   Add the inner voices.

   Refine the harmonization by the careful addition of nonharmonic tones, appropriate to the style.

   Add a harmonic analysis.

   After completion, play the harmonization several times.

Example 275

a.

b.

c.

d.

2. Make a thorough analysis of *Wir Singen Dir, Immanuel* (Example 276), including
   the following:

   Harmonic and structural analyses; the role and function of nonharmonic tones
   The nature and purpose of the instrumental interludes
   Cadence plan
   Possible figured-bass realizations

Example 276

WIR SINGEN DIR, IMMANUEL

Christmas Oratorio

Bach

lords,_ the _ vir - gin_ born.

Chapter 17

TONAL COUNTERPOINT

In the previous discussions of the chorales, functional harmonic progressions were shown to have partial contrapuntal implications as the result of careful control of each contributing line. Similarly, compositions that were conceived linearly (e.g., canons, fugues) are rarely observed to be without a strong harmonic basis.

SPECIES COUNTERPOINT

Current systematic study of contrapuntal techniques often begins with an investigation of *species counterpoint*. Here Johann Fux must be acknowledged for his treatise *Gradus ad Parnassum* (1725), which recommends an orderly course of study.

There are many reinterpretations of Fux—ranging from the rigorously disciplined to the nearly casual. The procedure set forth in Fux's treatise is appropriate for either the sixteenth-century or the eighteenth-century style. In the following discussion of species counterpoint, which is at once cursory and to a certain extent unorthodox, the examples are drawn from a single movement of a Bach *Suite* (see Example 282).

Example 277 (first species)

extracted from Bach

Counterpoint:

Cantus firmus:

OBSERVATIONS:

1. First species consists of a motion of one note of counterpoint for each note of *cantus firmus.*
2. Each line has a specific and independent contour.
3. Contrary motion is predominant.
4. Maximum sonority is achieved by the use of the intervals of thirds and sixths.

NOTE: Perfect consonances and dissonances are, of course, also acceptable. Octaves and fifths are sparingly used in two-voice texture because of the "thinness" of sound; the dissonance of seconds, sevenths, and tritones should be resolved—preferably by the use of contrary or oblique motion.

Example 278 (second species)

extracted from Bach

Counterpoint:

Cantus firmus:

OBSERVATIONS:

1. Second species consists of two notes of counterpoint for each note of *cantus firmus.*
2. Each line is independent and contoured.
3. Imperfect consonances predominate; ninths and sevenths are resolved; the tritone is approached and quitted in contrary motion; perfect fifths are followed by sixths or tenths.

NOTE: In Fux, the first note on a downbeat (two half notes to a whole note) was invariably a consonance.

Example 279 (third species)

extracted from Bach

OBSERVATIONS:

1. Third species consists of 3 or more notes (4,6,8,9, etc.) of counterpoint to 1 note of *cantus firmus* (in Fux, third species meant 4 to 1).
2. All intervals are employed; dissonances are resolved.
3. Contrary motion to the *cantus firmus* occurs typically on the first beats.

Example 280 (fourth species)

extracted from Bach

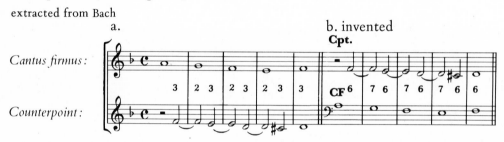

OBSERVATIONS:

1. Fourth species consists of 2 notes of counterpoint for each note of *cantus firmus* and further includes the use of tied notes and a particular device called *suspension*. In each instance (in Fux, called *ligature* or *syncopation*), a consonance is tied over the bar, creating a dissonance (second or seventh), which then is resolved on the weak beat to a consonant third or sixth. An explanation of suspension is found on page 166.
2. Tied notes and suspensions may alternate with "free" counterpoint.

Example 281 (fifth species)

extracted from Bach

OBSERVATIONS:

1. In fifth species, a free number of notes are invented for each note of *cantus firmus* or, as in the above example, the *cantus* and counterpoint are coequals.
2. Control of line, dissonance, and rhythmic interest is maintained.

One of the most engaging movements of Baroque keyboard literature is the Minuet II from the *French Suite in D Minor* of Bach (Example 282). The subtle changes in rhythm, texture, register, and tonality enhance the symmetrical proportion. The middle voice, with the exception of measures 5 and 6, has a sustaining, or "pedal," role; the outside voices are essentially curvilinear—balancing conjunct-disjunct motion, tension and repose.

Example 282

FRENCH SUITE NO. 1 (excerpt)

The contrapuntal ideal is an interwoven web of sonority, propelled by rhythmic thrust, and controlled by harmony, texture, and color. No composition is completely lacking in contrapuntal implication—be it a single-line melody or a series of block chords. The strength and quality of the counterpoint, real or implied, is often a decisive factor in determining the aesthetic value of a composition.

CANON

The concept of a circle of fifths within a key to control progression (III, VI, II, V, I) might well be expanded to embrace a rotating or circular composition such as the Kirnberger *Canon* (Example 283), which modulates through all twelve major keys. In this composition, the 5-measure subject modulates from its tonic to its dominant; concurrently, each subject entry is at the perfect fifth above the preceding entry; further, after a 1½-measure rest, each voice reenters at a major third above its starting note, eventually returning to the original note (an octave higher) and to the original key.

One may become fascinated primarily by the contrapuntal and modulatory aspects of this short composition; however, Kirnberger has built the work on a solid harmonic basis. Analysis of measures 1-5 illustrates:

1. C: I (ii vi)
2. V_6 — vi I
3. V_2^4 of V vii I iii
4. $vi^7 =$
   G: ii^7 V^7 I iii
5. $vi^7 =$
   D: ii^7 V^7 I iii

Example 283

CANON

(Modulating through all twelve major keys)

Johann Philipp Kirnberger (1721-1783)

C major: I (ii vi) V6 — vi I V4/vii°I iii vi7=V I iii vi7=V I iii
2/V G: ii7 V I iii D:ii7

Quoted in Imogene Horsley, *Fugue: History and Practice* (New York: Free Press, 1966), pp. 28-29. Used by permission.

It is recommended that the entire composition be analyzed harmonically, with particular attention to the points of *enharmonic change*. Copying (or transposing up a half step) will provide further insights.

J. S. Bach's formidable technique is nearly without peer in the history of Western music. It is not just a matter of writing counterpoint that can be performed "upside down and backwards"; it is, rather, the beauty of the music that emerges as contrapuntal devices are used—all with the ease of breathing or walking. Both his *Musical Offering* and *Goldberg Variations* contain incredibly inventive canons. Two notational versions of the same canon from the *Musical Offering* are shown in Examples 284 and 285. Compare and study both, paying particular attention to measures 19 and following of Example 285.

Example 284

MUSICAL OFFERING (excerpt)

Canon 1. a2

Bach

Example 285

CANON 1. A2

Canon Cancrizans

Bach

FUGUE

Composers in the late Baroque turned their attention to a procedure called *fugue*. The most famous collection of fugues is, of course, J. S. Bach's 48 preludes and fugues entitled *Das Wohltemperierte Klavier,* which may be correctly translated as: *The Well-tempered Clavier* (i.e., "keyboard").

TERMINOLOGY OF FUGAL ANALYSIS

Certain terminology is commonly used in fugal analysis:

Exposition is the initial portion of a fugue, in which all voices have an opportunity of presenting the main melodic idea, called:

> *Subject (dux, leader)*: the designation for a pitch group or "theme"; and
> *Answer (comes, follower)*: the term denoting that the subject has been transposed, typically to the level of the dominant.
> A *real answer* is an exact transposition, interval by interval;
> A *tonal answer* adjusts certain notes (particularly the melodic perfect fifth) in order to remain in the principal tonality;
> *Modified real answers* or *modified tonal answers* are best described collectively as *hybrid.*

Entry group describes subsequent entries of the subject (after the exposition).

Episode is the term that describes the free or developmental portions of a fugue. An episode typically does *not* contain a full statement of the subject; rather, a part of the subject is used in fragmentation, sequence, or other developmental guise.

Close and *coda* describe the final portions of the fugue.

Stretto (It., narrow, close, tight) is a term denoting an overlapping technique (i.e., a second entry of the subject or answer prior to the completion of the first entry). Fugues in which this device is employed prominently are often referred to as *stretto fugues.*

Voice refers to the number of contrapuntal lines employed in any given composition. The *WTC* contains fugues from two-voice texture (a 2) to five-voice textures (a 5), with three- and four-voice fugues being the most numerous.

Two fugues from the *WTC,* Volume I, are quoted in their entirety for the purpose of showing two architectural types.

Example 286

WELL-TEMPERED CLAVIER, Vol. I

Fugue 1

Bach

SUBJECT-STRUCTURED FUGUE

Fugue 1 (Example 286) is a *subject-structured* fugue. Other terminologies, such as "subject-centered" and "subject-oriented," are synonymous.

OBSERVATIONS:

1. The subject (in brackets) is 1½ measures long; it is answered at the perfect fifth above (real answer), continues with another answer (which is unusual) at the perfect fourth below the original subject, and concludes the exposition with the subject an octave below the original.

2. Thereafter, the contrapuntal procedure is such that the subject (or answer) is presented in all measures except 23 and 26-27. Hence the term: *subject-structured*.

3. In lieu of episodes, Fugue 1 contains two stretto sections—becoming increasingly complex in the number of simultaneous presentations of the subject.

4. Finally, in measure 24, the subject appears again in the tonic (and subdominant), indicating the conclusion or *close* of the composition.

A structural diagram of Fugue 1 would be as follows:

Measures:	1-6	7-13	14-22	23	24-27
Description or function:	exposition	stretto 1	stretto 2	LINK	close
Tonality:	C	G a	a D G C		C

Sophisticated in vocabulary and structure, Fugue 1 entices a kind of speculative theory, or the discovering of relationships and associations that penetrate beyond the purely surface features. A few additional observations may suggest further analysis:

1. The circled notes of measures 1 and 2 seem to define important aspects of the whole fugue:

   a. The basic tonal plan of the entire fugue: C G a (D) G C.
   b. The basic harmonic progression that, at different rhythmic rates, seems to pervade much of the fugue: I V vi ii V I
   $$\text{(II}\sharp)$$

2. The note f^i in measure 1 displays its structural importance in measures 5-6, and again in measures 24-26.

Example 287

WELL-TEMPERED CLAVIER, Vol. I

Fugue 2

Bach

EPISODE-STRUCTURED FUGUE

Fugue II (Example 287) differs substantially from *Fugue I* in the character of the subject and, assuredly, in its structuring. *Fugue II* is an example of an *episode-structured* fugue.

OBSERVATIONS:

1. The subject of measures 1-2 is answered tonally at the perfect fifth above. It is observed that the original interval of a perfect fourth is now modified to a perfect fifth.
2. Prior to the entry of the subject in the bass, a two-bar *episode* is inserted (measures 5-6). These bars contain a sequential treatment of the opening motive. The restatement of the subject in measures 7-8 brings the exposition to a close.
3. Thereafter, the structuring of Fugue 2 consists of an alternation of "strict" and "free" presentations, as shown in the accompanying table:

Measures:	1-2	3-4	5-6	7-8
Description/ function:	Subject	Answer	Free sequence	Subject
Structure:	Exposition		Episode 1*	Completion of exposition
Tonality	c	c to g	g to c	c

*This first episode might be considered as a structural link.

9-10	11-12	13-14	15-16	17-19
Free sequence	Subject "strict"	Free sequence	Subject	Free, but inversion of measure 5
Episode 2	Entry group II	Episode 3	Entry group III	Episode 4
c to Eb	Eb	Eb	g	g to c

20-21	22-middle of 26	26 (beat 3)- 29 (beat 3)	29-31
Subject	Expansion of material from measure 9	Subject (close)	Subject coda
Entry group IV	Episode 5	Entry group V	
c	Eb, c	c	c

FURTHER OBSERVATIONS:

1. Hence, the basic tonal plan is: c (g) c E♭ g c (E♭) c. Those areas marked ( ) are nonstructural tonal areas but are nevertheless interesting in terms of balance and symmetry.

2. With the exception of the coda, each subject entry is accompanied by a consistent and persistent musical idea, marked〰〰〰〰. This accompanying counterpoint is referred to as a *countersubject*.

3. An additional counterpoint, initially observed in measure 8 (marked X—X—X —X) may be considered either as a second countersubject or possibly as a contrapuntal associate. Although its appearance is persistent throughout the remainder of the composition, its musical role seems subservient to the subject and principal countersubject.

4. The gradual lengthening of the episodes from 2 measures to 3 measures (17-19), to 4½ measures (22-26), provides for asymmetry and nonpredictability of structure. In fact, it might be argued that Bach really effected a metrical change in measure 22—where the third beat might become the first beat of a new measure.

5. Bach provides for variety of color and register by his judicious control of each entry of the subject.

Example 288

Per item 4 above, observe the expanding arithmetical series.

6. Once again the subtleties of Bach's technique, which are revealed with each successive analysis, are nearly inexhaustible.

CHAPTER SUMMARY

Systematic study of contrapuntal techniques often begins with an investigation of species counterpoint, derived from the treatise *Gradus ad Parnassum* (1725), by Johann Fux. There are five species of counterpoint, composed to a *cantus firmus*. Each "step" becomes progressively more difficult.

Canon and fugue were the principal contrapuntal procedures used by Baroque composers. Certain terms are commonly used in the analysis of fugues. These include: *subject, answer, exposition, entry group, episode, stretto, voice.*

There are two principal categories of fugues in Bach's *Well-tempered Clavier*: subject-structured fugues and episode-structured fugues. Each category is analyzed in detail in this chapter.

SUGGESTED STUDIES

1. Be prepared to discuss Baroque melodic types, contours, and harmonic outlines from the examples presented in the text.
2. Study and be able to sing any of the fugue subjects from the *WTC*.
3. Write the *exposition* of a fugue a 3, using *Fuga II* (Example 287) as a model.
4. Write a short expository paper on the development of fugue from c. 1600 to 1750.
5. Examine two-voice examples for observation of the composer's control of motion and dissonance.
6. Write an example of each species, above or below the given *cantus firmus*. (The original form may be found in Bach's *Art of the Fugue*.)

Example 289

NOTE: Although it is not expected that the student be proficient in writing counterpoint after this brief introduction, the shaping of a good line and the control of consonant and dissonant intervals are reasonable expectations.

Chapter 18

THE CLASSICAL ERA
Theory and Practice

In many ways, the individual parameters of music are of lesser complexity in the Classical era than in the preceding Baroque period. "Classical" is generally defined as a style that achieves an objectivity, a clarity of form, and a balanced emotional expression—whether in literature, painting, or music. The period of c. 1750-1820 is commonly denoted as the Classical period or, by some writers, as the "Viennese Classical period" of music.

Rhythms were straightforward, typically including two or three different note values within the phrase, for example:

Borrowed divisions, syncopations, and hemiola are, of course, employed, but with a restraint that partially defines the style.

The new melodic style in general attains a simplicity not unlike that of folk music; it often assumes a singable quality, with phrase lengths about the duration of one breath.

Both melodically and harmonically, the pitch materials are typically diatonic. Chromaticism is reserved for very special points of tension (Haydn) or for embellishment (Mozart), or for the exceptionally evocative composition such as Mozart's *Dissonant Quartet* or distinct passages from the late string quartets and piano sonatas of Beethoven.

This homophonic style relied heavily on the primary triads. Modulations were made to closely related keys. Haydn was fond of using the parallel minor within a major-key context; late Haydn works and those of Beethoven show some preference for *third relationships*—that is, C major to E major, or C major to A♭ major.

Texture achieved great clarity. Tempi were rarely exaggerated. Robert Schumann's famous indication "as fast as possible" and, a few bars later, "faster still" would not have been conceivable in Haydn's time except as a point of humor—a quality all the Viennese composers possessed in good measure. Typical tempo markings used by Classical composers were *Adagio* (It., comfortable, easy), *Andante* (It. *andare,* to go, i.e., moderate), *Allegro* (It., cheerful), and *Presto* (It., fast). Similarly, dynamics ranged from *p* to *f*, with occasional *pp* and *ff*.

The mature classical style emerged from several interwoven chains of influence that included the French florid style, the North German "sensitive style," Italian operatic traditions, including *bel canto,* and folk materials. From these diverse and seemingly contradictory influences developed an exceptionally cohesive style that was vibrant and innovative.

The classical composers' contributions to musical form and to standardization of instrumental ensembles are discussed in some detail in this chapter and should be considered a part of a student's knowledge of the basic materials of music.

STRUCTURAL HARMONY

Rhythm, melody, texture, color, and harmony are usually significant only in a syntactical framework. Depending upon the emphasis designed by the composer, these elements either define or contribute to the organic whole. The study of melodic and harmonic *rhythm* may reveal the composer's pacing of musical events; *melody* may suggest the composer's attitudes toward expression and meaning of music; *texture* and *color* may suggest the musical environment; finally *harmony* (obviously in compositions where this element is a contributing parameter) may provide important clues regarding musical architecture. Structural harmony refers to groups of sonorities or chords. Such a group, by reasons of function or interrelation, may define phrase or periodicity. Larger harmonic groupings may confirm tonality as well as a basic structure. One studies the parts (harmony) in order to comprehend the whole (structure and form).

In the time-space continuum, a single pitch (already a "chord" by virtue of its overtones) may be viewed in several of its horizontal dimensions. By way of illustration, consider a single tone in its relationship to a three-movement sonata:

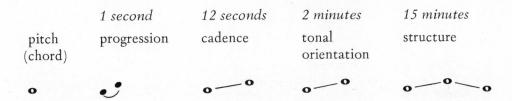

1 second	12 seconds	2 minutes	15 minutes
pitch (chord)	progression	cadence	tonal orientation	structure

The internal relationships of *chord-tonality-structure* were perhaps in their most perfect agreement during the Classical era.

Example 290

SONATA NO. 1

Haydn

CLASSICAL DESIGN

Example 290 quotes in its entirety the *Piano Sonata* No. 1* by Franz Joseph Haydn (1732-1809). *Sonata* (It. *suonare,* to sound) is the term frequently applied to compositions (typically for one or two performers) in which structural organization and unity are of prime importance. Obviously, trios, quartets, quintets, symphonies are "sonatas" for varying instrumental combinations. Although there exist keyboard sonatas of one movement (Scarlatti) and five movements (Brahms), two- to four-movement works are more common. During the late eighteenth century, the three-movement, fast-slow-fast sonata became the norm. The internal design of each movement was primarily limited to the following:

Binary	Theme and variations
Ternary	Menuet (typically with trio)
Rondo	Sonata-allegro

Nearly without exception, "form" resides in, and results from, the careful control of tonal organization in all the above categories. A given movement may be made up of themes or of motives; it may involve strongly contrasting ideas or, conversely, may be *monothematic.* Although proportions, repetitions, and the spacing of events are obviously important considerations in any musical design, the most constant and predictable factor in relation to Classical forms would seem to be the tonal organization of each movement and of the composition as a whole.

The brief digest of Classical forms listed below is intended as a general guide for initial studies.

BINARY (BIPARTITE PRINCIPLE):

A		B		
I	to V	V	to I	Repeats and repetitions vary from movement to movement.
i	to III	III	to i	V (or III in a minor key) may be actual tonal levels or simply a chordal emphasis. There are exceptions, of course, to the I to V (III) schemata.

---

*Early Haydn sonatas bore diverse titles such as Divertimento or Partita. These compositions are now included, however, in the complete Sonatas. (See Vienna Urtext Edition, 1965.)

Balanced proportions are important for the bipartite principle, although an expanded B section is very common. (For a simple binary form see Example 290, *Andante*.)

TERNARY (TRIPARTITE PRINCIPLE):

A   B   A   or A BA   or Aa Bb Aa
I to V to I   etc.

Typically the B section emphasizes a chord or tonal center other than the tonic.

RONDO (PRINCIPLE OF RETURN):

A B A B A   Small (or second) Rondo
         C

A B A C A B A   Large (or third) Rondo

In both versions of the rondo, thematic and tonal digressions are consistently observed. The B sections are typically in the dominant or mediant tonality; C sections provide for further tonal digression—often to the subdominant or submediant or to the parallel mode. Haydn frequently employed the principle of variation for his returning or repeated sections, thus fusing form and procedure.*

VARIATION:

The most frequently observed technique of variation in the Classical period is that of thematic elaboration within a set structural and harmonic framework. The "theme" and its initial harmonization usually define a simple binary or simple ternary design. This set structure is then typically maintained for each variation; similarly, the basic harmonic progression supporting the theme is commonly retained (with or without disguise) throughout the entire movement—or independent composition.

MENUET AND TRIO:

The menuet (typically with trio) is one of the durable designs of the Classical era. The term *menuet* describes a dance and possibly suggests the character and tempo of the composition. Depending on the temperament of the composer, the terms *song* or *scherzo* (see Mendelssohn and Beethoven) are substituted. The basic structure remains the same, however. The most typical appearance is as shown below:

Menuet	Trio	Menuet	
			(most often indicated *Da capo* after the Trio section).
A:‖ BA:‖	C:‖ DC:‖	ABA	(in the return, internal repeat signs are not observed).

The B sections typically achieve a tonal variety; similarly, the trio rarely remains in the same key or mode as the menuet. The design as a whole, of course, forms a *compound ternary*. Compare Haydn's *Menuet* (Example 290) to the above structural plan.

*There are surprisingly few examples of *Rondo* or *Theme and Variations* in the piano sonatas of Haydn and Mozart.

SONATA PRINCIPLE

SONATA-ALLEGRO:

By far the most widely employed structure of the Classical era—in sonatas, quartets, concertos, and symphonies—is the so-called *sonata-allegro,* also, unfortunately, referred to as the *first-movement form.* Of all the names assigned to Classical forms, *sonata-allegro* (to sound, cheerfully) or *first-movement form* are the most misleading, inadequate, and initially confusing. This design, the *sonata principle,* appears in all moods and tempos; it serves as a first, middle, or last movement; it has a few or many themes; and, despite these seeming ambiguities, it is basically the most vibrant, flexible, and energizing organizational premise to emerge from the Classical era. Early appearances of this organizational premise (mid-eighteenth century) bear a close resemblance to the binary form of the Baroque era; thereafter, its most distinguishing feature is that of a clearly delineated middle section, termed "development," thus changing the proportions to ternary. A brief outline of the sonata principle follows:

EXPOSITION	DEVELOPMENT	RECAPITULATION
Statement of ideas	Elaboration of ideas	Restatement and summation of ideas
Duality of tonalities (I to V is typical)	Multiplicity of tonalities	Unity of tonality emphasis on I
Group I (first tonal area) *transition* or connective link; typically modulates. Group II (second tonal area) Repeat of exposition.	Development sections vary from movement to movement. With some frequency one observes several key areas related by fifths and a clear preparation (by dominant pedal) for the return of the opening material.	In the recapitulation, it is typical that Group I and Group II remain in the tonic key. Indications for repetition of the development and recapitulation vary.

None of the Haydn or Mozart keyboard sonatas have a slow *introduction,* as is the case in some symphonies; a few sonatas do have a final summation, however, which is referred to as a *coda. Hybrid forms* are beyond the discussions of this text. The crossing of sonata and rondo principles, the menuet with variation techniques, etc., are occasionally observed.

The musical structure described above inherently provides for unity and diversity, predictability and surprise, event and the connection of events. Pacing as well as dramatic shape are the physiological and the psychological factors involved in the successful rendering of the sonata form—or preferably, the sonata principle.

Haydn's *Sonata No. 1* is a model of simplicity. The first movement employs, perhaps in its embryonic stage, the sonata principle—satisfying the tonal requirements in the exposition and again in the recapitulation. The equivalent of the development section functions as a free fantasy and connection to the return. The *Menuet* movement, without *Trio,* is a simple binary; the same structural principles are used in the *Andante* movement. Haydn's final *Allegro* is a simple ternary, with sufficient digression (B) to provide interest for the repetition of A.

The harmonic vocabulary is as straightforward as the structure, with primary triads providing the basis of the harmonic language. Further, selected chords define both phrase and periodicity; finally, structure emerges from harmonic manipulation. A Baroque feature is retained: all movements are in the same key. Most other sonatas, however, have a tonally contrasting middle movement.

Haydn's melodies are direct and almost as simple as folk songs. Short rhythmic cells or motives engage in a free exchange and stimulate an interesting dimension.

The third movement of Mozart's *Eine kleine Nachtmusik* illustrates the balanced Minuet-and-Trio structure. It is diagramed as follows:

MENUETTO:

A	:	B	A'	:
8		4	4	

G major   G (slight reference to e minor)

TRIO:

C	:	D	C	:
8		4	8	

D major

MENUETTO DA CAPO:

A	B
8	8

G major

Performance practice today normally observes the repeat signs; therefore, from 36 written measures, a total of 88 bars of charming music result.

Example 291

EINE KLEINE NACHTMUSIK (excerpt)

Third movement

Mozart

Menuetto da Capo.

Beethoven's dramatic *C minor Sonata*, Op. 13, shows several deviations from classical norms and suggests that a new era is in the offing. A basic structural analysis is provided in the score. The design of each movement is as follows:

I. INTRODUCTION: MS. 1-10
    Sonata principle
        Exposition: ms. 11-132
        Development: ms. 133-194
        Recapitulation: ms. 195-310

II. SMALL RONDO

A	ms. 1-16
B	ms. 17-28
A'	ms. 29-36
C	ms. 37-52
A''	ms. 53-73

III. LARGE RONDO

A	ms. 1-24
B	ms. 25-61
A'	ms. 62-78
C	ms. 79-120
A''	ms. 121-133
B'	ms. 134-170
A'''	ms. 171-186
Coda	ms. 186-210

A striking feature of this great work is its unification of materials. Themes, tonalities, and structure seem derivative of the opening motive:

Example 292

Principal key levels for each movement.   ● = minor;   𝗈 = major.

Example 293

PIANO SONATA IN C MINOR, OP. 13 (*PATHÉTIQUE*)

Beethoven

I. SONATA PRINCIPLE

INTRODUCTION

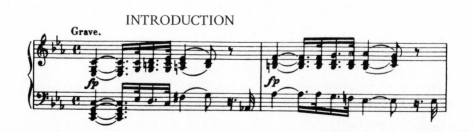

attacca subito il Allegro.

EXPOSITION

Closing, Eb

DEVELOPMENT
Tempo I. return of introductory material

attacca subito Allegro molto e con brio.

II. SMALL RONDO, A B A' C A''

Dominant pedal and preparation

CLASSICAL ORCHESTRATION

In common usage, the term *orchestra* describes a large instrumental ensemble, as distinct from small groups such as quartets and quintets. It may be of interest to trace the origins of the term: "Orchestra (Gk., literally 'dancing place', i.e., that portion of the Greek theater—situated between the auditorium and the stage, as in the modern opera—which was reserved for the dancing of the chorus and also for the instrumentalists)."[1]

Instruments have, throughout the history of Western music, played a substantial role in sacred, secular, and folk traditions of all eras. Brasses, woodwinds, organs, and percussion instruments were vital to Medieval concepts; consorts of viols and recorders gave both homogeneity and variety of color to Renaissance instrumental music; the double brass choirs of the late sixteenth and the seventeenth centuries splendidly expressed the grandeur of church and court; the emergence of the great string-instrument makers such as Amati, Stradivari, and Guarneri from c. 1625 to c. 1735 responded to the new instrumental idiom. The large ensemble was not completely standardized in the Baroque era, however, as suggested by the fact that each of J. S. Bach's six Brandenburg Concertos calls for a slightly different instrumentation. Not until the latter half of the eighteenth century did a set instrumentation for the orchestra begin to be standardized. Jean-Philippe Rameau (1683-1764), Johann Stamitz (1717-57), and C. P. E. Bach (1714-88) made important contributions both to the ideals of modern orchestration and to the development of the large instrumental group as a "set" ensemble.

Initially the orchestra comprised:

1 or 2 flutes*
2 oboes
1 or 2 bassoons*
2 French horns
Strings: violins I, II
       violas
       celli
       double basses

To this basic complement, gradual additions were made: 2 trumpets, 2 or 4 horns, and timpani. In the late works of Haydn and Mozart 2 clarinets were added. Beethoven included trombones for his Fifth Symphony; he also utilized both the piccolo and the contrabassoon.

Twelve measures from the opening of Beethoven's Symphony No. 8 are quoted for study of a late-Classical score format, of instrumental combinations, and for observation of the principles of orchestral balance.

---

[1]Willi Apel, *Harvard Dictionary of Music* (Cambridge, Mass.: Harvard University Press, 1944), p. 519.

*In very early Classical orchestras, flutes and bassoons were frequently omitted.

Example 294

SYMPHONY NO. 8 (excerpt)

First movement

Beethoven

INSTRUMENTAL COMBINATION

In traditional scoring, several principles are observed, each of which requires considerable knowledge and experience before it is completely mastered and used with sophistication. These principles include: vertical balance, horizontal balance, textural balance, pedals, and disposition in relationship and in opposition to the overtone series.

VERTICAL BALANCE

Vertical balance is achieved by specific combination of instruments, agreement with the overtone series, dynamic adjustments, and placement in terms of range. Example 295 illustrates.

Example 295

SYMPHONY NO. 8 (excerpt)

The opening chord

Beethoven

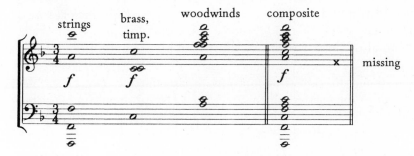

The chord is balanced in terms of tone color, strength of each instrument group, dynamics, and agreement with the overtone series.

HORIZONTAL BALANCE

Horizontal balance in traditional scoring involves at least three different considerations:

1. Equal voicing in a contrapuntal texture.
2. Careful voice leading in general, including the resolution of dissonant intervals and the maintenance of a logical line, appropriate for the style.

3. The development of a musical logic in each part and for the instrumental design as a whole.

TEXTURAL BALANCE

Textural balance provides for both contrast and unity. Passages employing the full orchestra (*tutti*) are typically contrasted by sections for fewer instruments or for specific colors.

CHAPTER SUMMARY

In many ways, the parameters of music are of lesser complexity in the Classical era than in the preceding Baroque period. Rhythms were straightforward, typically including two or three different note values within the phrase; Classical melodies often attain a simplicity not unlike that of folk music; both melodically and harmonically, the pitch materials are typically diatonic.

The homophonic style of the period relied heavily on the primary triads. Modulations were made to closely related keys. Texture achieved great clarity; tempi were rarely exaggerated.

The Classical period is noted for its clarity of musical designs. Principal forms of the period include: binary, ternary, rondo, theme and variations, menuet and trio, and sonata-allegro. Several of these designs are illustrated by examples from Haydn, Mozart, and Beethoven.

The concept of a standardized instrumentation for large instrumental ensembles emerged in the latter half of the eighteenth century. The Classical orchestra consisted of flutes, oboes, bassoons, horns, and strings. To this basic complement, gradual additions were made: trumpets, additional horns, and timpani. In the late works of Haydn and Mozart, clarinets were added. Beethoven included trombones, as well as piccolo and contrabassoon.

SUGGESTED STUDIES

1. Analyze and perform a Classical composition written for your instrument. If none exist (contrabassoon, tuba, percussion, etc.) make an appropriate substitution. The analysis should include the following:

   large, overall structure
   indication of transitions and connective passages
   unusual phrase structuring, if any
   principal tonal levels

selected harmonic analysis, paying particular attention to secondary dominants, modulations, and altered chords.

2. Compose a trio section for Haydn's Menuet, Example 290, for piano. The length should be about 16 measures, and the musical materials should be closely related to those of the Menuet.

Chapter 19

HARMONIZATION OF FOLK MELODIES

One of the most satisfying accomplishments of the theory student is the ability to harmonize an invented or given melody. Folk songs offer a wealth of melodic materials that are musically engaging and technically challenging. Arthur Honegger once remarked that the complex was accomplished easily while the simple required much time and thought. His reflection is apt for the study of folk-song harmonization. To achieve interest and variety from a highly limited and selective vocabulary requires compositional skills, aural experience, and an appreciable sense of style.

During the nineteenth and twentieth centuries, many composers used folk melodies as *one* basis of their pitch materials in some of their works. Dvořák, Tschaikovsky, Vaughan-Williams, Bartók, and Copland are prominent examples. The collection of oral traditions and transcription into notated versions became an important artistic obligation. These endeavors were pursued in the first part of this century and still continue—to try to preserve this rich heritage from total extinction on all continents.

Certainly the student is familiar with contemporary folk singers, folk-rock, and art music that incorporates folk song. The choice of placing folk-song harmonization in this text after the Classical era and before a discussion of Romantic music was made on the basis of appropriate vocabulary. Most folk-song harmonizations consist of primary chords I, IV, V, with occasional coloration of II and VI and, less frequently, III, except when the folk song is in a minor key.

Generally one will find in these melodies that:

Root-position chords are prominent, yet first-inversion chords will help effect an interesting counterpoint to the melody.

Seventh chords are to be used sparingly.

A judicious use of passing tones, suspensions, and other nonchord tones is appropriate.

Chromaticism is generally alien to the simple, diatonic melodies.

The basic melodic rhythm should be observed and supported.

Rhythmic motion at points of internal cadencing is advised—for example:

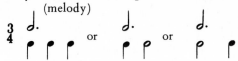

Several examples are provided for the student's perusal. Study of additional sources is invited and encouraged.

Example 296a

JOHNNY HAS GONE FOR A SOLDIER

American alteration of an Irish song, seventeenth century

Fireside Book of Folk Songs (New York: Simon & Schuster, 1947).

This is probably an American alteration of an Irish song dating to the seventeenth century.

Example 296b

JOHNNY HAS GONE FOR A SOLDIER

Basic four-part choral version

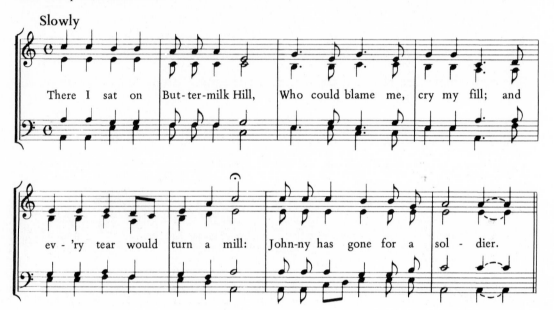

Example 297

a. *THE RIDDLE*

(Kentucky Folksong)

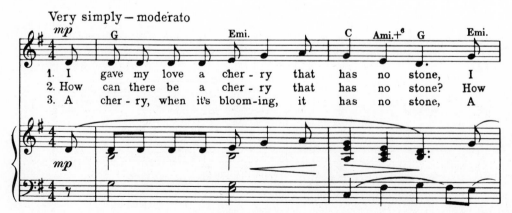

Example 298

b. *STEAL AWAY*

(Spiritual)

Fireside Book of Folk Songs.

A folk song from the Kentucky mountains. An earlier version has been discovered in a fifteenth-century English manuscript.

Example 299

I AM A POOR WAYFARING STRANGER

(Spiritual)

Fireside Book of Folk Songs.

After the Revolutionary War, this spiritual sprang up all through the Southern mountains. It was sung by Negroes: it was sung at camp meetings and revivals, and appears in the old shape-note hymnbooks of the period. This is a version sung by the early settlers of De Kalb County, Texas.

CHAPTER SUMMARY

One of the most satisfying accomplishments of the theory student is the ability to harmonize an invented or given melody. Folk songs offer a wealth of melodic materials that are musically engaging and technically challenging. Most folk-song harmonizations consist of primary chords: I, IV, V, with occasional coloration of II and VI and, less frequently, III, except when the folk song is in a minor key.

No new theoretical concepts or vocabulary have been introduced in this chapter. Rather, the student is encouraged to sing, analyze, and harmonize several folk songs in a variety of ways (keyboard accompaniment, choral, etc.) in order to gain complete fluency in basic part writing.

SUGGESTED STUDIES

1. Sing and analyze the following folk songs. Some melodies contain suggested chordal backgrounds (G, Am, D⁷, etc.) while other songs are presented with melody and text only. For those melodies without chordal indications, decide on an appropriate harmonization based on agreement with the notes of the melodic line and on a logical harmonic progression.
2. Provide a keyboard accompaniment for two or three of the given melodies; arrange two or three additional melodies for SATB or as suitable for classroom performance.

Example 300

IŠLA DĚVEČKA (THE COOL, SWEET WATER)

(Czechoslovakia)

1. Išla Děvečka	1. Down by the lakeside
Do jazerečka	Fetching the water
Pro vodu;	One fine day,
Vyžádala si	I heard a young girl,
Od panímámy	Sent by her mother,
Slobodu.	Softly say:

2. Vodička čistá,	2. Clear running water,
Studeňul'ička	So sweet and cooling,
Jako l'ed,	Yet I will
Moja hubička	Give my beloved
Je slad'ul'ičká	Kisses and kisses
Jako med.	Sweeter still.

3. Co by hubička
   Má slad'ul'ičká
   Nebyla?
   Šak mne ju moja
   Mamička stará
   Sladila.

3. Tell me, O, tell me,
   Why should my kisses
   Not be so?
   For my old mother
   Sweetened my kisses
   Years ago.
                    E. V. de B.

Example 301

CHILDREN DO LINGER

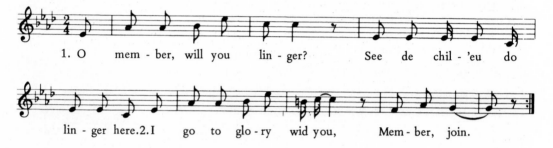

1. O mem - ber, will you lin - ger? See de chil - 'eu do lin - ger here. 2. I go to glo - ry wid you, Mem - ber, join.

3. O Jesus is our Captain.
4. He lead us on to glory.
5. We'll meet at Zion gateway.*
6. We'll talk dis story over.
7. We'll enter into glory.
8. When we done wid dis world trials.
9. We done wid all our crosses.
10. O brudder, will you meet us?
11. When de ship is out a-sailin'.
12. O Jesus got de hellum.
13. Fader, gader in your chil'en.
14. O gader dem for Zion.
15. 'Twas a beauteous Sunday mornin'.
16. When he rose from de dead.
17. He will bring you milk and honey.

*Heaven portal.

Example 302

MANY THOUSAND GO

1. No more peck o' corn for me, No more, no more;

No more peck o' corn for me, Man-y tou-sand go.

2. No more driver's lash for me.   4. No more hundred lash for me.
3. No more pint o' salt for me.   5. No more mistress' call for me.

Example 303

KERSTLIED (ALL IN A STABLE)

(Carol, Belgium)

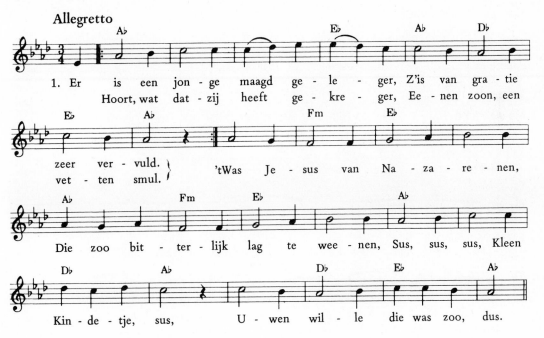

1. Er is een jon-ge maagd ge-le-ger, Z'is van gra-tie
   Hoort, wat dat-zij heeft ge-kre-ger, Ee-nen zoon, een

zeer ver-vuld.)
vet-ten smul. / 'tWas Je-sus van Na-za-re-nen,

Die zoo bit-ter-lijk lag te wee-nen, Sus, sus, sus, Kleen

Kin-de-tje, sus, U-wen wil-le die was zoo, dus.

From E. Closson, Volksliederen der Belgische Provinc, Vol. 1, Schott Frères, Brussels.

1. Er is een jonge maagd gelegen,
   Z' is van gratie zeer vervuld,
   Hoort, wat dat zij heeft gekregen,
   Eenen zoon, een vetten smul.
   't Was Jesus van Nazarenen,
   Die zoo bitterlijk lag te weenen.
       Sus, sus, sus, Kleen Kindetje, sus,
       Uwen wille die was zoo, dus.

2. Sint Joseph stond in benauwen,
   Met zijn hoedje in zijn hand,
   Nevens onze Lieve Vrouwe,
   't Was droefheid ten allen kant.
   En alwaar hij hem wendde,
   Hij en zag niet als ellende.

3. Sint Joseph die moest gaan zoeken,
   Barrevoets en zonder schoen;
   Hout en kolen moest hij zoeken,
   En het was zeer wel van doen.
   En er was noch doek noch luiermande,
   't Kindetje lag te kleppertanden.

1. All in a stable lay a maiden,
   Blest was she and full of grace.
   God to her a gift had given;
   'Twas a son, a bonny babe.
   It was Jesus there a-lying
   There in the manger helpless crying.
       Hush, O hush, my little babe, hush,
       'Tis God's will, and so be it, thus.

2. St. Joseph stood in awe and wonder
   With his hat all in his hand
   By the blessed Virgin Mary,
   Sore perplexed he there did stand.
   He saw everywhere around him
   Nothing but misery abounding.

3. Abroad St. Joseph went a-walking
   Barefoot in the frost and snow,
   Wood and coal he went a-seeking,
   It was well that he did so.
   Without clothing, without firing,
   Trembling with cold the babe was lying.

M. K.

Example 304

NA BYERYEZHKU U STAVKA (ON THE MILL POND SHORE SHE STOOD)

(Ukraine, English text by Herbert Haufrecht)

rib - tsi - na. Tai u - pa - la vstav nye - bo - go
on the ground. Then she tripped when some - thing caught her,

i nye - ma - ye tut ni - ko - go Ta ni - ko - mu
She fell right in - to the wa - ter. Was there no one

pid - big - tih, shcho b div - chih - nu vin - tyag - tih. Krih - tsit pro - bu
stand - ing_ 'round, who could save her, or_ she'll_drown. Hear her moth - er

i i___ ma - tih shcho b div - tsih - nu rya - tu - va - tih,
give _ a _ shout: "Who will pull my daugh - ter___ out?"

ka - zhe shcho za pra - tsyu tu - yu ya div - tsih - nu po - da ru - yu.
Then a young man saved her life, And he claimed her for his wife.

© Copyright 1963 by Hollis Music, Inc., New York, N. Y.

Example 305

SULIRAM

(Indonesia, English text by Herbert Haufrecht)

Moderately slow, flowing

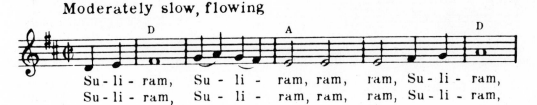

Su - li - ram, Su - li - ram, ram, ram, Su - li - ram,
Su - li - ram, Su - li - ram, ram, ram, Su - li - ram,

Example 306

LA RANA, LA ARAÑA, Y LA MOSCA (THE FROG, THE SPIDER, AND THE FLY)

(Mexico, English text by Henrietta Yurchenco and Herbert Haufrecht)

Es - ta - ba la ra - na can - tan - do de ba - jo del
There once was a frog who did love to sing un - der the

a - gua, ___ cuan - do la a - ra - ña se pu so a can-
wa - ter, ___ There came a spi - der, de - cid - ed to

tar, vi - no la mos - ca y la hi - zo ca-
try it; Then came a fly, it made him be

llar. ___ Ca - lla - ba la mos - ca la
qui - et. ___ The ver - y same fly stopped the

ra - na que es - ta - ba can - tan - do de ba - jo del
ver - y same frog who was sing - ing there un - der the

a - gua; ___ cuan - do la mos - ca se pu so a can-
wa - ter; ___ Then when the fly her - self want - ed to

tar,   vi - no laa - ra - ñay la hi - zo ca - llar. __
try it, Back came the   spi - der, made her be qui - et. _

Example 307

NÄVERVISAN (THE BIRCHBARK SONG)

(Sweden)

1. E - ja mitt hjär ta, hur in - ner - lig är fröj - den.
Den lust och gläd je som un - nas mig av höj -

den. När jag be - tän - ker alt dö - dens län - ker Har

Chris - tus bru - tit och li - vet skän - ker Av nå - de.

1. Eja mitt hjärta, hur innerlig är fröjden,
   Den lust och glädje som unnas mig av
      höjden.
   När jag betänker att dödens länker
   Har Christus brutit och livet skänker
      Av nåde.

2. Beredder håll mig, o Jesus Christ, att vänta
   Den nadens stund, då du till dig vill hamta
   Ut sorgen, kvalen, fran jämmerdalen
   Din brud till dig uti himnasalen,
      Ja amen!

1. My heart, with inward peace, adores
      creation,
   Redeemed, my spirit goes to sure salvation.

   For Christ lives now, his grace will show
   That death is conquered, its pow'r brought

   low for ever.

2. Let me be ready, the hour of grace is nearing,
   To bring me home to see Christ's face
      appearing.

From sorrow, pain and grief set free,

From Heaven gather thy bride to thee
for ever.

U.W.

Example 308

SCHOON LIEF, HOE LIGT GIJ HIER

(Maying Song, Belgium)

Andante

1. Schoon lief, hoe ligt gij hier en slaapt In uwen eersten drome? Wilt opstaan en den mei ontvaan: Hij staat hier alzo schone.

1. Schoon lief, hoe ligt gij hier en slaapt
   In uwen eersten drome?
   Wilt opstaan en den mei ontvaan:
   Hij staat hier alzo schone.

2. Ik zou voor genen mei opstaan,
   Mijn vensterken niet ontsluiten:
   Plant uwen mei, waar 't u gerei:
   Plant uwen mei daarbuiten.

3. Waar zou 'k hem planten, of waar doen?
   't Is al op 's Heren strate;
   De winternacht is koud en lang,
   Hij zou zijn bloeien laten.

1. Arise, dear love, shake off your dream
   This May morning so early;
   Accept, I pray, this tree for May,
   That here stands flowering so rarely.

2. My window I shall not unbar,
   Nor rise the May to greet, sir;
   Go plant your may where'er you please,
   Go plant it out in the street, sir.

3. But if all on the Lord's highway
   I set it up to flourish,
   This winter's night is cold and long,
   The tender flowers they will perish.

4. Schoon lief, laat hij zijn bloeien staan,
   Wij zullen hem begraven
   Op 't kerkhof bij den eglantier
   Zijn graf zal roosjes dragen.

5. Schoon lief, en om die rozekens
   Zal 't nachtegaaltjen springen,
   En voor ons bei in elken Mei
   Zijn zoete liedjens zingen.

4. And if they die, dear love, the tree
   To churchyard shall be carried,
   And laid beneath a briar rose,
   Shall blossom where it lies buried.

5. And on the briar the nightingale
   Shall sit and sing so clear, love;
   She'll sing for us her sweetest songs
   As May comes round every year, love.

R.H.

Example 309

THE LAME SOLDIER

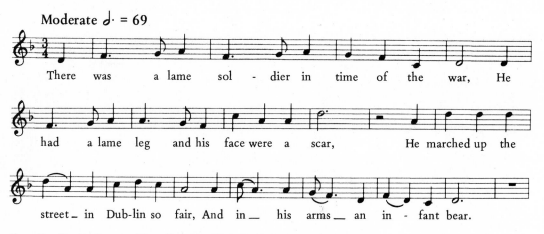

There was a lame sol - dier in time of the war, He had a lame leg and his face were a scar, He marched up the street — in Dub-lin so fair, And in — his arms — an in - fant bear.

From *Our Singing Country* (Macmillan, New York, N. Y., 1941.)

Example 310

SUR LE GAZON (ALL ON THE GRASS)

(Un Cramignon, Belgium: Walloon)

Allegretto ma non troppo

1. Nous somm's ci dans u - ne dans' tout' rem - pli' de jeu - nes

gens. Ce qui me dé-plait le plus, mon a - mant n'est pas de - dans.

Refrain

Sur le ga - zon, la - fa - ri - don - daine, Ve - nez, mou -

tons, la - fa - ri - don - don.

1. Nous somm's ci dans une dans' tout'
      rempli' de jeunes gens.
   Ce qui me déplaît le plus, mon amant n'est
      pas dedans.
      Sur le gazon, lafaridondaine,
      Venez, moutons, lafaridondon.

2. Ce qui me déplaît le plus, mon amant n'est
      pas dedans.
   Je le vois venir de loin sur un ch'val qu'est
      blanc et noir.

1. Here we dance all hand in hand, men and
      maids on the green grass.
   I am sad because my love in the dance
      cannot be found.
      All on the grass, a roodle dum day,
      Come, lambkin, dance, a roodle dum
      dee.

2. I am sad because my love in the dance
      cannot be found.
   But I see him from afar riding on a piebald
      horse.

Example 311

HORA HANEGEV

(Israel, English text by Herbert Haufrecht and David Gerlich)

Lively

Ze - mer ze - mer lach,   ze - mer ze - mer lach,
We shall sing a song,   We shall sing a song,

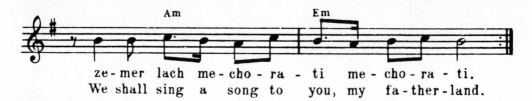

ze - mer lach me - cho - ra - ti me - cho - ra - ti.
We shall sing a song to you, my fa - ther - land.

Ha - ra - ra - ich he - ma yis - ma - chu
Then will glad - ness cov - er your moun - tains

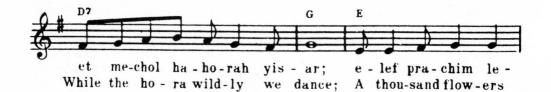

et me - chol ha - ho - rah yis - ar; e - lef pra - chim le -
While the ho - ra wild - ly we dance; A thou - sand flow - ers

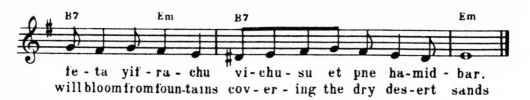

fe - ta yif - ra - chu vi - chu - su et pne ha - mid - bar.
will bloom from foun - tains cov - er - ing the dry des - ert sands

Example 312

AY LA LE LO

(Spain: Galicia)

Lento

Ay la le lo ay la le lo,

Example 313

NUN ZIRADE (WHERE ARE YOU, MY BELOVED?)

(Spain: Basque)

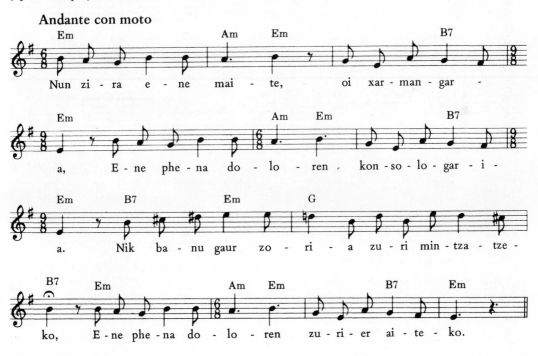

Where are you, my beloved?
On me you've cast your spell.
Were your arms but around me
You would my grief dispel.
Were I but with you, dearest,
Comfort you'd bring to me,
And from my pains and troubles
Evermore I'd be free.

M. K.

Example 314

POR UN BESO (FOR A KISS)

(Colombia, English text by Henrietta Yurchenco and Herbert Haufrecht)

Por un be - so de tu bo - ca yo no
For a kiss from your most sweet lips, I'd give up

sé lo que da - ri - a; tal vez en me fie - bre
ev - 'ry-thing I cher-ish; May-be in my burn-ing

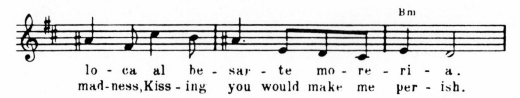

lo - ca al be - sar - te mo - re - ri - a.
mad-ness, Kiss - ing you would make me per - ish.

No se que me pa - sa - ri - a por un
Would fate bring me joy or sad - ness For a

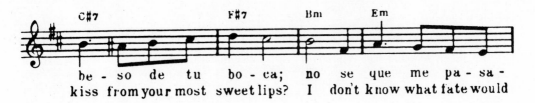

be - so de tu bo - ca; no se que me pa - sa-
kiss from your most sweet lips? I don't know what fate would

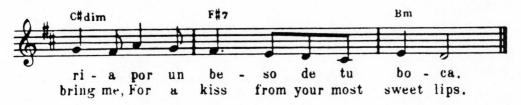

ri - a por un be - so de tu bo - ca.
bring me, For a kiss from your most sweet lips.

Example 315

EWE FOLK SONG (*I DIDN'T DO IT*)

(Ghana, from the singing of Prospera Atsu)

Lively

Nye me woe ne - be me woe. No - si dzo - dzo ge -
No, I did - n't do＿ it. You say I did, Well, ＿

- ne dzo mi kpo, No - si dzo - dzo ge - ne dzo mi
＿ let come what may, You say I did, Well, ＿ let come what

(Repeat ad libitum)

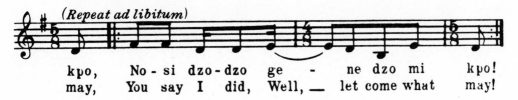

kpo, No - si dzo - dzo ge - ne dzo mi kpo!
may, You say I did, Well, ＿ let come what may!

Example 316

NIGHEAN DUBH 'S A NIGHEAN DONN (MAIDEN OF THE DARK BROWN HAIR)

(United Kingdom, Scotland, The Hebrides (Oran Luadhaidh), Waulking Song)

Moderato

Nigh-ean dubh 's a nigh-ean donn Shiubhl-ainn leat far m'eòl-ais;

Nigh-ean dubh 's a nigh-ean donn. 1.'S mis-e tha gu mul-a-dach Air

m'uil-inn anns an i-seòmb-ar.

Nighean dubh 's a nighean donn,	Maiden of the dark brown hair,
Shiubhlainn leat far m'eòlais	Far with her I'd wander,
Nighean dubh 's a nighean donn.	Maiden of the dark brown hair.
1. 'S mise tha gu muladach	1. Long have I been waiting here
Air m'uilinn anns an t-seòmbar.	Alone and full of sorrow.
2. Mise muigh air cùl na tobhta,	2. I outside behind the house
'S tusa staigh a còrdadh.	While you inside are courting.
3. Shiubhlainn leat an ear 's an iar,	3. East and west I'd walk with you
Gun each, gun strian, gun ròpa.	Without my horse and bridle.
4. Rachainn ro' Chaol Muile leat,	4. Through the Sound of Mull I'd go,
Gun fuireach ri mo bhrògan.	Nor wait to put my shoes on.
5. Rachainn gu Cinn-tìre leat,	5. To Kintyre I'd go with you,
's dha'n tir 'san robh mi eòlach.	Where I was well acquainted.
6. Rachainn leat a dh'Uibhist,	6. I would go to Uist with you
Far am buidhicheadh an t-còrna.	Where barley ripens golden.
7. Rachainn do na runnagan,	7. I would reach the stars with you,
Nam biodh do chuideachd deònach.	If your own folk were willing.
8. Rachainn-sa dha'n a' ghealaich leat,	8. I would reach the moon with you,
Nan gealladh tu mo phòsadh.	If you would say we'll marry.
	M. S. C.

Example 317

PERDIKITZA (LITTLE PARTRIDGE)

(Greece)

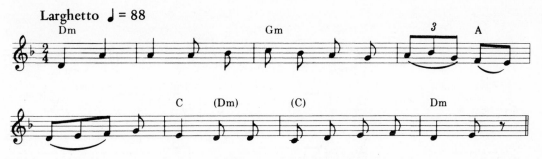

Η ΠΕΡΔΙΚΙΤΣΑ

1. Little Partridge, our greetings we are bringing,
   Songs of joy on this bridal morn we're singing.

2. Like a bird in her nest your young ones bearing,
   May you tenderly for their needs be caring.

3. Though your nest be by wind and tempest shaken,
   Yet your young ones must never be forsaken.

4. May your children be like the summer flowers
   Shedding fragrance amongst the shady bowers.

1. Καλῶς ὦρσες, περδικίτσα

   μέ σ'αὐτὴν τὴν γειτονίτσα.

2. Ἐδαδῶ πουλὰ νὰ βγάλης,

   ἐδαδῶ νὰ ξεπουλάσης.

3. Ἀστραπαὶς, βρονταὶςκι' ἂν κούσης

   τὰ πουλά σ' μὴν τάφήσης.

4. Νάναι καὶ τά συντεκνάκια

   μόσχος καὶ γαρουφαλάκια.

M. K.

The three first syllables of each line in the Greek text are always sung twice.

Example 318

PKIASTE KOPELLES, STO CHORO (O DANCE, YOU MAIDS)

(Cyprus, Dance Song)

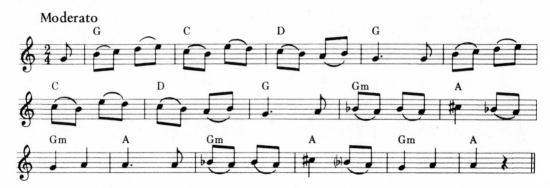

ΠΚΙΑΣΤΕ ΚΟΠΕΛΛΕΣ ΣΤΟ ΧΟΡΟ

1. O dance, you maids, be blithe and gay, (*bis*)
   When you are young, 'tis time to play,
   O dance, you maids be blithe and gay.

2. O dance, while you have time to spend (*bis*)
   Before you have a babe to tend. (*bis*)

3. Before your toil it does begin (*bis*)
   O that's the time to dance and sing (*bis*)

4. When you your single life do quit (*bis*)
   Then in your corner you must sit. (*bis*)
   M. K.

1. Πκιᾶστε κοπέλλες στόχ χορόν (δίς)
   Τώρα πού ἔοιετε τζιαιρόν,
   πκιᾶστε κοπέλλες στόχ χορόν

2. Πκιᾶστε χορέψετε τωρά
   Τζι'ἔθ θά σᾶς φίνουν τά μωρά.

3. Ἔθ θά σᾶς φίνουν οἱ δουλειές,
   νά πᾶτε τζιεῖ ποῦν'οἱ χαρές.

4. Ἔθ θά σᾶς 'φίνν' ὁ ἄντρας οας
   τζι ἔν νᾶσαστιν στήν πάντα σας.

Example 319

DRENOVARE (THE MAID FROM THE MOUNTAINS)

(Albania, Korça)

shko — Nje dit shko - va nga — Dre - no - va Gje - ta

një vaj - zë të re, — Gje - ta një vaj - zë të re.

1. Një dit shkova nga Drenova,
   Një dit shko—
   Një dit shkova nga Drenova
   Gjeta një vajzë të re.   (bis)

2. Ish e bukur, ish e mitur,
   Ish e bu—
   Ish e bukur, ish e mitur
   Dukësh ishte fort e ngjitur.

3. Dhe më thotë me zë plotë.
   Zot që më vë kaqë re.

4. Në do udhënë t'a gjeshë
   Haj me mua dhe mos qeshë.

5. Jam i lodhur thashë fare,
   Drenova, moj Drenovare.

6. Rimë pakë në lëndinë
   Të flasin për dashurinë.

7. Se ti zëmërën m'a more
   Malëso maj, malësore.

8. Tani kemi pesë vjet
   Që po rojmë të gëzuar.

9. Dy fëmijë, bir e bijë,
   Zoti na i ka dhuruar.

1. One fine morning I rose early,
   One fine morn,
   One fine morning I rose early
   And I met a fair young maid.   (bis)

2. She was fair and she was modest,
   She was fair,
   She was fair and she was modest
   And she seemed just made for love.

3. She did smile and ask me kindly:
   Why do you thus stand and stare?

4. If this pathway you would follow,
   Pray, kind sir, do not delay.

5. O, fair maiden, I am tired;
   Let me stay and rest awhile.

6. In this green and pleasant meadow,
   Let us sit and talk of love.

7. O fair maiden from the mountain,
   You have won my heart and hand.

8. Now my love and I are married
   We are happy and content.

9. First a son and then a daughter,
   God has given unto us.

                                        M. K.

Chapter 20

HARMONIC EXPANSION
OF
THE NINETEENTH CENTURY

"Melody, unexhausted, nay inexhaustible, is pre-eminently the source of musical beauty. Harmony, with its countless ways of transforming, inverting, and intensifying, offers the material for constantly new developments; while rhythm, the main artery of the musical organism, is the regulator of both."[1] Hanslick, one of the most reknowned spokesmen of nineteenth-century music, not only states a credo and a hierarchical order of music for his time (about 1850) but also provides numerous clues concerning the spirit and philosophy of the nineteenth century.

In the main, the first half of the century espoused an optimistic philosophy. Man was a free spirit, noble, best of all creatures, capable of infinite invention, and in control of his own destiny and of his creations. This spirit pervaded the totality of music. Individualism produced both simple and complex rhythms, diatonic and chromatic melodic and harmonic styles, one-line textures and massive forces, and miniature "sketches" as well as a cycle of music dramas lasting *days*.

Since the actual sound of nineteenth-century music is familiar to all students of music, these chapters address themselves to the technical aspects of harmonic expansion, chromatic alteration, enharmonic modulation, and other specifics of the style that are, although aurally taken for granted, nevertheless quite elusive. Analysis of several works can, perhaps, assist in illustrating and clarifying what Hanslick had in

---

[1] Eduard Hanslick, *The Beautiful in Music,* trans. Gustav Cohen (New York: Liberal Arts Press, 1957), p. 47.

mind in expressing his admiration for the "countless ways of transforming, inverting, and intensifying."

NINTH CHORDS

The harmonic vocabularies of the principal composers of the Classical era—including Haydn, Mozart, and Beethoven—were primarily confined to triadic and seventh-chord structures, secondary functions, and occasional altered chords such as the augmented sixth, Neapolitan sixth, and diverse seventh chords involving one or more alterations. Each of the above-named composers became quite experimental, however, in his mature and late works, and jointly they contributed to new concepts in harmonic language, chordal and tonal relationships, and general musical syntax.

Ninth chords may be observed in Baroque compositions—but mainly as contrapuntal coincidences involving *appoggiature* or other nonchord tones; most of these appearances seem to suggest a lack of independence as an individual chord. The principal exception would be the vii°⁷, functioning as an *incomplete dominant ninth*. This chord is incomplete in the sense that the root of the chord is absent. Implied by Rameau's theory and affirmed by distinguished theorists since that time, the question of *implied* roots prompts serious and provocative discussion of a composer's intent. Example 320 briefly illustrates:

Example 320

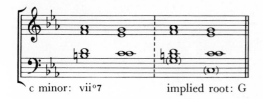

c minor: vii°7   implied root: G

The *complete* ninth chord was used with considerable frequency in the nineteenth century. As a *dominant* ninth the sonority achieved a special vogue, although its appearances were certainly not limited exclusively to dominant function. Succinctly—to any triad, or triad with seventh, a chordal ninth may be added (Example 321):

Example 321

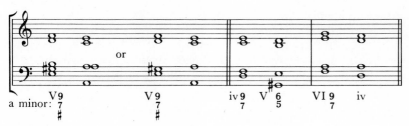

a minor: V9 7 #   V9 7 #   iv9 7   V 6 5   VI9 7   iv

In most instances of ninth-chord usage, the chordal seventh also appears, and typically both the ninth and the seventh resolve stepwise down. In a four-voice texture, the chordal fifth is omitted.

DIMINISHED SEVENTHS

The *diminished seventh chord,* with at least two names—diminished-diminished, or doubly diminished—is also observed in Baroque music, but its widest adoption came during the Romantic era. The diminished-diminished seventh is poignant in sonority; it fits the keyboardist's hand remarkably well; and it holds a special theoretical fascination because of its makeup of equidistant minor thirds, its *aural* noninvertibility, and its great flexibility in resolution. Further, the basic sonority is capable of only *two* transpositions—thereafter, duplication takes place. Example 322 illustrates:

Example 322

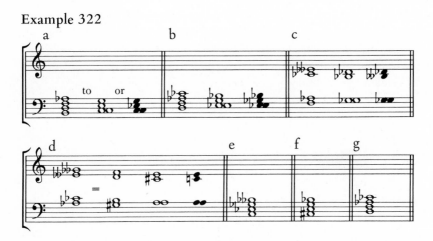

a. Basic chord in C major or c minor.
b. Same sonority, using original chord third as new root.
c. Same sonority, using original chord fifth as new root.
d. Same sonority, using original chord seventh as new root.
e. Basic chord transposed up a half step.
f. Basic chord transposed up a whole step.
g. Observe that chord *g* is a duplication of chord *b*.

As indicated above, the diminished-diminished seventh may resolve to either a major or a minor triad, which effects eight possible resolutions for each of the basic forms of the chord. Further, the half-step alteration of any *one* chord member will result in a dominant-seventh (Mm) formation (Example 323):

Example 323

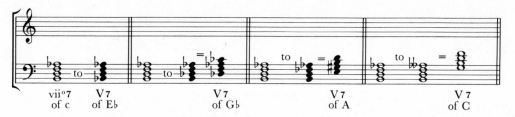

Finally, as a negotiator for quick modulations, the diminished-diminished seventh is without peer in the tertian vocabulary. From C major to e♭ minor or from c minor to f♯ minor, each of which are six degrees removed, the processes are simple—even if sometimes blatant (Example 324):

Example 324

An excerpt from Schubert's *Du bist die Ruh'* (Example 325) shows a nonmodulatory use of the diminished-diminished seventh sonority (measure 41). The same song contains an excellent example of a subtle change of mode. As will be recalled, the terminology for this process is *interchangeability of modes,* or *bimodality* (see measures 55-57).

Example 325

DU BIST DIE RUH' (excerpt)

Franz Schubert (1797-1828)

THIRD RELATIONSHIPS

Bimodal third relationships are observed as early as the sixteenth century. Sometimes presenting multiple cross-relations, the pungency and freshness of sound obviously fascinated many generations of composers.

From the late eighteenth century through the late nineteenth century, harmonic and tonal relationship by third held a special interest for composers. Additional examples will serve to illustrate:

Example 326

As in Haydn

Example 327

As in Robert Schumann (1810-1856)

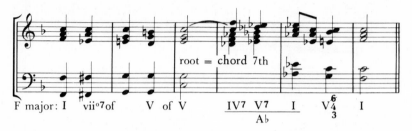

ANALYTICAL PROBLEMS

ENHARMONICISM

As previously explained, *enharmonic modulation* involves a respelling from sharps to flats, or the reverse. When confronted by analytical problems that include enharmonicism, the visual aspect of the page can often supply important clues. Example 328 below serves as a case in point.

Example 328

PIANO SONATA, OP. 13

Second movement *Adagio*

Beethoven

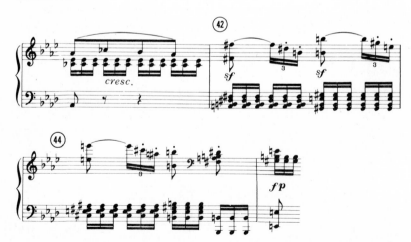

OBSERVATIONS:

1. The key of the entire sonata (*Pathétique*) is c minor; the principal tonality of the *Adagio* movement is A♭ major (i.e., a relationship of a major third).

2. At the juncture shown above (measures 41-44), the mode has changed to a♭ minor and, as notated, a modulation has been made to E major.

3. Therefore, as notated, an a♭ minor triad (measure 44) is enharmonically a g♯ minor triad: old key i equals new key iii.

4. Further, one should consider two somewhat contradictory views of the tonality of this passage:

   a. In relationship to c minor, E major is the bimodal third above.
   b. In relationship to A♭, not E but rather F♭ is the bimodal third below.

Obviously, notation in E is easier to read than in the theoretical key of F♭ (eight flats).

An additional example of enharmonic change is shown in Hugo Wolf's song, *Das Verlassene Maegdlein,* measures 17-21.

Example 329

DAS VERLASSENE MAEGDLEIN

Measures 17-21

Hugo Wolf (1860-1903)

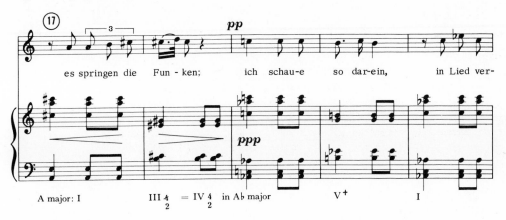

CHROMATICISM

Throughout the nineteenth century, composers felt free to alter any or all chord members of a given tertian structure according to their compositional needs and dictates. Pronounced or continuous chordal alteration resulted in *chromaticism*. Chromaticism, together with frequent modulations and an abundance of nonchord tones, initially effected an expansion of the tertian system; the overuse of the procedures late in the century forewarned of the decline and near collapse of the system.

ALTERED CHORDS

It is certainly not necessary to identify the profusion of altered chords employed throughout the nineteenth century. Altered chords are typically easy to distinguish in analysis and, similarly, easy to imitate in writing. A few alterations do, however, merit special consideration. Example 330 demonstrates several common formations.

Example 330

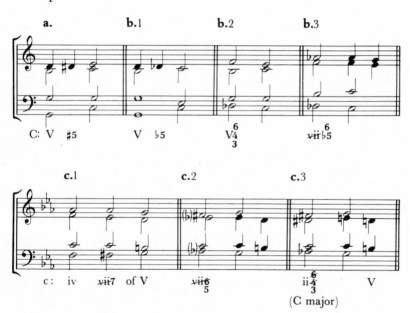

a. Raised fifth of the chord.
b1. Flatted fifth of the chord.
b2. The same sonority as b1 becomes a *dominant* augmented sixth chord when inverted.
b3. Similarly, an augmented sixth chord may be built from the *leading-tone triad*.
c1. Raised root of the chord.
c2. c1, when inverted, again produces an augmented sixth chord.

c3. c1 may be (and in practice often is) respelled as a *doubly augmented sixth* chord.

It is generally true that an alteration of the chord third does not change the function of the chord. Observe the alterations in Example 331:

Example 331

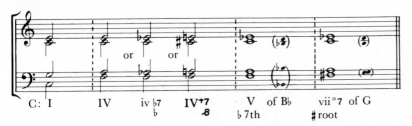

An excerpt from *Ich will meine Seele tauchen* by Robert Schumann (Example 332) illustrates actual usage of altered chords in the first part of the nineteenth century.

Example 332

ICH WILL MEINE SEELE TAUCHEN (excerpt)

Schumann

OBSERVATIONS:

1. Alteration of iv^7 to include the flatted fifth (measure 13).
2. A chain of major-major seventh chords (measures 13-14) adds diatonic interest.
3. The subdominant "region" is explored in measures 17-18.
4. The mediant triad III$^6_3$ functions as a passing dominant (measure 19)—or simply as a melodic function between IV$_6$ and II$_6$.

One of Schumann's most eloquent and interesting *lieder* is the opening song of his *Dichterliebe* cycle, *Im Wunderschönen Monat Mai* (Example 333). Harmonic analysis of this composition reveals an absence of the tonic chord. Tonality per se is nevertheless firmly entrenched, resulting from the unambiguous functioning of the dominant chord at two important cadences. The dominant seventh in the final measure serves as a preparation for the next song in the cycle.

Example 333

IM WUNDERSCHÖNEN MONAT MAI

Schumann

For obvious musical reasons, Chopin's *Prelude in E Minor,* Op. 28, No. 4, is performed by most keyboard students. Yet, despite its familiarity, it is probably rarely analyzed because of the quite formidable problems it presents (Example 334).

Example 334

PRELUDE IN E MINOR, OP. 28, NO. 4

Chopin

CHORDAL MUTATION

The fluid and harmonically evasive left hand of Chopin's *Prelude* employs a technique common to the nineteenth century, which, for lack of a better term, will be called *chordal mutation*. The term is used to describe a gradual harmonic change, or perhaps evolution, of a given starting sonority. The first 5 measures—as well as the remainder of the *Prelude*—illustrate this technique.

Example 335

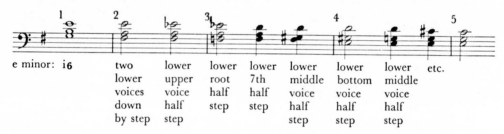

| two lower voices down by step | lower upper voice half step | lower root half step | lower 7th half step | lower middle voice half step | lower bottom voice half step | lower middle voice half step | etc. |

While a modest amount of insight may be derived from a chord-by-chord analysis of the *Prelude* (Example 334), the results reveal neither the procedure nor the basic harmonic structure of the composition. Chopin eschews traditional chordal relationships and suggests perhaps a kind of nonfunctional harmonic movement. A Schenker-type analysis (Example 336), however, gives considerable insight into the basic structures.

Example 336

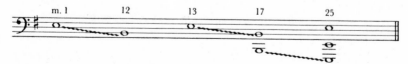

Further, a reduction of the expressive upper line of the composition (Example 337) begins to unravel Chopin's enigma.

Example 337

*Approximate durations are shown (𝅝 = 4 measures) to illustrate Chopin's control of time span.

OBSERVATIONS:

1. The dramatic high point is found in measure 17—achieved by a dominant ninth that supports a flamboyant melisma; an *appoggiatura chord* further heightens the tension in this measure.

2. The basic melodic structure would appear to be derived from two descending scale fragments that together utilize all pitches from e^i to b^i, with the exception of $f\natural^i$.

3. Measure 23 contains a very interesting sonority. In many editions, the bass note is written as B♭ rather than A♯. In a theoretical sense, A♯ (i.e., the leading tone to V) is preferred to B♭. At least two interpretations of the chord are possible:

   a. B♭ C♮ e^i g, a substitution for B♭ C♯ e^i g, vii°⁷ of V;
   b. A♯ C e^i g, a German augmented sixth chord in *root position*.

4. The turn in measure 16 is precisely at the golden proportion (.618) of this work.

Example 338

ETUDES IN THE FORM OF VARIATIONS, OP. 13

Schumann

ETUDE I (VARIATION 1)

ETUDE IV (VARIATION 3)

Edited by Harold Bauer. Dedicated to his friend William Sterndale Bennett. Original edition: "Les notes de la mélodie sont de la composition d'un amateur." This amateur was the father of Schumann's friend Ernestine von Fricken (Estrella).

Schumann's *Etudes in the Form of Variations,* Op. 13, is one of his finest works for solo piano. The composer successfully and adroitly uses his gifts as a "miniaturist" to form a large and substantial work.

OBSERVATIONS:

1. The Etudes are based primarily on the original 16 measures. (The theme itself is a borrowed one.) These 16 measures form a double period: a a' (first period)

   b a" (second period)

   Each phrase is 4 measures in length; yet the internal variety and variety of cadence prevent the work from becoming either static or square.

2. The harmonic vocabulary is straightforward—that is, basically diatonic chords and a few secondary dominants. A modulation to E major is effected in measures 7-8.

3. In Etude I, the accompaniment figure is derived from the theme; it provides an interesting melodic and rhythmic counterpoint for the entry of the theme in measure 5. The form of the Etude I remains the same as the theme except for the repetition of the final 8 measures.

4. Etude IV (Variation 3) illustrates Schumann's treatment of canon, made not of single notes but of full 4-note chords. Although some chords are modified to accommodate the principal harmony, the imitation is both effective and aurally exciting.

Example 339

INTERMEZZO (RÜCKBLICK)

Complete from the Sonata in F Minor, Op. 5

Brahms

Brahms' eloquent and reflective *Intermezzo* from the *Sonata in F minor* is based principally on two gestures, each presented in the first two measures of Example 339. The right-hand motive underscores the melodic/harmonic element, while the left hand figure is rhythmic in both its makeup and its function. The two ideas are developed with logic and consummate technical mastery.

OBSERVATIONS:

1. The central tonality of Bb minor is varied by slight references to F minor and Eb minor. Chords that contain accidentals are primarily secondary dominants.

2. Measures 19-23 are of interest because of the composer's use of two sets of consecutive fifths (mostly parallel perfect fifths). This technique foreshadows perhaps the textures used by the Impressionists later in the century.

3. Musical events occur at quite specific mathematical points: measures 1, 2, 3, 5, 8, 13, (21), and 34. This additive arithmetical series is known as the Fibonacci Series. Analysis of music from diverse eras reveals a remarkable correlation between the series and the internal events, high points, loudest dynamic, and so forth in a piece of music. Further, the golden mean of the Intermezzo is precisely at the *ff* of measure 33! As Tovey once remarked about Brahms, "he profited from the luck that goes with genius."

FOUR-VOICE, NONCHROMATIC TEXTURE

Example 340 illustrates an essentially nonchromatic passage from *Ein Deutsches Requiem* by Brahms. The orchestral accompaniment is omitted.

Example 340

EIN DEUTSCHES REQUIEM (excerpt)

Brahms

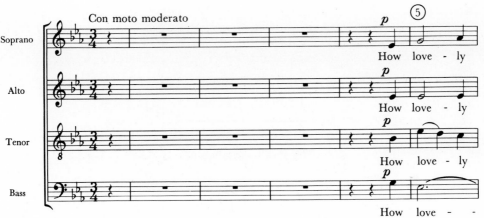

OBSERVATIONS:

1. Each of the four lines is expressively contoured—suggesting a contrapuntal-harmonic conception.
2. The bass line has a particular independence as well as a special relationship to the soprano line (i.e., suggested mirror, nonstrict imitation).
3. The overlapping phrase structure between the upper three voices and the basses in measures 8-9 relates to Renaissance practice.
4. The phrase structure of three bars plus five bars (measures 16-23) is an architectural feature of interest.
5. The stability of E♭ major and the eventual modulation to the dominant (via c minor) suggests a conservative view of tonal relationships.

CHAPTER SUMMARY

The chapter is concerned with the technical aspects of harmonic expansion, chromatic alteration, enharmonic modulation, and other specifics of style of the nineteenth century.

Ninth chords may be observed in Baroque compositions—but mainly as contrapuntal coincidences involving *appoggiature* or other nonchord tones. The complete ninth chord was used with considerable frequency in the nineteenth century. As a *dominant* ninth the sonority achieved a special vogue, although its appearances were certainly not limited to dominant function.

The diminished seventh chord is also observed in Baroque music, but its widest adoption came during the Romantic era. The diminished-diminished seventh is poignant in sonority; it holds a special theoretical fascination because of its makeup of equidistant minor thirds, its aural noninvertibility, and its great flexibility in resolution.

Enharmonic modulation involves a respelling from sharps to flats, or the reverse. Pronounced or continuous chordal alteration produces chromaticism. Chromaticism, together with frequent modulations and an abundance of nonchord tones, effected an expansion of the tertian system.

Chordal mutation is a term used to describe gradual harmonic change—that is, alteration of one or two chord tones consecutively to produce a new sonority. Thereafter the process is repeated.

In an analysis of a movement of Brahms' F Minor Sonata, observation was made of musical events that occur at specific mathematical points: at measures 1, 2, 3, 5, 8, 13, (21), and 34. This additive arithmetical series is known as the Fibonacci Series.

SUGGESTED STUDIES

1. Provide a harmonic analysis for the following excerpt. Include a short expository amplification of your analysis.

Example 341

INTERMEZZO, OP. 116, NO. 6 (excerpt)

Brahms

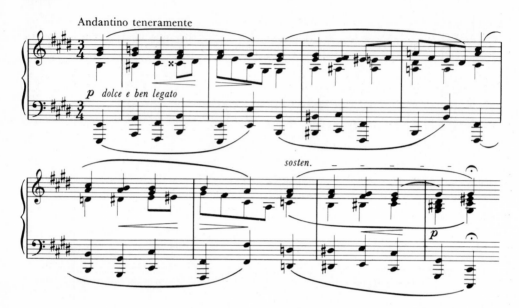

2. Write a short composition for piano using diminished-diminished seventh chords for purposes of modulation. Include one or more examples of enharmonic modulation.

3. On a text in English, write a short song (about 20 measures), using the melodic, harmonic, rhythmic vocabularies typical of Schumann, Chopin, or Brahms.

Chapter 21

CHROMATIC HARMONY OF THE NINETEENTH CENTURY

CHROMATIC ANALYSIS

Detailed harmonic analysis of nineteenth-century compositions poses problems that demand both a critical judgment and considerable tenacity. However veiled the composer's intent may seem initially, a system is always discernible, and not infrequently one finds behind the surface complexity rather simple organizational premises.

Example 342

VARIATIONS SYMPHONIQUES (excerpt)

César Franck (1822-1890)

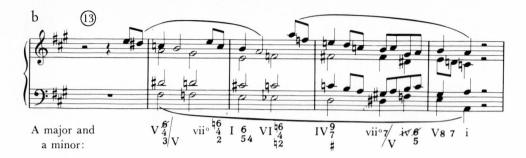

The analyses included in this chapter offer possible solutions, to which others should be added. Subjective, at least in part, the observations are perhaps appropriate to the *Zeitgeist,* or spirit of the times, of high Romanticism.

OBSERVATIONS ON EXAMPLE 342:

1. The two excerpts illustrate parallel phrase construction: the first in f♯ minor, the second in A major-minor.
2. Chordal structures in measures 6, 7 and 14, 15 are partially resultants of the descending bass lines.
3. Chromatic evasiveness internally in the phrases is countered by cadence strength and clarity.
4. In both phrases, observe the chromatic but resolute movement from V of V to V to I.

HARMONIC SEQUENCE

The harmonic structure in Example 343 is governed quite consistently by a convergence of the outside voices:

Example 343

DIE WALKÜRE

Sleep motive

Wagner

Implied bass line

OBSERVATIONS:

1. The upper voice descends by half steps; a two-bar rhythmic pattern effects a sequence in which the repetition occurs a major third lower for each presentation.

2. The lower voice similarly is a two-bar sequence, ascending, in which the repetition is at the minor sixth above. Observe the interval inversion of the soprano sequence—that is, E_1 up to C; C up to G♯; G♯ up to the final e.

PLURALITY OF TONAL AXES

One possible approach to the harmonic analysis of this passage is to consider a *plural* or *multiple* tonal axis—that is, tonal axes or tonal centers that function concurrently.

G♯ (A♭) ———————————— is the upper parallel axis

E ———————————— is the principal tonal axis (center)

C/c ———————————— is the lower parallel axis

Observe that by using the above concept of plurality of tonal axes, all chords in the excerpt function with reasonable clarity in a traditional sense.

ANALYSIS BY CHORD NUMBER:

1. I in E
2. V in G♯ (A♭); also III in c
3. x (B♭ and E♭ are suspensions to the next chord)
4. vii[7] in C

5. I in C
6. III in c; also V in G♯ (A♭)
7. V/V in C
8. I$^6_4$ (plus flatted chordal seventh); actually a mispelled vii[7] of G♯—that is, F𝄪 A♯ C♯ E

9. I in G♯
10. V in E
11. V/V in G♯ (A♭)
12. vii[7] in E

13. I in E

Alternate analyses to the above are encouraged. Too often analysis of chromatic music of the late Romantic period is purely descriptive, with little attention directed toward melodic and harmonic movement, and the relationships that form its basis.

MOTIVIC CONSTRUCTION

The fact that the musical fabric is formed from motives or, in the Wagnerian term, *leitmotifs* (G., leading or guiding motive) that represent characters, moods, aspirations, and philosophical commentary need not deter one from technical analysis of the composer's methods of controlling the horizontal-vertical time span. Prior to the study of a chordal analysis of the first 24 measures of the Prelude to *Tristan und Isolde* (Example 344), a few explanations are pertinent:

EXTENDED APPOGGIATURA

1. A scheme of plural tonal axes again seems to be implied:

$$A/a \overset{\displaystyle E/e}{\underset{\displaystyle C/c}{\rule{4cm}{0.4pt}}} \text{ principal axis, both major and minor}$$

2. The *appoggiature* in this work (and many others) are lengthened to the extent that often the duration is several times longer than that of the chord tone to which they resolve (as examples, see measures 1 and 2).

3. Altered chords, especially augmented sixth chords, are coequal in importance with diatonic sonorities.

4. Harmonic and melodic sequences are abundant.

5. Cadence evasion, elision, and deception are facets of the compositional process.

Example 344

TRISTAN UND ISOLDE

Prelude, measures 1-24 (piano reduction)

Wagner

ENHARMONIC SPELLINGS

Enharmonic spellings are common in the music of the late nineteenth century. Sometimes the spellings are theoretically precise, and at other times they result from a consideration for ease of reading—that is, the avoidance of a large number of double sharps or double flats.

The opening of Dvořák's *Largo* from his Ninth Symphony is aurally very familiar. It is quite elusive in analysis, however, partly because of its strange mixtures of sharps, flats, and enharmonic spellings. The previous movement of the symphony concludes in E major; the first chord of the excerpt below, Example 345, is the same sonority.

Consider the passage to be in both C♯ major *and* C♯ minor (alternating) with both tonic notes enharmonic to D♭ (major). The enigma disappears, and Dvořák's fine sense of harmonic progression emerges both aurally and intellectually.

Example 345

LARGO (excerpt)

From Symphony No. 9 (piano reduction)

Antonin Dvořák (1841-1904)

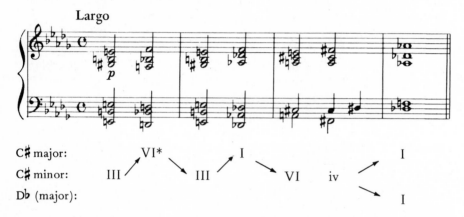

*That is, A♯, C✕, E♯ —thus being the only "altered" chord, using the analysis suggested above.

CHAPTER SUMMARY

Detailed harmonic analysis of nineteenth-century compositions poses problems that demand both a critical judgment and considerable tenacity. A compositional system is always discernible, and not infrequently one finds behind the surface complexity rather simple organizational premises. One possible approach to harmonic analysis is to consider a plurality of tonal axes, such as major and minor modes in rapid succession or axes that are a major third apart.

Enharmonic spellings are common in the music of the late nineteenth century. Sometimes the spellings are theoretically precise, and at other times they result from a consideration for ease of reading.

An extensive analysis of the Prelude to *Tristan und Isolde* of Wagner is included in the chapter.

SUGGESTED STUDIES

1. Using Example 346b as a model and guide, realize the figured bass (Example 346a) in four parts. Appropriate chromatic passing tones, auxiliary tones, and

suspensions may be freely utilized, provided the general style and vocabulary are maintained.

Example 346a

Example 346b

INTERMEZZO (excerpt)

Concerto No. 3 (piano reduction)

Sergei Rachmaninoff (1873-1943)

2. Provide a motivic and harmonic analysis of measures 25-44 of the Prelude to *Tristan und Isolde* (Example 344).

3. Using primary or secondary sources, write a short expository paper on the use of the *leitmotif* for compositional unification in nineteenth-century music. See: Berlioz, Liszt, Wagner, Franck.

Example 347

TRISTAN UND ISOLDE

Prelude, measures 25-44 (piano reduction)

Wagner

Chapter 22

ELEVENTH AND THIRTEENTH CHORDS PARALLEL HARMONY ADDED-TONE TECHNIQUE

ELEVENTH AND THIRTEENTH CHORDS

In the latter part of the nineteenth century, not only did harmonic practice include chordal and melodic chromaticism, frequent modulations to distant key centers, and prolongation of nonharmonic tones, but the tertian system itself expanded to encompass sonorities beyond seventh and ninth chords. A new phase began, of increased use of nonharmonic tones that gradually became harmonic. The resulting eleventh chords, and especially thirteenth chords, were used with some frequency in the continuing search for new resources within the major-minor system. Example 348 illustrates several common formations.

Example 348

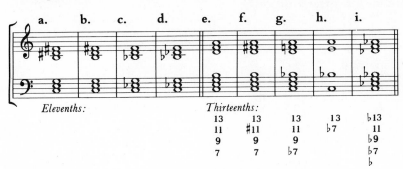

OBSERVATIONS:

1. The eleventh chord may be considered as an expansion beyond the ninth; or as two triads, superimposed vertically, and related by an interval of a third. In Example 348a, the eleventh chord consists of a C major triad and a B major triad producing, in effect, a *polychord*.

2. Similarly, as in Example 348i, the thirteenth chord may comprise a seventh chord (Cmm^7) plus a triad (Db major).

3. Although a kind of artificial figured bass may be devised—by simply taking an inventory above the bass note—the practice is not recommended, since composers ceased using this musical shorthand about 1750.*

4. Perhaps the most common usage of these chords was the dominant thirteenth (Example 348g), which is a V^7 with diatonic expansion. Example 348h shows a four-voice version that includes a root, third, seventh, and thirteenth. This disposition is typical. Most often the chordal seventh will resolve stepwise down, but the thirteenth is free to

    a. remain stationary
    b. move down
    c. leap up

Example 349

Resolutions:

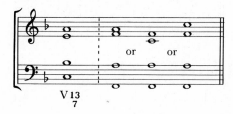

$$V\,{}^{13}_{7}$$

    Of interest, as a theoretical point, is that the complete seven-voice thirteenth chord is noninvertible. Any attempt at first, second, and so forth, inversion simply produces a new chord with a different root.

Example 350

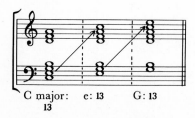

C major: e: 13   G: 13
  13

---

*In some sacred music, however, figured bass practice continued well into the nineteenth century.

A poignant example of the dominant thirteenth is observed in César Franck's D Minor Symphony.

Example 351

SYMPHONY IN D MINOR (excerpt)

First movement, measures 175-178

Franck

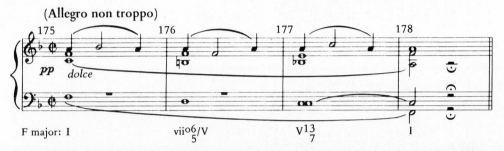

The following excerpt from Alexander Scriabin's *Prelude,* Op. 48, No. 4 (Example 352), shows an extensive use of expanded tertian sonorities derived from linear considerations.

Example 352

PRELUDE, OP. 48, NO. 4 (excerpt)

Alexander Scriabin (1872-1915)

OBSERVATIONS:

1. Although most vertical sonorities include the seventh, ninth, eleventh, or thirteenth, the basic harmonic progressions are strongly anchored to the concept of root movement by fifths.

2. Two examples of root movement by tritone (measures 17-18, Db-G and the same notes in measures 19-22) are supportive of a certain dissonant character of this *Prelude*.

3. The chordal dispositions covering 5½ octaves (measure 23) further indicate the expansiveness of concept and mood.

Scriabin's *Prelude,* Op. 11, No. 9, further illustrates expanded tertian sonorities.

Example 353

PRELUDE IN E MAJOR, OP. 11, NO. 9

Scriabin

iv (from E minor)   I (ist inv., chord 3rd raised)

ii⁹   V¹³

PARALLEL HARMONY

In the two decades from about 1890 to 1910, several musical cross-currents rather radically influenced the direction of Western music. The highly expanded tertian system, illustrated above, was modified by numerous composers by the introduction of one or more of the following influences:

1. Medieval and Renaissance music, and reuse of a modified modal system.
2. Use of folk-song materials, which resulted in a certain simplification of the tertian system.
3. Interest in certain exotic elements such as the pentatonic scales, Iberian rhythms, and quasi-Oriental clarity of texture. In orchestral music these items were frequently coupled to a highly coloristic scoring.
4. Reexamination of the traditional major-minor syntax, effecting nonfunctional harmonic progression—that is, progression and root movement *not* determined by a circle of fifths.

Claude Debussy's Sarabande from *Pour le Piano* (Example 355), composed during the years 1896 to 1901, illustrates several of the above influences. Anchored in the aesthetic of Impressionism, the chordal structures remain tertian in their spelling and disposition; yet the relationships from one chord to the next approach a return to nonfunctional harmonic movement. Although a harmonic analysis may be devised, the results do not seem altogether germane. For example, measures 1-2 would read:

In c♯ minor and modal:

ii°⁷   iv⁷   ♮VII⁴₂   iv⁷   ii°⁷ │ III   v   v │

The chord-to-chord progression seems to be determined by means of *parallelism* or *planing*—generated from the opening sonority. Debussy's parallel harmony and Medieval organum would appear to share a common denominator. One may also speculate (see observations below) that the opening chord defines the tonal structure of this excerpt.

Example 354

Example 355

SARABANDE

From *Pour Le Piano*

Debussy

OBSERVATIONS:

1. Although Debussy's harmonic progressions appear to be nonfunctional in a chord-to-chord relationship, the chords do relate, and function, in a larger time span. A middle-ground, or second harmonic dimension, analysis is given in Example 354.

2. Consider most carefully the organizing progression

$$\text{ii}^7 \qquad \text{v (minor)} \qquad \text{i}$$

3. The Aeolian mode is used for both melodic and harmonic formations.

4. The avoidance of the raised leading tone (minor dominant) is observed quite frequently in Impressionist music.

5. The whole-tone scale appears in measures 12-13: d e f♯ g♯ a♯ (in the bass line).

6. These 22 measures form a small ternary: a b a'. (Compare measure 19 to measure 5.) The excerpt, in turn, is the A section of a larger tripartite design.

Modal parallelism, abrupt tonal shifts, fluid rhythms, and open-fifth sonorities are eloquently fused in this short composition (Example 356), entitled *Canope* (*Second Book of Preludes*). Of particular interest is measure 3, in which a shift to the flat side takes place without benefit (or perhaps distraction) of a modulation formula. Rather, a tritone relates the a minor triad to the e♭ minor triad, while the bass line assumes a temporary independent role. The *color* of sonorities held a special fascination for the Impressionist composers; and the relationships between painting, poetry, and music during this era are particularly striking.

Example 356

CANOPE

From *The Second Book of Preludes*

Debussy

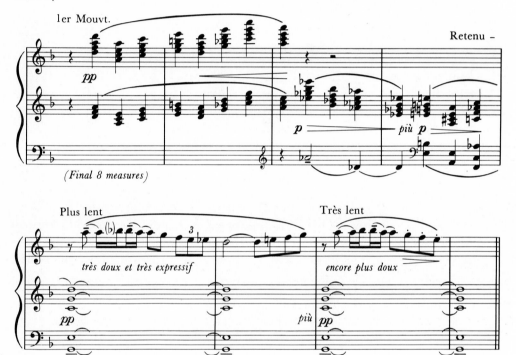

ADDED-TONE TECHNIQUE

The technique of adding a second, fourth, or sixth to a basic triad offers additional color resources in music. Usually referred to as the *added-tone technique*, this additive process is commonly associated with the Impressionist composers. Appearances occur much earlier, however, and the tendency of late-nineteenth-century composers to leave *appoggiature* and suspensions unresolved is a closely allied compositional technique. Example 357 illustrates the most basic formations.

Example 357

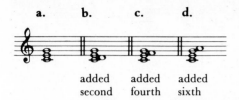

It is immediately apparent that these sonorities might be subjected to two or more views of analysis. Why is Example 357b not a ninth chord, 357c an eleventh chord, and 357d either a thirteenth chord or the first inversion of a seventh chord with A as its root? Most analytical judgments must be based on style, context, function, and chordal disposition. A few subjective analyses are provided below.

Example 358

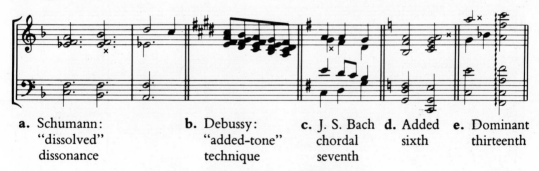

a. Schumann: "dissolved" dissonance b. Debussy: "added-tone" technique c. J. S. Bach chordal seventh d. Added sixth e. Dominant thirteenth

Impressionist composers addressed themselves to the question of texture, color, and vertical spacing with particular adroitness.

The first movement of Ravel's *String Quartet in F* illustrates how striking and luminous a d minor triad (with ninth) can sound. The first violin line is "registered" two octaves below in the viola (a technique Ravel probably discovered in the scores of Mozart). This spacious melodic scoring is stabilized by the harmonic and textural tremolos of the second violin. And, not least, the pizzicato cello buoys, punctuates, and provides harmonic clarification for the upper voices (pp. 52-62).

A basic structural and tonal analysis is annotated in the score of the First Movement of Ravel's elegant *String Quartet*. Additional commentaries and analyses are provided at points of particular interest.

Example 359

STRING QUARTET

First movement

Ravel

Allegro moderato–Très doux (♩ = 120)

Violin I

Violin II

Viola

Cello

Exposition, Group I, F major

f (modal)

6

cresc.   poco   a

12

poco

part 2

F major

Transition, preparation for Group II

Observe change in texture

Group II, d (modal)

Development:
note whole-tone
bass line

Preparation for recapitulation

Recapitulation (F major)

again, whole-tone movement in bass line

CHAPTER SUMMARY

In the latter part of the nineteenth century, not only did harmonic practice include chordal and melodic chromaticism, frequent modulations to distant key centers, and prolongation of nonharmonic tones, but the tertian system itself expanded to encompass sonorities beyond seventh and ninth chords. A new phase began, of increased use of nonharmonic tones that gradually became harmonic. The resulting eleventh chords, and especially thirteenth chords, were used with some frequency in the continuing search for new resources within the major-minor system.

In the two decades from about 1890 to 1910, several musical cross-currents rather radically influenced the direction of Western music. The highly expanded tertian system was further modified by: use of modal materials, folk-song materials, exotic elements such as the pentatonic scales, Iberian rhythms, and so forth, and re-examination of the traditional major-minor syntax, effecting nonfunctional harmonic progression.

Modal parallelism, abrupt tonal shifts, fluid rhythms, and open-fifth sonorities are some of the resources of Impressionistic music.

A basic analysis of the First Movement of Ravel's *String Quartet* (1902-1903) is provided in this chapter.

SUGGESTED STUDIES

1. Make a basic structural analysis of a short Impressionistic piano composition (see Debussy: *Preludes,* Books I, II). Comment on techniques used, scale resources, harmonic dispositions, and treatment of color and texture.
2. Using Debussy's *Canope* (Example 356) as a point of departure, write a short composition of about 20 measures for piano, in a similar style.
3. Using the following fragment (Example 360), compose a short piece for solo flute (or similar instrument) that continues with modal and whole-tone scale interplay.

Example 360

4. Using primary and secondary sources, write a short expository paper discussing the relationships between Impressionist painting, poetry, and music.

PART IV

MUSIC OF THE TWENTIETH CENTURY

"Mankind are very odd Creatures: One
half censure what they practise, the
other half practise what they censure;
the rest always say and do as they
ought."

—Benjamin Franklin

Chapter 23

ELEMENTS OF TWENTIETH-CENTURY MUSIC

The first half of the twentieth century witnessed numerous changes in the inherited systems of Western music. Some innovations served as further expansions or modifications of the existing major-minor-tonal system; other developments, however, were antithetical to the conventions of the past and eventually produced a rethinking of the aesthetics and mechanics of music. Each parameter was scrutinized with a view to extracting its fullest potential. Rhythm, color, timbre, orchestration, texture, form—as well as melody and harmony—were each in turn used as the focal point of the composer's aural postulations.

RHYTHM

A new rhythmic vitality is characteristic of many works. Syncopations, asymmetrical groupings, and free or rhapsodic rhythms are frequently observed. One of the most extraordinary compositions of the twentieth century that emphasize the elements of rhythm and timbre is Edgar Varèse's *Ionisation* of 1931, Example 361.

Example 361

IONISATION (1931) (excerpt)

Edgar Varèse (1883-1965)

The question of durations was often coupled to the metric organization in a "war against the tyranny of the bar line." Such considerations led to several schemes of time organization, a few of which are cited below:

1. *Odd meters:* $\frac{5}{8}$ $\frac{7}{8}$ $\frac{11}{4}$

2. *Changing meters:* $\frac{2}{4}$ $\frac{3}{8}$ $\frac{3}{4}$ $\frac{1}{16}$ $\frac{5}{8}$

3. *Variable metrics—a predetermined scheme of metric organization:*

   $\frac{2}{8}$ $\frac{4}{8}$ $\frac{6}{8}$ $\frac{8}{8}$ $\frac{8}{8}$ $\frac{7}{8}$ $\frac{5}{8}$ $\frac{3}{8}$ (expansion by even meters and compression by odd meters)

Example 362

THE RITE OF SPRING (1913) (excerpt)

Stravinsky

Rite of Spring, Igor Stravinsky. Copyright 1921 by Edition Russe de Musique. Copyright assigned 1947 to Boosey & Hawkes, Inc. Reprinted by permission of Boosey & Hawkes, Inc., and Boosey & Hawkes (Canada) Ltd.

MELODY

Melodic lines are frequently more disjunct than in the nineteenth century. Occasionally, voices imitate instruments (Webern, *Kantate*) and, conversely, instruments imitate voices (Bartók, *Music for Strings, Percussion and Celesta*).

Example 363
KANTATE, OP. 31 (excerpt)
Bass solo, II
Anton Webern (1833-1945)

Universal Edition UE 12486.

Example 364
MUSIC FOR STRINGS, PERCUSSION, AND CELESTA (1936)
First movement
Bartók

Boosey & Hawkes. Used by permission.

Example 365

SYMPHONY OF PSALMS (excerpt)

Second movement

Stravinsky

Example 366

THIRD PIANO SONATA (excerpt)

From the fourth movement

Paul Hindemith (1895-1963)

Example 367

PIANO CONCERTO, OP. 42 (excerpt)

From the first movement

Schoenberg

COLOR AND TIMBRE

The possibilities of color and timbre were rather consistently explored by most composers. Two concepts are of particular importance—both of which may provide new life for a series of pitches.

1. *Klangfarbenmelodie* literally means tone-color melody. A particularly striking passage is shown in Example 368.

Example 368

FIVE PIECES FOR ORCHESTRA, OP. 16, III FARBEN (excerpt)

Schoenberg

Reprinted from *Five Pieces for Orchestra* by Arnold Schoenberg, III—Summer Morning by a Lake (Peters Nr. 6061). © 1952 by Henmar Press, Inc., New York. Reprint permission granted by the publisher.

2. *Pointillism* is a term borrowed from painting. It refers to points of color that collectively effect a representational or semirepresentational likeness of the painter's subject matter. (See Examples 369, 405.)

In a facetious vein, the following example uses a well-known tune and subjects it to a free rhythmic arrangement, *octave displacement* (i.e., substitution of a different octave for the given note), and a pointillistic treatment.

Example 369

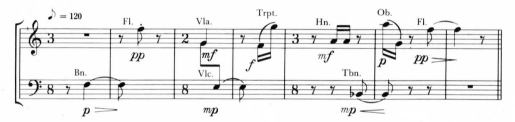

OBSERVATIONS:

1. Points of instrumental color create a constantly changing texture. In viewing a pointillistic painting, one should stand at some distance in order to perceive the whole; similarly, one should "stand back" aurally in order to absorb the totality of pointillistic musical fabric.
2. The use of different orchestral timbres evokes a *tone painting* of nearly infinite potential.

QUERIES:

1. What is the paraphrased melody?
2. Is the example within a given tonality?

TEXTURE AND DENSITY

Texture is often a significant facet of composition, providing depth and dimension and contributing to the organization of time span. Texture per se *may* be used as a form-producing parameter, especially in the control of density.

Example 370

PIANO VARIATIONS (excerpt)

Aaron Copland (1900-   )

Copyright 1932 by Cos Cob Press, Inc.; renewed 1959. Copyright and renewal assigned to Boosey & Hawkes, Inc.

ORCHESTRATION

One of the most radical departures from previous practice can be observed in the instrumentation and orchestration that has been employed by twentieth-century composers. From among the numerous innovations, a few are cited:

1. A complete and independent use of four orchestral choirs: winds, brasses, percussion, and strings.
2. Scoring for special combinations of instruments, such as thirteen diverse colors or eight 'celli and voice.

FORM

As with the "shape" of the universe, any discussion of musical form of this century is out of date before it has even been verbalized. Philosophy aside, the reader is advised to consider at least two principal categories for twentieth-century musical form:

1. Modifications of eighteenth- and nineteenth-century principles of musical design
2. Structural innovations and practices that relate specifically to the twentieth century.

The principles of binary, ternary, sonata, rondo, and variation have been freely utilized by twentieth-century composers. These parent forms, however, have been modified substantially—particularly with regard to repetition. The psychological impact of sound and of experience from sound have been carefully considered. A hypothetical comparison will serve to illustrate:

TERNARY PRINCIPLE (NINETEENTH-CENTURY):

A	B	A
16 measures	12-16 measures	exact repetition

TERNARY PRINCIPLE (TWENTIETH-CENTURY):

A	B	A'/(B)
15 measures	11 measures	13 measures comprising short quotations from A and B; possibly in inverted or retrograde form.

Some writers refer to this twentieth-century foreshortening of the repeated portions as *dynamic symmetry*—a symmetry resulting from the weight of musical event and experience rather than from a symmetrical proportioning of the time span.

Arch forms are used to structural advantage by several composers. As examples, in Bartók's *String Quartet No. 4,* 1928, and Stravinsky's *Cantata,* 1950, the arch serves to unify structure and is clearly recognizable aurally. The ageless premises of unity and variety are underscored with new vocabularies.

A hypothetical arch form is shown in Example 371.

Example 371

Arch: 1 2 3 4 5

Sections 1 and 5 related; 2 and 4 related; 3 independent

As in any of the previous eras of change (Ars Nova, c. 1300, Nuove Musiche, c. 1600, and the new music of c. 1900), the old and the new continue in tandem, with the older traditions often influencing some composers to a major degree. As a broad generalization that can, however, be substantiated, *some* of the influences on major composers of the first half of the century are shown below:

Bartók: Impressionism and Eastern European folk song

Hindemith: Medieval theory and philosophy; Baroque counterpoint

Schoenberg: Eighteenth- and nineteenth-century musical form; nineteenth-century philosophy and literature

Stravinsky: Late Renaissance and early Baroque music; literature of antiquity

Webern: Renaissance (Isaac) clarity of sound and structure.

Dmitri Shostakovitch's Fifth Symphony is an excellent example of nineteenth-century compositional procedures adapted to the twentieth century. In many ways, it is a traditional piece, yet the specifics of vocabulary could have been produced only in the twentieth century. The work as a whole comprises four movements with a decidedly classical format:

I Moderato   II Allegretto   III Largo   IV Allegro non troppo

Eighteenth- and nineteenth-century forms are utilized within tonal frameworks. As an example of modified key plan, the principal tonal levels of measures 1-122 of the first movement are shown below:

First Movement, Fifth Symphony, Shostakovitch

Group I
    d minor
        motive x   ms. 1-4
        motive y   ms. 5-8
        motive x^1 ms. 9-12
        motive x   ms. 13-20
        connective ms. 21-33
        motive x   ms. 34-41
        connective ms. 42-49

Group II
    Part 1
        eb minor-E major   ms. 50-69
        connective   ms. 70-74
    Part 2
        g minor, Eb major   ms. 75-105
    Part 1 varied
        b minor modulating   ms. 106-121
    Part 3
        bb minor   ms. 122-. . .

Similarly, the composer's themes are seemingly scale-derived, but not from traditional major-minor formations. Two principal themes are reduced to scalar forms from measures 1-4 and 50-68:

Example 372

Rhythmic motives are highly contributive to the musical fabric—for example,

 or

The composer's orchestration is varied—from quiet scoring for strings and harp of Group II, measure 50, to the brassy passage for four horns with piano and low string pizzicato, measure 122.

Example 373
SYMPHONY NO. 5, OP. 47 (excerpt)
First movement
Dimitri Shostakovitch (1905-1975)

416

Edwin F. Kalmus, Publisher of Music, Scarsdale, N.Y.

CHAPTER SUMMARY

The first half of the twentieth century witnessed numerous changes in Western music. A few of the most important changes are cited below:

Rhythm:

A new rhythmic vitality is characteristic of many works. Syncopations, asymmetrical groupings, and free rhythms are frequently observed. The question of durations was often coupled to metric organization, such as the use of odd meters, changing meters, and variable metrics.

Melody:

Melody is frequently more disjunct than in the nineteenth century. *Klangfarbenmelodie* literally means "tone-color melody." The technique was used to enhance the coloristic and timbral possibilities of melody. Pointillism is another possible treatment of melodic lines.

Orchestration:

One of the most radical departures from previous practice is observed in instrumentation and orchestration. A complete and independent use of four orchestral choirs—winds, brasses, percussion, strings—is commonly observed.

Form:

Two main categories for discussion of musical form include: modifications of eighteenth- and nineteenth-century principles of musical design and structural innovations and practices that relate specifically to the twentieth century. Foreshortening of repeated portions is sometimes referred to as dynamic symmetry. Arch forms are used to advantage by several composers.

An analysis of an extended excerpt from Shostakovitch's Fifth Symphony is made in this chapter.

SUGGESTED STUDIES

1. Suggested reading:

Leon Dallin. *Techniques of Twentieth Century Harmony*. Dubuque, Iowa: Wm. C. Brown Company Publishers, 1957.

Allen Forte. *Contemporary Tone-Structures*. New York: Columbia University Press, 1955.

G. Welton Marquis. *Twentieth Century Music Idioms*. Englewood Cliffs, N. J.: Prentice-Hall, 1964.

Vincent Persichetti. *Twentieth Century Harmony*. New York: W. W. Norton Company, 1961.

2. Write a short composition for percussion instruments (or sound-producing objects) in which variable metrics and a wedge design are employed.

3. Paraphrase a familiar folk song for four or five different instruments, employing the techniques of octave displacement and pointillism.
4. Using the excerpt from the song *Serenity,* by Charles Ives (Example 374), prepare an analysis providing three or four points on each of the following: harmony, melody, rhythm/meter, structure/repetition, texture/dynamics.

Example 374

*SERENITY**

Text by John G. Whittier, 1807-1892

Charles Ives (1874-1954)

*About 1919, according to the Catalogue of Ives Manuscripts, compiled by John Kirkpatrick.

Chapter 24

PANDIATONICISM

DEFINITION

A vocabulary used extensively by American and French composers in the second and third decades of this century consisted of a linearly conceived, nonfunctional diatonicism. Sometimes referred to as "white-key music," it is perhaps more aptly termed *pandiatonicism* (i.e., an all-inclusive, essentially nonchromatic pitch series). Often, one or more of the convergent lines will suggest a mode, freely employed. Phrygian, Dorian, and Aeolian characteristics seem to have been particularly popular.

The independence of each line, within the tonal/modal restrictions set by the composer, can scarcely be overemphasized. The linear process contributes to the nonfunctionalism of chords. As a result, modulation in the traditional sense is un-necessary—since a freedom of tonal orientation and of cadence already exists. To illustrate, the cadence in measure 6 of Stravinsky's *Dithyrambe* (Example 375a) is shown rewritten four times (375b-e) not as improvements, but as possible alternatives within the style:

Example 375

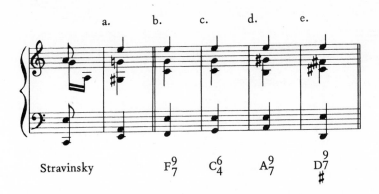

Stravinsky

Example 376

DITHYRAMBE

Stravinsky

Copyright 1933 by Edition Russe de Musique. Printed by arrangement, Boosey & Hawkes, Inc., New York. Used by permission.

OBSERVATIONS:

1. Stravinsky's structure of *Dithyrambe* (Example 376) suggests more than a simple ABA. The A sections serve as introduction and conclusion and "frame" to the middle section, which in turn is divided into two parts: B1, the expansive, unmeasured *parlando;* followed by B2, the chordal focal point and climax.

2. The tonal orientation is to C, with a tritone relationship to the climax.

3. Except for the chordal climax, the texture moves freely from four to six voices, including the solo violin. Control of range and of register create the movement's dramatic shape.

4. Examination of the vertical sonorities reveals an expanded tertian vocabulary. As a typical sampling, chord structures *a* through *e* (the latter, see analysis below,

certainly the most ambiguous of these five chords) on the second page of the example would seem to indicate the absence of a systematized root movement.

a. F_9^{11} b. C_9^{11} c. D_9^{13} d. C^7 e. D_{+6}^9
     $_7$ $_7$

Example 377

SYMPHONIES OF WIND INSTRUMENTS (excerpt)

Final 19 measures

Stravinsky

B &H 17144

B.&H.17144   BHMP 10/76

Example 378

SYMPHONY OF PSALMS (1930) (excerpt)

First movement

Stravinsky

Stravinsky's *Symphony of Psalms* is one of the most significant works of the twentieth century. The materials of pitch and duration are masterfully controlled; musical events are ingeniously scheduled with perfect agreement between micro-rhythm and total proportion; its dedication "to the glory of God" clearly confirms the composer's philosophical intent.

The entire work of three movements may be approximately diagrammed as follows:

```
I   ——————————
    e           G
II  ————————————————————
    c       (double fugue)      E♭
III ——————————————————————————————
    c                               C
```

The proportions are premised on expansion from one time unit, to two, to three time units in the last movement. The excerpt of 16 measures also illustrates the concept of expansion:

```
        4          6         10
      beats      beats      beats

   chord      chord      chord      chord
```

Observe: 4 to 6 = golden ratio (approx.)
            6 to 10 = golden ratio (approx.)
            4 + 6 to 10 = perfect symmetry

Similarly, the pitch materials of the opening gestures predict the total tonal form:

Example 379

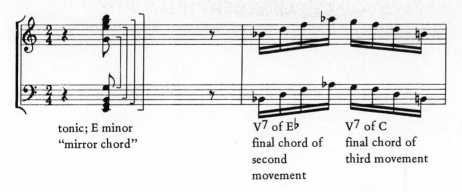

tonic; E minor
"mirror chord"

V^7 of E♭
final chord of
second
movement

V^7 of C
final chord of
third movement

The *Symphony of Psalms* as a whole is a tonal composition, but the triads (with or without tertian expansion—i.e., sevenths, ninths, etc.) do not function in a circle of fifths or other systematic way. In some respects the pandiatonicism Stravinsky employed from about 1920 to 1950 bears a striking resemblance to early-seventeenth-century music, especially to some works of Monteverdi, where modal-tonal mixtures and associations effected a logical succession of sound—but one that is rarely predictable.

CHAPTER SUMMARY

A vocabulary used extensively by American and French composers in the second and third decades of this century consisted of a linearly conceived, nonfunctional diatonicism. This process is called pandiatonicism. Several pandiatonic compositions of Stravinsky are analyzed in this chapter.

SUGGESTED STUDIES

1. Analyze and perform the following excerpts from Stravinsky's *Ave Maria* (Example 380). Study the contour of each line, the vertical coincidence, and the cadence practice.

Example 380

AVE MARIA (excerpt)

Stravinsky

a.

b.

2. As an experiment, continue the five-voice fragment in Example 381 for an additional 9 measures. Use no accidentals; write one line at a time, considering the

contour and musicality of each line. Cover each completed line before writing a new voice. After all five voices are completed, play or perform the total composition. Carefully study the pandiatonic, nonfunctional results.

Example 381

3. Write a short composition with the following requirements:

> Piano, four hands
> Phrygian or Dorian characteristics (essentially white-key)
> Phrase design: A (9 measures), B (7 measures), A' (5 measures)

4. Prepare a basic structural/tonal analysis of the Second Movement of Stravinsky's *Symphony of Psalms.* Comment on the unique features of this work.

Chapter 25

QUARTAL HARMONY

In Western music, vertical sonorities are produced primarily by three different kinds of harmony:

Secundal: spelling of chords in interval of seconds
Tertian: spelling of chords in thirds
Quartal: spelling of chords in fourths

All other spellings are formed from interval inversion, and there exists a modest debate among writers as to whether these three kinds of harmony coexist or are, rather, mutually interchangeable. Example 382 illustrates:

Example 382

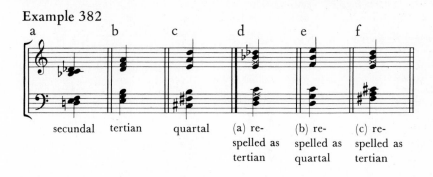

| secundal | tertian | quartal | (a) re-spelled as tertian | (b) re-spelled as quartal | (c) re-spelled as tertian |

QUARTAL HARMONY

Paul Hindemith's chanson *Since all is passing* (Example 383) provides an excellent example of combined tertian-quartal harmony. The interplay produces a fresh and appealing sonority within a tonal and traditional framework.

OBSERVATIONS:

1. Deliberate quartal (or the inverted, quintal) dispositions are to be found in each of the 17 measures.
2. Parallel perfect fourths or perfect fifths provide for open, quasiarchaic sonorities.
3. The composition has a tonal orientation to G, although chord-to-chord progressions are nonfunctional in the traditional sense.
4. Cadences are exceptionally clear: on B, G, C, G—achieving internal variety; the cadences are typically approached by a strong bass line that ascends or descends diatonically.
5. The four phrases (a b c b) contain only one nonsymmetrical feature—that of the elongation of the third phrase.

Example 383

SINCE ALL IS PASSING
Text by Rainer Maria Rilke, English version by Elaine de Sinçay
Paul Hindemith (1895-1963)

(b)

by   us. That which as - sua - ges when nigh us Shall_ a -
gè - re; cel - le qui nous dés - al - tè - re au - ra_ de

by_ us. That which as - sua - ges when nigh us Shall_ a -
gè - re; cel - le qui nous dés - al - tè - re au - ra de

by_ us. That which as - sua - ges when nigh us Shall a -
gè - re; cel - le qui nous dés - al - tè - re au - ra de

by_ us. That which as - sua - ges when nigh us Shall a -
gè - re; cel - le qui nous dés - al - tè - re au - ra de

(c)

- lone,_ re - main. Let us sing what will leave us With our
nous,_ rai - son. Chan - tons ce qui nous quit - te a - vec a -

- lone, a - lone re - main. Let us sing what will leave us With our
nous, au - ra_ rai - son. Chan - tons ce qui nous quit - te a - vec a -

- lone, a - lone re - main. Let us sing what will leave us With our
nous, au - ra_ rai - son. Chan - tons ce qui nous quit - te a - vec a -

- lone, a - lone re - main. Let us sing what will leave us With our
nous, au - ra_ rai - son. Chan - tons ce qui nous quit - te a - vec a -

ANALYTICAL SYSTEM (Hindemith)

Hindemith set forth his analytical concepts in Volume I of *The Craft of Musical Composition: Theory*. He attempted to reach a system of analysis that could accurately describe the root of any chord (however complex), harmonic value, strength and fluctuation, and tonality at any given moment. His many suggestions included the following:

1. Construction in thirds should no longer be the basic rule for erection of chords.
2. An all-embracing principle should be substituted for the description of chordal invertibility.
3. The thesis that chords are susceptible to a variety of interpretations should be abandoned.

Hindemith classified all chords into two groups: *Group A:* chords without a tritone; *Group B:* chords containing a tritone. Group A is further divided into two series: (1) melodic, and (2) harmonic, according to the relationship to the "progenitor tone."

Example 384

Hindemith also suggests that for both series the fifths, fourths, thirds, and sixths are "first-generation descendants" of the progenitor tone (the tone C in the example above), while seconds and sevenths form a "second-generation" relationship.

Although disputed by some theorists, Hindemith's concepts contain valuable insight into melodic (intervalic) relationships as well as harmonic function and determination of roots. Of special interest is his *Table of Chord Groups*, which prescribes the method of determining chord roots. Best intervals and roots of selected chords are shown in Example 385.

Example 385

CHAPTER SUMMARY

In Western music, vertical sonorities are produced primarily by three different kinds of harmony:

Secundal: spelling of chords in intervals of seconds
Tertian: spelling of chords in thirds
Quartal: spelling of chords in fourths

Several composers have used quartal dispositions to good effect, producing fresh and appealing sonorities.

Of several systems that deal with analysis of twentieth-century music, Paul Hindemith's is one of the most detailed. Set forth in Volume I of *The Craft of Musical Composition,* Hindemith attempted to reach a system of analysis that could accurately describe the root of any chord (however complex), harmonic value, strength and fluctuation, and tonality at any given moment. Of special interest is his *Table of Chord Groups,* which prescribes the method of determining chord roots.

SUGGESTED STUDIES

1. Compose a short (about 21-28 measures) composition which incorporates the following passage of tertian-quartal harmonic counterpoint:

Example 386

2. Determine the chord roots of Hindemith's *Since all is passing* (Example 383) by consulting the composer's *Table of Chord Groups* (p. 445). Be prepared to discuss the following questions:

   a. Does the information on chord roots assist in understanding the harmonic structure of the composition?
   b. What are the areas of agreement and disagreement between Hindemith's system and traditional root analysis?

3. Sing, play, and analyze Example 387, *The Cat,* by Darius Milhaud. Observe the combination of tertian and quartal (quintal) harmony. In this simple and un-

assuming piece, the composer demonstrates a sophisticated technique. How is variety achieved? What principles of variation are observed? Is the piece tonal? (Be prepared to defend your answers specifically.)

Example 387

THE CAT

From *The Household Muse*

Darius Milhaud (1892-1968)

Permission for reprint granted by Elkan-Vogel Co., Philadelphia, Pa., copyright owners.

Chapter 26

SYNTHETIC SCALES MELODIC METAMORPHOSIS HARMONIC RESOURCES OF THE TERTIAN SYSTEM

SYNTHETIC SCALES

Synthetic scales of all varieties have either formed or complemented the pitch materials of numerous twentieth-century compositions. It is presumed, theoretically, that three different pitches are sufficient to qualify as a *scale*—hence, the possibilities are abundant, even within the equal-temperament octave. An excellent example of scale employment and development is observed in Walter Piston's expressive *Passacaglia* (Example 389). The passacaglia theme, or "ground," may perhaps be considered derivative from a scale formed by two slightly asymmetrical tetrachords. Obviously, the scale is freely deployed and represents a reduction of the "theme." A reduction of each 4-measure section reveals a very interesting scalar evolution or metamorphosis. Example 388 illustrates:

Example 388

a. Reduction of theme

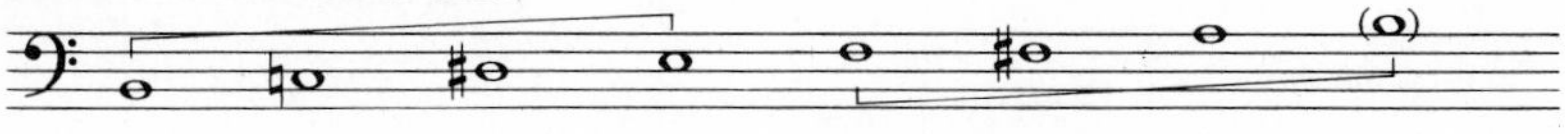

b. Version I: measures 1–4 (upper voice)

c. Version II: measures 5–8

d. Version III: measures 9–12

e. Version IV: measures 13–16

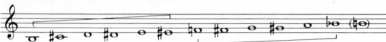

Example 389

PASSACAGLIA (excerpt)

Walter Piston (1895-1976)

OBSERVATIONS:

1. The gradual introduction of chromaticism subtly effects a musical tension.
2. The $\frac{5}{8}$ meter provides for a rhythmic asymmetry; the phrase overlaps cover the structural seams.
3. Changes in register (range) and texture secure a logical unfolding of these continuous variations.

QUERIES:

1. What similarities and differences are observed between this passacaglia and an eighteenth-century passacaglia?
2. Could the first 4 measures constitute the beginnings of a chaconne?

Bartók's sophisticated *Children's Song* from the *Mikrokosmos* is quoted in its entirety (Example 391). The 44 measures constitute a consummate study in the control of line and motive, modal combinations, phrase expansion, and arch form.

OBSERVATIONS:

1. Bartók's arch structure in *Children's Song* (Example 391) is as follows:

Designation:	A	B	A′	B′	A″
Measures:	1-8	9-18	19-26	27-36	37-44
Number of bars:	8	10	8	10	8

2. The composition seems to be derived from two forms of a single motive, which appears in measures 1-2.
3. Interest is achieved by the interaction of opposing tetrachords. For example, measures 1-8, left hand: the upper tetrachord from A melodic minor (or major) opposes a Dorian tetrachord centered on D.
4. Measures 9-10, right hand, illustrate a melodic variant of measures 1-2, right hand.
5. Measures 19-26 are the transposed, inverted, and modified version of measures 1-8.

6. Measures 27-36 invert and modify measures 9-18.

7. Measures 37-44 present the final version of measures 1-8.

8. The basic harmonic/tonal structure may be diagramed as in Example 390.

Observe that the analysis in Example 390 shows a tonal orientation to F♯, which is surrounded by thirds and leading tones. V through Z represents perhaps a chromatic ascension to an emphatic tonic.

Example 390

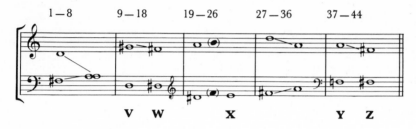

Example 391

CHILDREN'S SONG

From *Mikrokosmos,* Vol. IV, No. 106

Bartók

MELODIC METAMORPHOSIS

The gradual change of a motive or theme is commonly referred to as *melodic meta-morphosis*. Modifications of the original may include the devices of mirror, retro-grade, augmentation, and diminution, as well as transposition, interval expansion or contraction, truncation or fragmentation of themes and/or rhythms, and the succes-sive transformation of the original interval series. In short, the process of melodic metamorphosis is limited only by the composer's imagination.

A synthetic scale that alternates half steps with whole steps (previously quoted in Example 22) is employed in Example 392 to further illustrate melodic metamor-phosis and its harmonic use.

Example 392

a. Basic synthetic scale

b. Melody derived from scale

c. Retrograde, inversion, transposed; slight rhythmic and intervallic changes

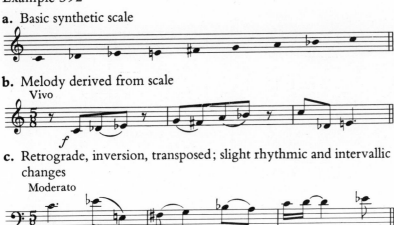

d. Inversion, augmentation, transposed, interval repetition

e. Used vertically, the same scale achieves new harmonic possibilities.
(The F♮ is extraneous to the scale.)

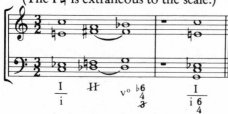

Melodic metamorphosis, also termed simply *transformation,* often plays an important role in unifying an entire composition. Halsey Stevens[1] traces the origins and metamorphosis of a motive in Béla Bartók's *Quartet No. 4.*

> This basic motive, when first heard in the seventh measure, is a simple rhythmic succession of semitones, moving up from B to D♭ and back down to B♭. On the following page it is inverted and cadences in a cluster-chord; then it assumes its diatonic form, expanded intervallically and extended by repetition of a fragment; this passage, which serves as subsidiary "theme," presents its materials in a sort of free perpetual canon or round. Further transformation occurs throughout the movement, and at the beginning of the finale the motive is cast in a dancelike rhythmic pattern, utilizing the diatonic form, which is itself immediately inverted, and then pulled apart intervallically so that the newly assumed rhythm becomes the recognizable element. These changes are tabulated in the example below:

Example 393

QUARTET NO. 4 (excerpt)

Bartók

[1]Halsey Stevens, *The Life and Music of Béla Bartók* (New York: Oxford University Press, 1953), p. 187.

HARMONIC RESOURCES OF THE TERTIAN SYSTEM

In several respects, the tertian harmonic system "reached the ceiling" (to borrow Olivier Messiaen's phrase) in the first half of the twentieth century. One may counter, however, that the possible combinations of the basic system are nearly inexhaustible —particularly when coupled to the resources of color and timbre, disposition, dynamics, and articulation. Arnold Schoenberg purportedly stated that there were still beautiful C major triads to be written. The following displacement of C E G is not an attempt to heed this admonition, but the scoring may suggest to the reader some perception of musical infinity.

Example 394

six violins, unison, harmonics, *ppp*

vibraphone, one alto flute, *ppp*

harp, four double basses, unison, *ppp*

"DISPLACED" BASS

In addition to scoring and pitch disposition, other items should be mentioned that further the harmonic resources of the tertian system. These would include:

1. *"Displaced bass"*
2. Bichordal and polychordal formations
3. Expansions beyond the thirteenth chord to 12-note chords
4. Expansion of clusters to the extent that each instrument plays a different note

An independent, or even "displaced," bass line is observed with some frequency in twentieth-century music. Two examples are shown (Example 395):

Example 395

a. *Lincoln Portrait,* by Copland.

b. *Rites of Spring,* by Stravinsky. Parallel MM seventh chords are countered by a seemingly "independent" bass line.

POLYTONALITY

Numerous twentieth-century composers have experimented with *bitonality* (two independent tonal centers functioning simultaneously) or with *polytonality* (several simultaneous tonalities). Multiple key signatures sometimes have been used to show the composer's intent; on other occasions no signatures have been used — rather, the individual accidentals provided the necessary information.

Example 396

a. Prokofiev   **b.** Bartók   **c.** Milhaud

If Example 396c continued to function at the levels of F, G, and A, the resultant would be *polytonal*. With the information given, however, the example should accurately be termed *polychordal*. The superimposition of chords a perfect fifth apart was considerably in vogue in the third and fourth decades of this century—particularly in French and American scores. There are obviously solid acoustical factors that support this interesting sonority, as Example 397 shows:

Example 397

12-NOTE CHORDS

Beyond the thirteenth chords lies a chromatic area of fifteenth, seventeenth, nineteenth, twenty-first, twenty-third chords. The author and reader will happily and mutually acknowledge that the "twenty-third chord" represents the limit of the tertian system in this particular theoretical sense. It is observed that, with all twelve tones utilized, additions simply result in unison or octave equivalents.

Example 398

TONE CLUSTERS

Disposition of pitches into *tone clusters* in twentieth-century music merits special consideration. Not infrequently, clusters have comprised tertian formations plus two or more added tones—resulting, of course, in blurred sonorities. Interestingly enough, the cluster was not devised in the twentieth century. Eighteenth-century examples are observed in the keyboard works of Domenico Scarlatti and, less boldly, in the A minor Piano Sonata of Mozart. An extraordinary example comes from Michel Corrette (1709-1795), a French composer who called for "thunder" to be produced on the organ by using a board that depressed several pedal tones simultaneously. In the twentieth century, Henry Cowell, Charles Ives, Béla Bartók, and more recently Krzysztof Penderecki, among numerous others, have explored the quite unique sound of closely spaced tones. The following fragment of Bartók's *Melody in the Mist, Mikrokosmos* (Example 399), illustrates a possible use of tone clusters.

Example 399

MELODY IN THE MIST (excerpt)

From *Mikrokosmos,* Vol. IV, No. 107

Bartók

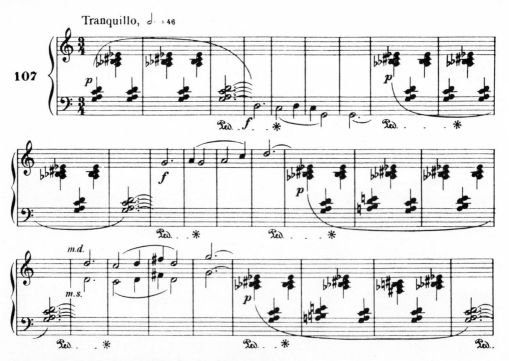

CHAPTER SUMMARY

Synthetic scales of all varieties have either formed or complemented the pitch materials of numerous twentieth-century compositions.

The gradual change of a motive or theme is commonly referred to as melodic metamorphosis. Modifications of the original may include the devices of mirror, retrograde, augmentation, and diminution, as well as transposition, interval expansion or contraction, truncation or fragmentation. Melodic metamorphosis, also termed *transformation,* often plays an important role in unifying an entire composition. Such a role is observed in Bartók's String Quartet No. 4.

Additional harmonic resources of the tertian system include: "displaced bass," bichordal and polychordal formations, expansions beyond the thirteenth chord to 12-note chords, and tone clusters.

SUGGESTED STUDIES

1. Make an independent analysis of at least one additional composition from the *Mikrokosmos,* Volumes IV, V, or VI.
2. Write a short composition (about 28 measures) for solo clarinet or similar instrument, using a synthetic scale and the process of melodic metamorphosis.
3. Write a consequent section to the two-voice incomplete composition in Example 400.

Example 400

Chapter 27

STRUCTUCTURAL ANALYSIS AND BASIC COMMENTARY
Béla Bartók, *Music for String Instruments, Percussion, and Celesta (1937), First Movement*

Bartók's *Music for String Instruments, Percussion, and Celesta* is one of this century's most eloquent musical statements. The First Movement, Example 401c, is particularly engaging in its synthesis of traditional procedures and twentieth-century techniques. Its proportions are meticulously controlled in terms of both real and psychological time; micro-macro correlations provide for logic, coherence, climax of events, denouement, and a totally satisfying aural experience.

The chromatic subject illustrates the growth potential of a 5-note cell: a b♭ c♯¹ c♮¹ b♮. Expansion of the cell is effected—first to e♭, then to e♮. Contraction of intervals follows—to e♭ again and to c♮. Expansion contraction is *the* shape of the whole movement. There are 36 time units (♪ and ♪ = 1 unit) in the subject, and the golden mean or golden proportion is reached precisely at the only E natural contained in the subject. Example 401a illustrates graphically.

Example 401a

Bartók uses the range of the subject, a perfect fifth, as an organizing premise. Each entry of the subject in this imaginative fugue is either a perfect fifth above or a perfect fifth below the preceding entry on ascending and descending axes. Expansion of range, tension, and dynamics pushes inexorably to the climax in measure 56. This arrival point is the golden proportion of the entire movement; it contains the only *fff* dynamic of the movement; it contains the most dissonant intervals: tritones and diminished octaves; the violin E♭ is, in itself, the most dissonant interval from the central tonic, A. The devices of mirror (melodic inversion) and stretto are used not as "devices" but as expressive tools in the crafting of a masterful work. A time chart, with basic analysis, is shown in Example 401b.

Example 401b

Example 401c

MUSIC FOR STRINGS, PERCUSSION, AND CELESTA (1937)

First movement

Bartók

2

4

INTRODUCTION TO PART II (MIRROR FORM)

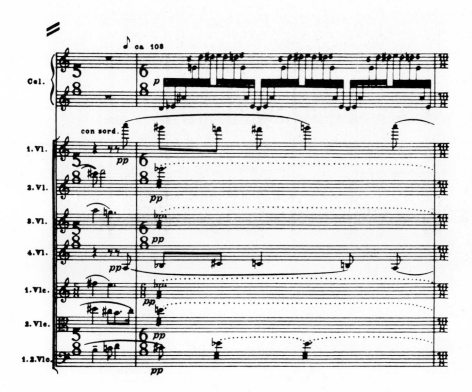

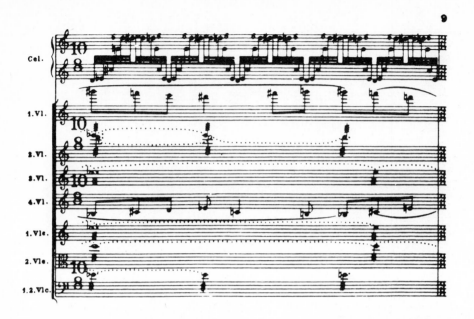

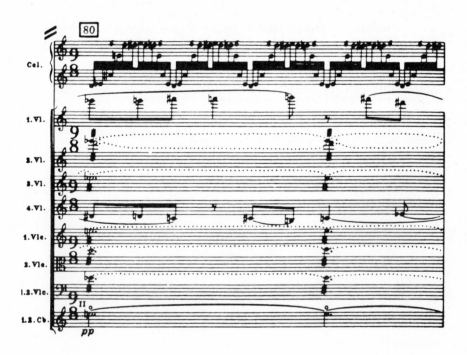

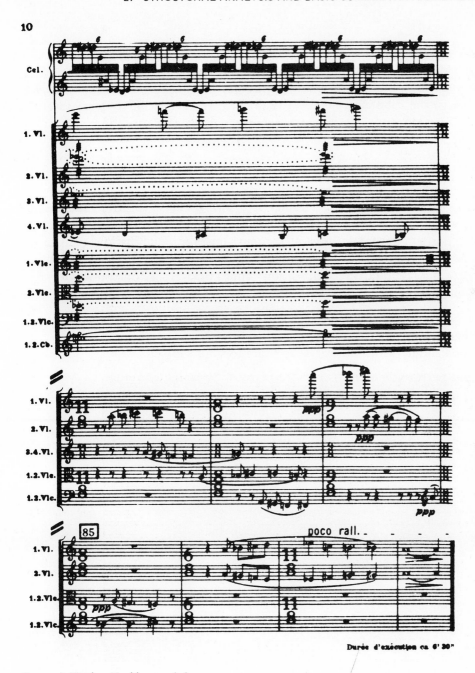

CHAPTER SUMMARY

Bartók's *Music for String Instruments, Percussion, and Celesta* employs traditional polyphonic procedures in new and exciting ways. The subject of this First Movement fugue is a microcosm of the entire movement. Proportions, particularly those related to the Fibonacci Series (1, 2, 3, 5, 8, 13, 21, 34, 55, 89), are carefully considered. Timpani and celesta entrances are delayed for specific clarifications of structure.

SUGGESTED STUDIES

1. Listen to a good recording of Example 401c several times, absorbing more detail with each repetition. Study the sections that use stretto and mirror. Be able to discuss the counterpoint (interval content, melodic combination, etc.) in the first 21 measures.
2. Compose a short imitative composition (approximately 12 measures) for four instruments:

   Use a 2-measure chromatic subject.
   Use changing meters (these must be integral to the music).
   Imitation should be at intervals that relate to your subject.

   If possible, perform in class.

Chapter 28

TWELVE-TONE METHOD

"After many unsuccessful attempts during a period
of approximately twelve years, I laid the foundations
for a new procedure in musical construction which
seemed fitted to replace those structural differentia-
tions provided formerly by tonal harmonies. I call
this procedure *Method of Composing with Twelve
tones which are related only with one another.*"

—Arnold Schoenberg

In architecture, expansion in height necessitates special building principles or materials. The pyramids of Egypt and, later, the temples of Greece and the Roman domes required interlocking, broadly based support; the flying-buttress concept made possible the lofty Medieval cathedrals; the Empire State Building is a reality because of the combined strengths of steel and concrete.

Similarly in music, expansion of a system requires a rethinking of the basic principles involved; new methods or materials are perhaps needed to serve as substitutes for the established ones; or perhaps an altogether new system has to be devised to replace the old system, which seems to be in disarray.

DEFINITION

Of the several attempts made in this century to find viable alternatives to the overly extended major-minor-tonal system, none has been more influential and controversial than Arnold Schoenberg's "method of composing with twelve tones." Schoenberg and others viewed with concern the tonal system they considered extended to its limits and capable of no further significant growth. In a desire to restabilize pitch materials of composition, Schoenberg suggested certain methods and procedures. A few of these procedures are paraphrased and interpreted below:

1. The twelve tones of the equal-tempered octave should contribute independently and as equally as possible to the musical structure and fabric.
2. The pitch resources of each composition (or movement) are to reside in a *tone row,* or *series,* that employs all twelve tones. The row is invented by the composer at a precompositional stage. (This process is not too dissimilar to the invention of a synthetic scale, used as a basis for melodic and harmonic vocabulary.)
3. Any series (row) has four forms, each of which is capable of eleven transpositions.

   a. Original row (O)
   b. Retrograde (R)
   c. Inversion (I), also called "mirror"
   d. Retrograde inversion (RI)

Example 402

4. The series can be used both horizontally and vertically.

5. A chart of transpositions, or *matrix* (see p. 483), will provide 48 different versions of the basic row. As an example, if the first 3 notes of a row (original form) are A B♭ G, then the first transposition would be A♯ B♮ G♯, the second transposition B♮ C♮ A♮, and so forth—ascending chromatically through eleven transpositions.

6. Certain considerations regarding the makeup of the series were postulated—and subsequently modified. These included:

  a. Avoidance of a return to a note of the series prior to the complete unfolding of the row form.
  b. Avoidance in the series of triadic outlines that might produce unintended tonal implications.
  c. Enharmonic equivalents as well as octave displacements were to be considered, in a theoretical sense, as identical to the original note of the series.

7. A row obviously gives clues to a particular composer's selective processes. Compare, for example, the following rows:*

Example 403

a. *String Quartet,* Op. 28, Webern

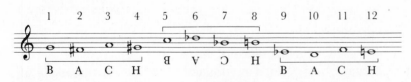

b. *Concerto for Violin and Orchestra,* Alban Berg (1885-1935)

*There are two principal ways of numbering serialized pitch: 1 through 12 and 0 through 11. 1-12 is used in most introductory discussions; 0-11 is appropriate for mathematical considerations (mod 12). Each has advantages.

c. *Variations for Orchestra,* Op. 31, Schoenberg

d. *Structures I,* for two pianos, Pierre Boulez (1925-   )

e. *Edge of Shadow,* for chorus and instruments, Finney

f. *Quaderno di Anna Libera,* for piano, Luigi Dallapiccola (1904-   )

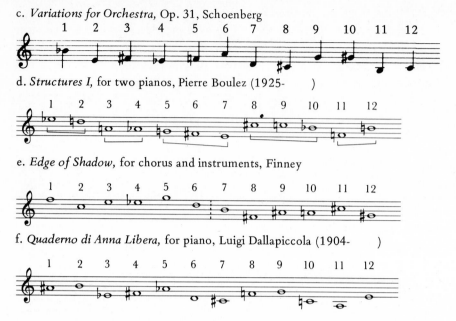

It is observed that a row may comprise quasi-motivic trichords or tetrachords (3-note or 4-note groupings), or may be divided as two symmetrical hexachords; it may be expansive—with a range of several octaves; it may be, in itself, melodically germinating, approaching what was traditionally called a *theme*.

PANTONALITY

Obviously, the *employment* of serial techniques is both personal and individual. Rows may be used to produce explicit tonalities, or the tonal orientation may be vaguely suggested. Finally, the seeming absence of any central or principal tonal center produces what is perhaps best termed *pantonality* (i.e., all-encompassing and variable tonal orientations, which, in turn, prescribe their own larger dimension).

Three twelve-tone analyses are offered on the following pages as an introduction to serial methods.

Schoenberg's *Variations for Orchestra,* Op. 31, is the first *orchestral* twelve-tone composition and represents a landmark not only for his method of composing but also for imaginative uses of timbre and color and for a masterful control of each parameter.

The Introduction and Theme are quoted in their entirety. A good recording is an essential aid to the study of this score. The row and its basic forms are cited on pp. 474-476; observations are presented on page 483.

Example 404

INTRODUCTION AND THEME
From *Variations for Orchestra*, Op. 31
Schoenberg

INTRODUKTION

478

OBSERVATIONS:

1. The first two notes of the row—the tritone interval Bb and E—establish the quiet atmosphere of the Introduction. Transposition of this interval as well as increase in rhythmic activity and expansion of texture lead to a climax (measure 22) and a return to the first tempo (measure 24). At this juncture, Schoenberg pays homage to another composer: B A C H (measures 24 and 25 in the trombone). Measure 28 contains the H and C (violin II) and measure 29 completes the motive with A and B in the horns. (In German, B is Bb and H is Bh.)
2. The Theme is divided into four phrases:

phrase a   ms. 34-38
      b   ms. 39-45
      c   ms. 46-50
      d   ms. 51-57

The alternation of 5-bar phrases with 7-bar statements is musically very satisfying. Clarification of the phrase structure is gained by careful use of pitch materials— that is, specific forms of the row:

phrase a: O (celli) in melodic format
          I (woodwinds) in harmonic format
phrase b: RI (celli)
          R (woodwinds)
phrase c: R (celli)
          RI (woodwinds, horns)
phrase d: I (violin I)
          O (celli) transposed
          O (woodwinds, horns)

3. As familiarity is gained with Schoenberg's vocabulary, it will be apparent that he was as natural and comfortable with his method of composing as Brahms was with the expanded tertian system.

An entirely different treatment of row technique is observed in Webern's Opus 28. (The row is given on p. 475.) The difference in density between the Schoenberg Variations and the quartet is not just a question of four players versus many; it is, rather, a question of attitude. In Webern every note is meant to be heard, and every nuance contributes to the total surface texture.

MATRIX

A matrix, constructed from the Webern row (Example 403a), follows:

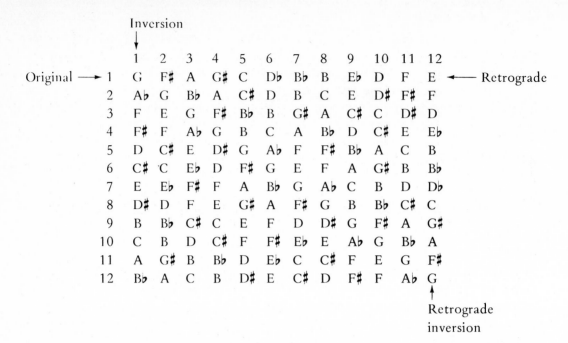

Example 405

STRING QUARTET, OP. 28 (excerpt)

Webern

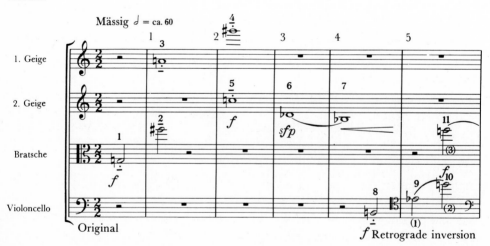

OBSERVATIONS:

1. Because of the symmetry of the row, duplications result. As examples: O1 is identical to RI 12; O2 to RI 11, and so on. Similarly, the row provides ample opportunity for "overlapping" technique (i.e., 9, 10, 11, 12 of one row-form will equal 1, 2, 3, 4 of a different form); also, 11, 12 of one form will be 1, 2 of a different form.

2. Webern's 15 measures (Example 405) constitute a "theme area," after which a set of variations follows.

3. Phrase and period equivalents are seemingly defined by a function in time—that is, *rests*—rather than by harmonic or melodic function.

4. Timbre, color, and register are explored within a constantly shifting one- and two-voice texture.
5. A reduction, without octave displacements (Example 406), reveals a fascinating relationship to tradition—one is tempted to suggest that a certain spirit of the Renaissance exists in the music.

Example 406

Since the mid-1920s, when serial techniques were initiated, numerous modifications and extensions of the original rationale have been made. A few of the modifications will serve to illustrate:

PERMUTATION

1. *Row permutation,* for example:
    1 3 5 7 9 11 12 10 8 6 4 2 of the original effects a new but related row.
2. *Use of hexachords, or partial series,* rather than twelve-tone series.
3. *Total serialization*—that is, serial techniques applied to the parameters of pitch, duration, dynamic, articulation, and so on.
4. *Free use.* There exists a large number of compositions in which serial methods were probably used at an early or precompositional stage but which in the eventual course of "working out" became so modified that a strict note-by-note analysis would be futile.

Clearly, the twelve-tone method, as used by Schoenberg, Webern, and Alban Berg, was a system that allowed for both flexibility and maximal personal expression. The excerpt from Berg's masterpiece, *Wozzeck* (Example 407), combines serial procedures with traditional techniques. One of the most poignant moments in the opera is Marie's "lullaby"; repetition, sequence, and tonal suggestion are all a part of Berg's process. The hauntingly beautiful solo line is set to essentially quartal harmonic dispositions; triads and seventh chords provide familiar sonorities. These imaginative juxtapositions, together with the extraordinary orchestration, yield one of the most eloquent passages in music literature.

Example 407

WOZZECK (excerpt)

Act I, Scene 3

Berg

Luigi Dallapiccola's *Quaderno di Anna Libera* (*The Notebook of Anna Libera*) is a set of eleven short pieces for piano based on a single row. The entire composition is further unified by traditional means of contrast and repetition of kind (i.e., types of texture, devices, structure). Dallapiccola's lyric and "thematic" treatment of serial methods serves to illustrate the procedure's flexibility. Number 7 of the *Quaderno* is a movement of singular beauty and amazing technical accomplishment. This canon cancrizans is quoted in Example 408.

Example 408

ANDANTINO AMOROSO E CONTRAPUNCTUS TERTIUS (excerpt)

From *Quaderno di Anna Libera,* No. 7 (Canon cancrizans)

Luigi Dallapiccola

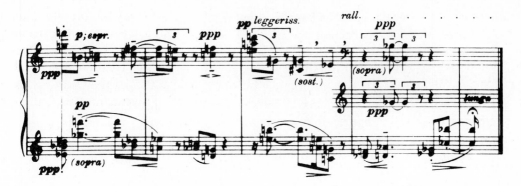

OBSERVATIONS:

1. The row of the *Quaderno* was previously stated (Example 403f).
2. The fact that serial techniques and polyphonic devices are employed in no way precludes the use of tertian formations—which are in considerable evidence.
3. There seems to be an elusive yet implied tonal orientation and a suggested function in this canon. Example 409 illustrates:

Example 409

4. Dallapiccola's *Quaderno* also exists in an orchestral version made by the composer —*Variations for Orchestra*—to which the reader is directed for further insight into the expressive twentieth century.

CHAPTER SUMMARY

One of the most influential methods of composing music in the twentieth century is Arnold Schoenberg's "method of composing with twelve tones." The method suggests that all twelve tones of the equal-tempered octave should contribute independently and as equally as possible to the musical structure and fabric. The pitch resources of each composition or movement reside in a tone row, or series, that employs all twelve tones. The row is invented by the composer at a precompositional stage. This process may be compared to the use of a scale that serves as the basis of melodic and harmonic vocabulary. The row has four forms: original, retrograde, inversion, and retrograde inversion. Each is capable of eleven transpositions.* A row obviously gives clues to a particular composer's selective processes.

Schoenberg's Variations for Orchestra, Op. 31, is the first orchestral twelve-tone composition; the work is noted for its imaginative uses of timbre and color and for a masterful control of each parameter. In Anton Webern's works every note is meant to be heard, and every nuance contributes to the total surface texture. Alban Berg employed serial techniques quite freely and not infrequently in an environment or form relating to previous traditions. Dallapiccola's lyric and thematic treatment of serial methods serves to illustrate further the flexibility of the procedure.

SUGGESTED STUDIES

1. Complete a row analysis of any of the other movements from the *Quaderno*. In addition, study the bipartite and tripartite structures, tertian formations, melodic writing, contrapuntal devices employed, and the implied broad tonal orientations.
2. Compose a set of miniatures for string quartet, using serial methods and pointillistic techniques.
3. Compose a short song or piano piece in which the row is thematic.
4. Suggested reading:

George Perle. *Serial Composition and Atonality*. 3d ed. Berkeley: The University of California Press, 1972.

---

*Certain symmetrical rows and rows consisting of symmetrical hexachords will produce duplications, therefore reducing the actual number of transpositions.

Chapter 29

MUSIC SINCE 1950

The effect of electronic communications—radio and television, together with phonograph and tape recording—on the arts of the twentieth century is pronounced and unique. The programs of major music festivals frequently are relayed in a matter of weeks, while recordings of new music often become available within a few months. The opportunities for the music student to become familiar with new music are simply without parallel in the history of music. A willingness to listen and an open and objective attitude toward the aesthetics of new music will bring great rewards. The difficulty of comprehension for the listener and for the music student stems from the rapidity of change, the seemingly conflicting and opposite views of music held by diverse composers, and the unfamiliar vocabulary and syntax. A wide-ranging and continuing acquaintance with new music will help to overcome these problems.

Two graphs may assist in understanding the various polarizations and syntheses of the twentieth century. Needless to say, given the thousands of active composers who form the composite profile of the twentieth century, only a sampling of the most influential can be indicated.

c. 1920 to 1950

Chromatic axis; 12-tone; Berg, Schoenberg, Webern

Elements of both: Bartók, Britten, Hindemith, Sessions

Diatonic axis; pandiatonicism; Copland, Milhaud, Stravinsky

c. 1950 to 1980

> Controlled axis; totally serialized, electronic, computer; Babbitt, Boulez, Davidovsky, Stockhausen, Xenakis
>
> Elements of both: Carter, Crumb, Dallapiccola, Finney, Ligeti, Lutoslawski, Nordheim, Penderecki
>
> Aleatoric axis; chance, improvisation; *musique concrète*; Berio Brown, Cage, Kagel

It is not the author's intent to suggest "schools" of composition or aesthetic "affiliations." The graphs may indicate, however, a certain fusion of ideals over a period of years. For example, Stravinsky embraced, during the 1950s, first serial procedures and then 12-tone methods, each technique employed in his own way; similarly, some of the last works of Schoenberg suggest this composer's reconsideration of pitch orientation. Since 1950 few Western composers could deny the influence on their music of postserial methods, electronic sounds, and improvisational techniques. Two decades of intense experimentation (c. 1945-1965) have produced, in the most recent major works, a fusion of concepts as well as an aesthetic focus—perhaps not too dissimilar to the Classical stride reached in the 1770s.*

RHYTHM

Two important facets of rhythm and meter are observed in this era. One is highly controlled, the other, free. Examples 410 and 411 illustrate. In Example 410 we see metric modulation—a systematized change of rate and pulse.

Example 410

CANARIES (excerpt)

From *Eight Pieces for Four Timpani* (1950-1966), (One Player)

Elliott Carter (1908-   )

---

*By definition, avant-garde remains distinct from any generalization regarding the "mainstream" of compositional trends.

C, N. R, DS, NS refer to ways of striking the drum to produce different timbres.

Example 411

INCENTERS (excerpt)
Flute part
Jacob Druckman (1928-   )

Melody and harmony have reflected the freedom and inventiveness of the first half of the century. One generalization might be permitted: since the intervals of a minor second, major seventh, and minor ninth formed the basis of dissonance in pre-1950 music, some composers have reconsidered the potential of perfect and imperfect consonances. Certain composers employ the harmonic cluster rather consistently and to good effect:

Example 412
THRENODY (excerpt)
Penderecki

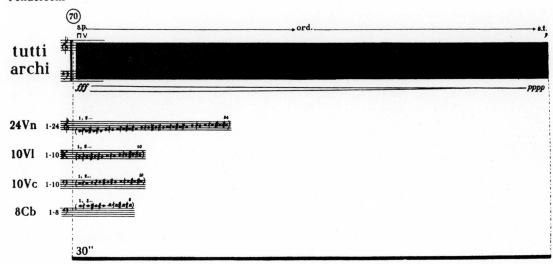

Texture, timbre, and density are most fully revealed in an orchestral environment. The luminous sonorities of Georg Ligeti's *Atmosphères,* the apposition of timbres in Elliott Carter's Double Concerto, the contrasts of densities in Krzysztof Penderecki's *Threnody,* offer important insights into scoring procedures. Two additional observations are made:

1. The use of extended ranges and new sound potentials such as the "prepared" piano, stringed instruments bowed beyond the bridge, use of wind-instrument mouthpieces.
2. The addition of diverse percussion and electronic instruments to the standard orchestral complement.

Form might appropriately be described as "the shape of content."* *Gesture, movement,* and *event* create designs in sound, and each of these components partially dictates both real and psychological aspects of time. Form, then, results quite inclusively from a sound-event series. In this category one must consider such items as improvisation, random and chance events, the "counterpoint of sound and silence," and noise in relationship to musical sound.

Some specific formal principles can be observed and aurally recognized. Among these are wedge-shaped designs and cantilever constructions, both of which are used with some frequency.

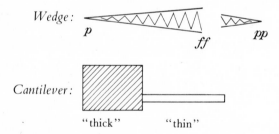

Aleatory (L. *aleatorius* and Fr. *alea,* chance, hazard, risk) and *free* improvisation in music veer from the traditionally accepted attitudes regarding form and the purposes of form. Perhaps one could venture the observation that form that results from a fully notated composition considers the physiological and psychological consequences of structure, whereas aleatoric composition addresses itself to the philosophical significance of the time continuum.

---

*The title of an excellent set of essays by the American artist Ben Shahn.

Example 413

THRENODY: TO THE VICTIMS OF HIROSHIMA (1959-1961)

Penderecki

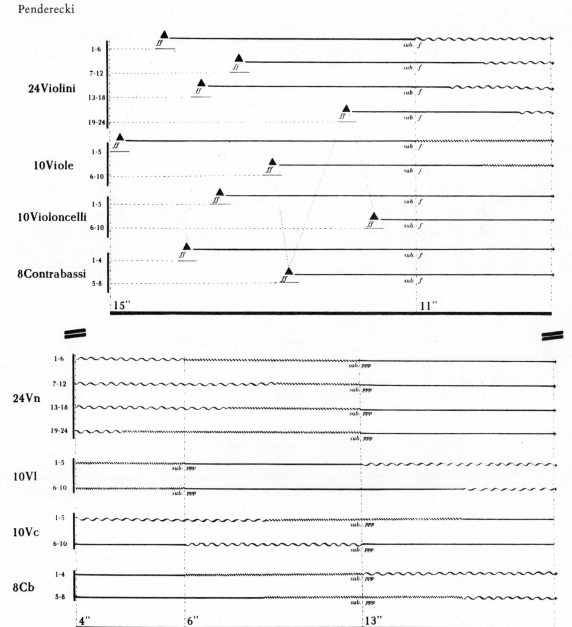

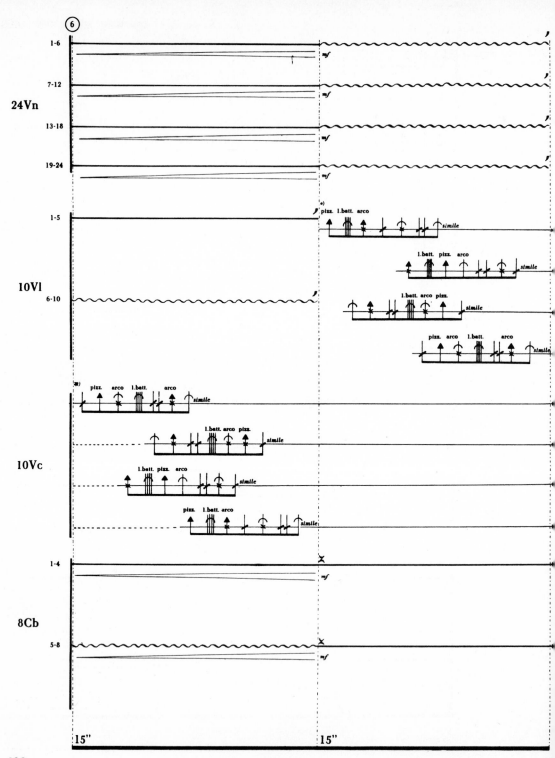

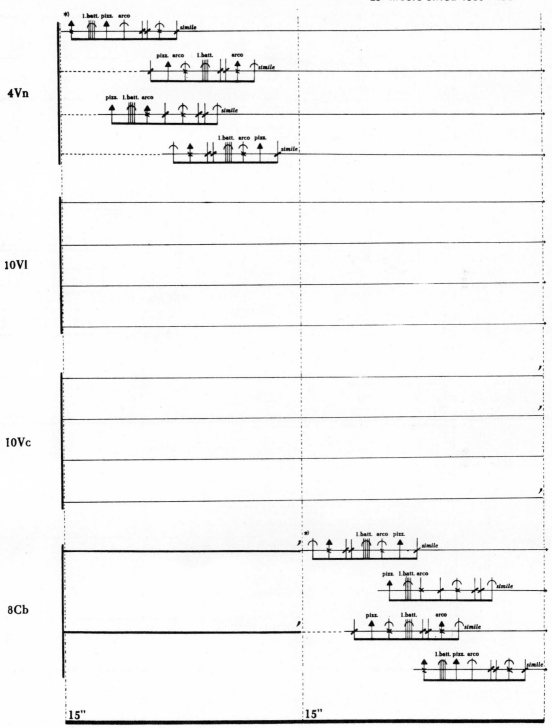

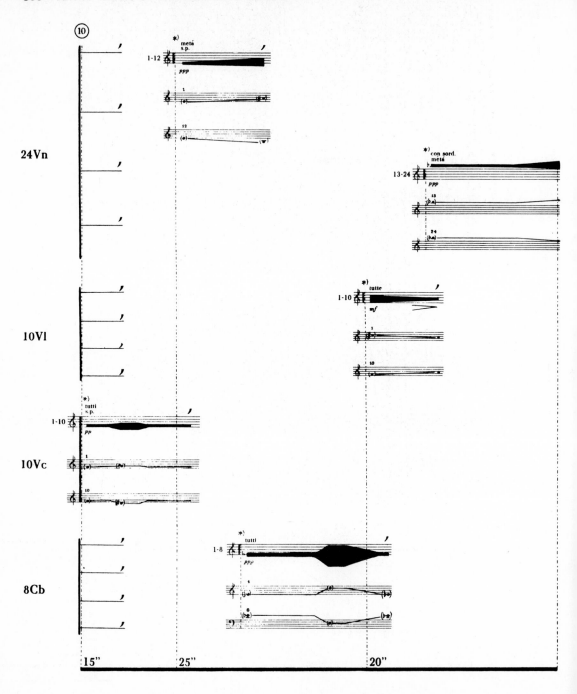

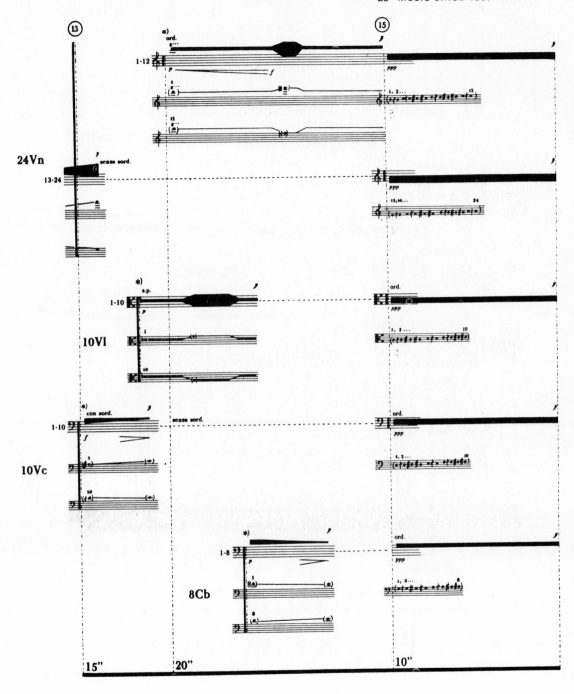

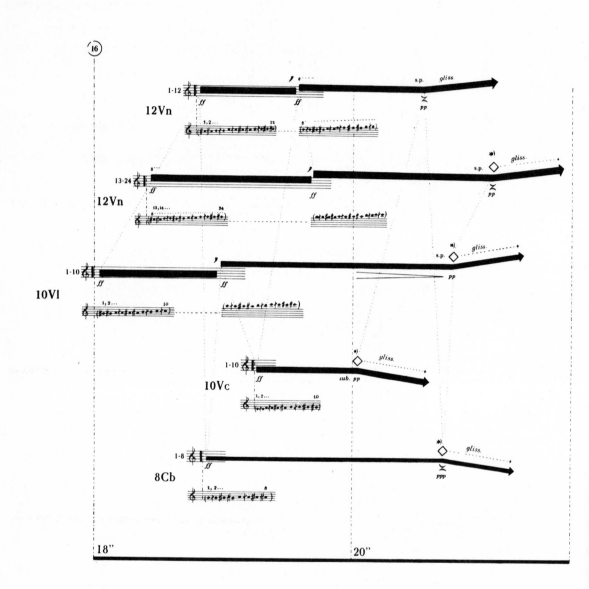

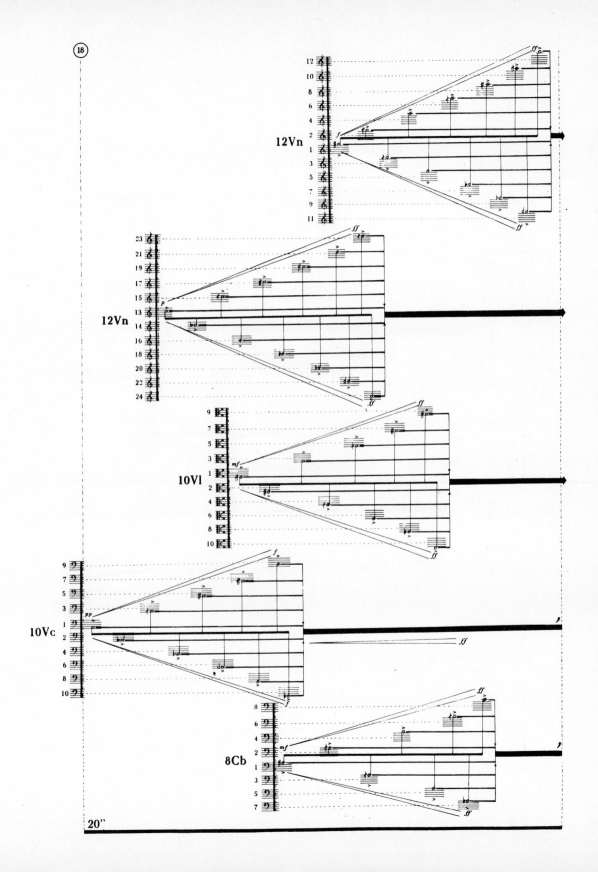

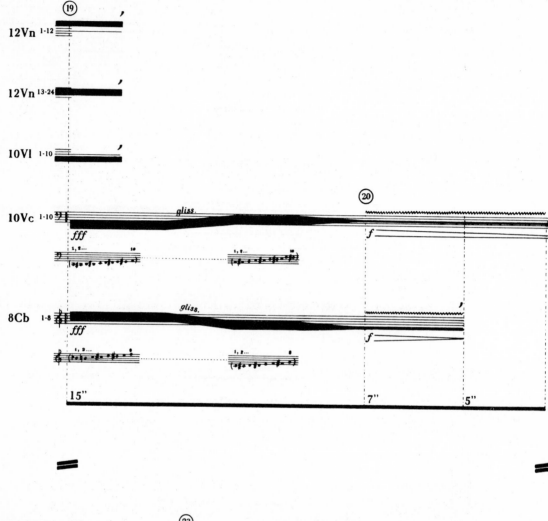

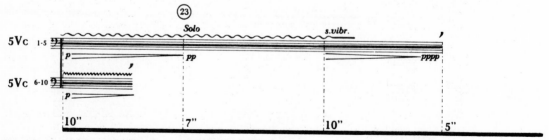

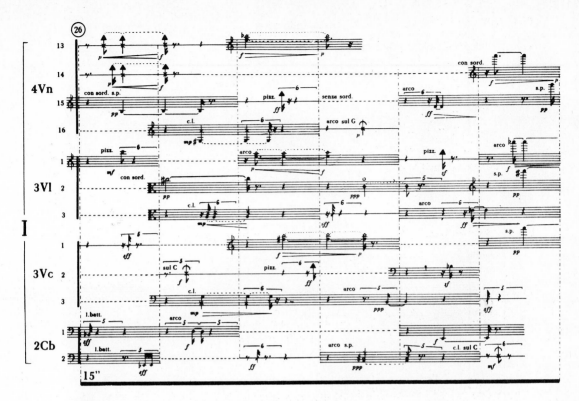

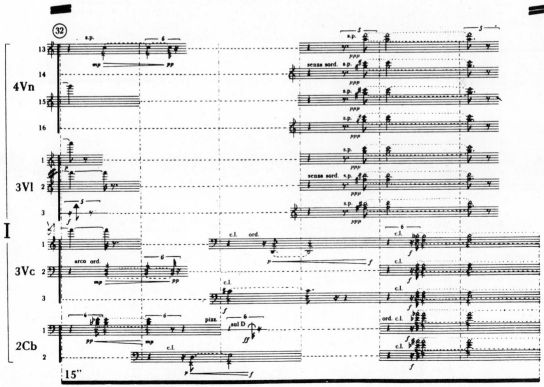

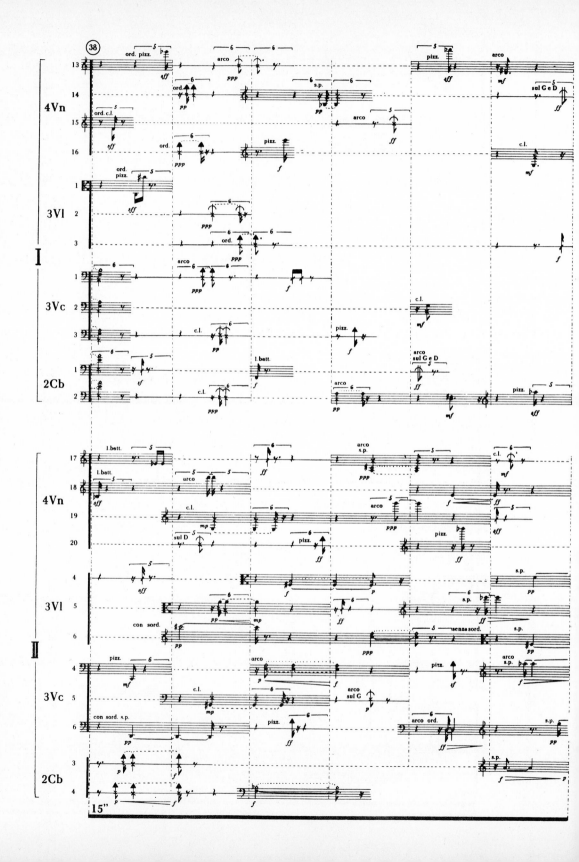

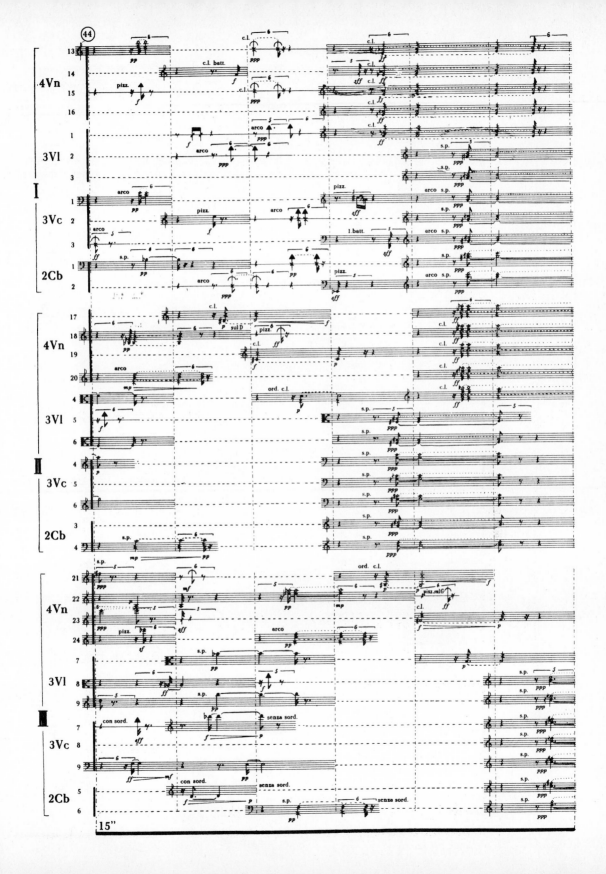

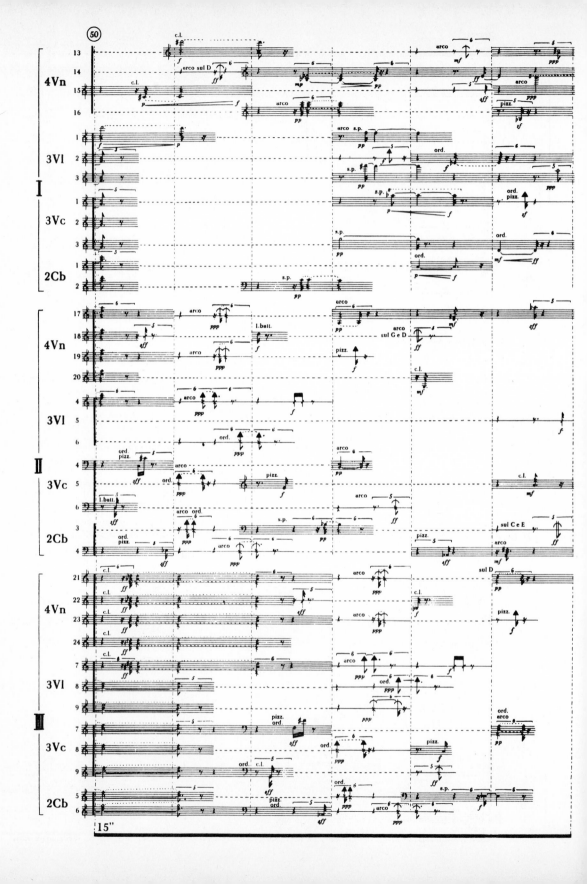

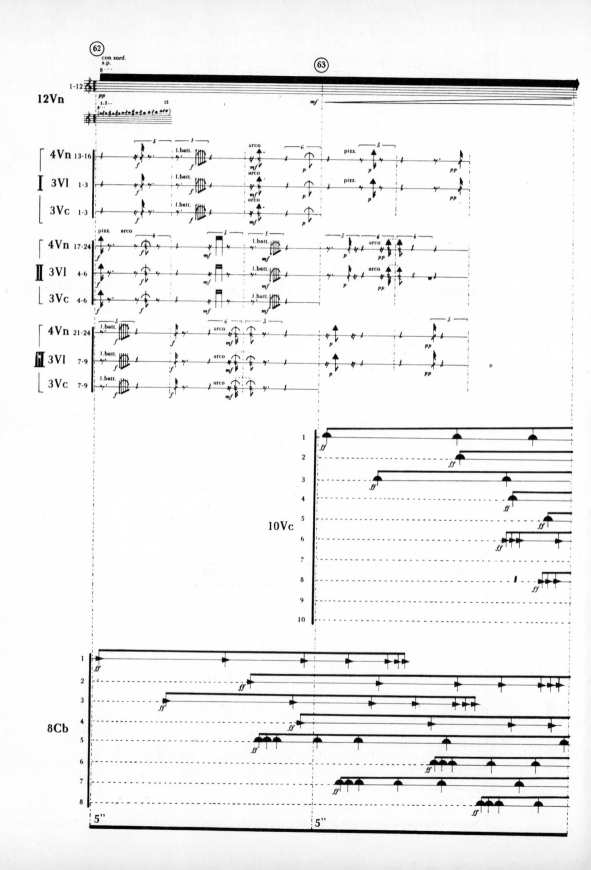

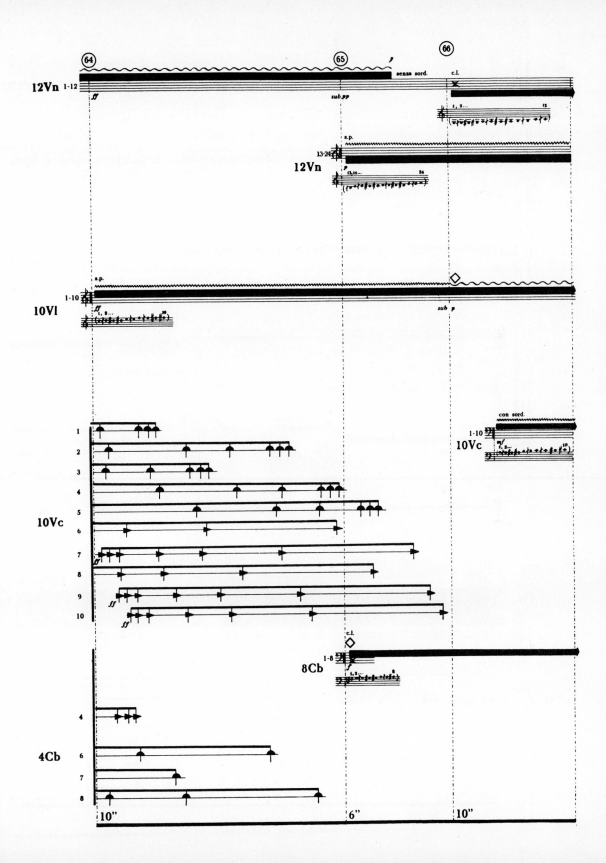

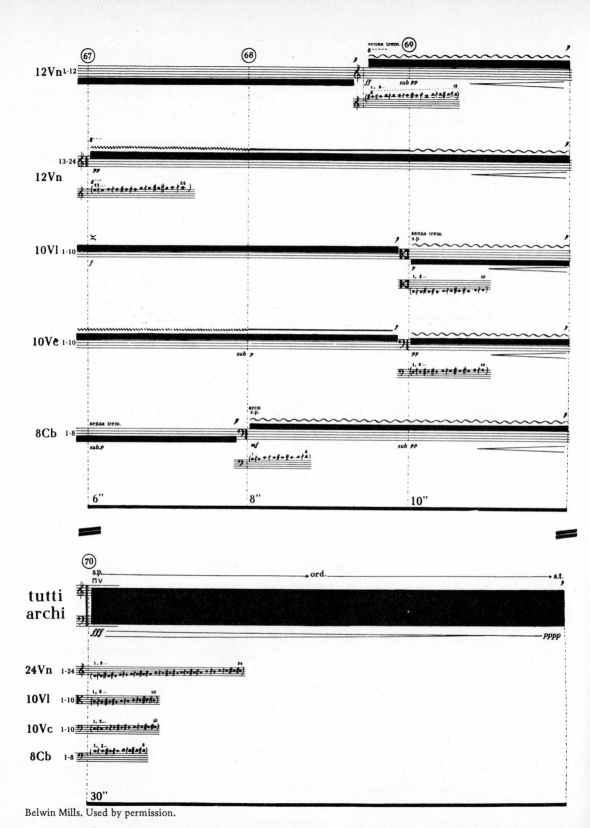

OBSERVATIONS:

1. Penderecki's *Threnody* (1961) has a very clear and basic shape: A B A'.

   A from the beginning to rehearsal 26
   B from rehearsal 26 to 63
   A' from 63 to the end

   Within this design, the composer has provided for sharp contrasts of unmetered sonic events to highly rhythmicized "canons" and a return to a kind of stream of consciousness. The total effect is extremely convincing.

2. Despite the appearance of the new notation, there are strong relationships to tradition. For example, the work opens with the following time sequence: 15″, 11″, 4″, 6″, 13″ etc. At each time interval a new sonority, dynamic, performance indication is introduced, producing period and phrase equivalents.

3. The composer adroitly "overlaps" textures, not too dissimilarly to the phrase overlapping of the sixteenth century or to the cadence evasion of the nineteenth century. The constantly changing sonorities are, in effect, linked together by transitions.

4. Certain kinds of sonorities, particularly clusters, appear several times, giving the work a sense of unity. Compare, for example, 16, 19, 66, and 70.

5. A and A' suggest a state of flux; B contains many elements of stability, traditional rhythmic patterns, and considerable energy.

6. Differences in performances are to be expected by reason of lack of specificity of graphic notations. Should any student be alarmed by these freedoms of performance, comparison of three or four recordings of a Prelude and Fugue of J. S. Bach is suggested.

Example 414

EACH AFTERNOON IN GRANADA, A CHILD DIES EACH AFTERNOON

Text by Garcia Lorca

George Crumb (1928-   )

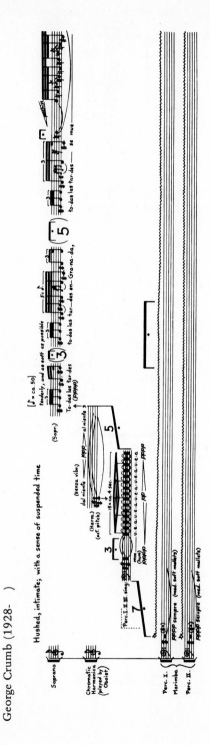

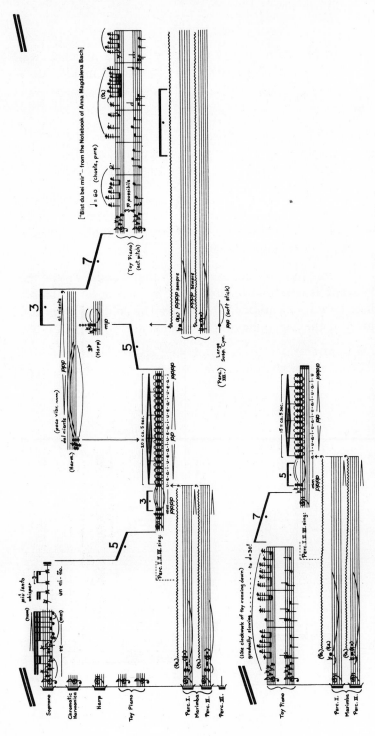

From *Ancient Voices of Children*, by George Crumb. Copyright © 1970 by C. F. Peters Corporation, 373 Park Avenue South, New York 10016. Reprinted with permission of the publishers, who published the score of the complete work under Peters Edition No. 66303.

OBSERVATIONS:

1. The excerpt provides abundant insight into both the technical and philosophical concerns of the composer. The work is based on two triads: C♯ major and G minor. The symbolic tritone again appears as the author/composer speaks of death.

2. To these two basic sonorities, the composer quotes eight measures from Bach: *"Bist du bei mir"* ("You are with me") as a personal statement, complementing Lorca's haunting "Each afternoon in Granada, a child dies each afternoon."

3. The simplicity of this portion of the work and the short duration of approximately two minutes stand in stark contrast to the typical complexities of the music of the 1950s. More important, the gentle scoring evokes moods, atmospheres, and experiential references to which large audiences can relate.

4. Time spans are carefully segmented into traditional period and phrase equivalents. Structurally, this movement is a simple binary: A B, with B occuring at the entrance of the G minor chord, just prior to the quote. The golden proportion is observed approximately at the beginning of "Bist du bei mir."

5. Although the notation is nontraditional, the composer exerts absolute control over each parameter. Time, rather than measure, controls temporal aspects of this extraordinarily beautiful work.

Example 415

SYNCHRONISMS NO. 1 FOR FLUTE AND ELECTRONIC SOUNDS (1963)

Mario Davidovsky (1934-   )

Flutter...

very short pause

STOP

32 sec.

Start this part right after electronic cue # 3 is finished.

START # 4

⊕ = Air + Percussion
+ = Percussion only.

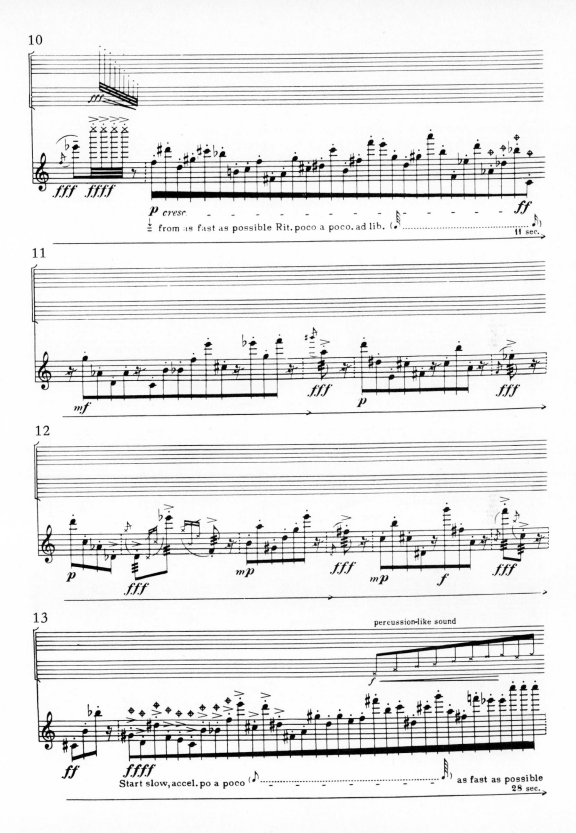

OBSERVATIONS:

1. An important contribution to electronic music literature is Davidovsky's series of *Synchronisms* for solo instruments or small groups of instruments with elec-

tronic sounds. A recording is obviously necessary for the study of these scores. Discussion is limited here to the solo flute part of *Synchronisms No. 1.*

2. In terms of pitch series, the work might aptly be called "postserial" in that although there is a clear indication of twelve-tone influence, the rendering is free; number analysis seems irrelevant. Rather, gestures, cells, organic growth, and the interplay of flute and tape effect a cohesive and very arresting entity.

3. Repose and fluidity serve as opposing and complementing forces. To these two basic premises, the composer adds a third idea, which stabilizes and unifies the whole; observe systems 4, 7, 10, 11, and 13.

4. In place of the traditional fast-*f,* slow-*pp,* and so on, the composer achieves these contrasts by a rapid succession of events, which by analogy, may seem to be a mosaic rather than a tableau. Lyric, dramatic, and virtuosic qualities are all in evidence and are a part of Davidovsky's expressive means.

CHAPTER SUMMARY

Thus far, the twentieth-century divides into two parts: c. 1920 to 1950 and c. 1950 to 1980. Each part seems to contain both polarizations and syntheses. Since 1950, intense reexamination of each parameter has been initiated. Two complete works and one movement of a larger work are presented for observation of rhythmic, melodic, textural, and timbral factors.

SUGGESTED STUDIES

1. Listen to a good recording of each of the examples in this chapter. Add two or three additional observations concerning: rhythmic and pitch control, texture and timbre, control of gesture, pacing of events, and overall structure.

2. Using Example 413 as a model, compose a short work (about two minutes in duration) for the instrumental and vocal resources in your class.

Chapter 30

FINAL PROJECTS

Nine diverse compositions dating from c. 1500 to c. 1930 are presented as examples for analysis and review of stylistic features, and as possible models for imitative composition. The basic rhythmic, melodic, and harmonic vocabularies are of sufficient scope to provoke challenging written or verbal discussion but are simple enough to be within the technical grasp of freshman/sophomore students of music theory.

SUGGESTED STUDIES

1. Analysis (for each example, or as assigned):

    a. Be able to discuss the overall form and "principles of organization" of the example (e.g., contrast, repetition, variation, contiguity).

    b. Study all elements as separate and as interdependent parameters of the composition.

    c. Attempt to describe the special musical qualities of each piece. Consider items of performance practice: tempo, dynamics, phrasing, cadencing; examine balances and dramatic shape.

2. Composition:

Each example may serve as a guide for a short, original composition using the vocabulary and texture of the given piece as a basic model.

Example 416

FROTTOLA

Bartolomeo Tromboncino (fl. 1500)

Cantus: Se ben hor non sco - - pro el

*Tenor: Se ben her non scopro el foco

Altus: Se ben hor non scopro el foco

Bassus: Se ben hor non scopro el foco

fo - co Ne la a-ma - ra pe - na mi - a,

Example 417

VOI VE N'ANDAT' AL CIELO

Madrigal

Jacob Arcadelt (c. 1514-after 1557)

Example 418

ICH LIEGE UND SCHLAFE

Heinrich Schütz (1585-1672)

526

Ich liege und schlafe, und erwache, denn der
Her hält mich.
Ich fürchte mich nicht für viel Hunderttausen-
den, die sich umher wider mich legen.

Auf, Herr, und hilf mir, hilf mir mein Gott.
Denn du schlagest alle meine Feinde auf den
Bakken und
zerschmetterst der Gottlosen Zahne.

Bei dem Herren findet man Hilfe, und deinen
Segen
uber dein Volk. Sela.

Example 419

ACH GOLGATHA

Arioso for alto, from the *St. Matthew Passion*

Bach

Der Herr der Herr - lich - keit muss schimpf-lich hier ver - der____ben,
The Lord of Glo - ry they in shame are cru - ci - fy____ing;

der Se - gen und das Heil der Welt wird als ein Fluch an's Kreuz ge -
the Blest Re-deem - er of Man-kind is spat on, tor - tured and ma -

stellt. Dem Schö - pfer Him - mels und der Er - den soll
ligned. Of earth and sky, from Him de - riv - ed, will

Example 420

QUARTET, OP. 76, NO. 3

Second movement

Haydn

Var. III

Var. IV

Example 421

SONATA, OP. 14, NO. 1

Third movement

Beethoven

Example 422

INTERMEZZO, OP. 76, NO. 7

Brahms

Moderato semplice.

Example 423

FROMM

Text by Gustav Falke (1853-1916)

Anton von Webern (1883-1945)

*From the collection of poems *Mit dem Leben,* by Gustav Falke, published by Georg Westermann Verlag, Braunschweig.

Example 424

SIXTH BAGATELLE

From *Bagatelles for Piano*, Op. 65

Bartók

Summary

In *Perspectives in Music Theory* the basic compositional concepts of Western music have been introduced as they emerged chronologically. The "mystery" of music should reside at the philosophical plane, not at the technical level; introduction should be followed by an ever-deepening analysis and by the acquisition of consummate skills in counterpoint and orchestration. For most practicing musicians, these skills and the insights that are engendered will require not just another course in music theory but, rather, a lifetime's work.

INDEX

80 81 82 83 84 9 8 7 6 5 4 3 2 1